Romulus

Romulus
The Legend of Rome's Founding Father

By Marc Hyden

PEN & SWORD
HISTORY
AN IMPRINT OF PEN & SWORD BOOKS LTD.
YORKSHIRE – PHILADELPHIA

First published in Great Britain in 2020 by
Pen & Sword History
An imprint of
Pen & Sword Books Ltd
Yorkshire – Philadelphia

Typeset in 11.5/14 Ehrhardt by Vman Infotech Pvt. Ltd.

Printed and bound in the UK by TJ International Ltd, Padstow, Cornwall.

Pen & Sword Books Limited incorporates the imprints of Atlas, Archaeology,
Aviation, Discovery, Family History, Fiction, History, Maritime, Military,
Military Classics, Politics, Select, Transport, True Crime, Air World,
Frontline Publishing, Leo Cooper, Remember When, Seaforth Publishing,
The Praetorian Press, Wharncliffe Local History, Wharncliffe Transport,
Wharncliffe True Crime and White Owl.

For a complete list of Pen & Sword titles please contact

PEN & SWORD BOOKS LIMITED
47 Church Street, Barnsley, South Yorkshire, S70 2AS, England
E-mail: enquiries@pen-and-sword.co.uk
Website: www.pen-and-sword.co.uk

Or
PEN AND SWORD BOOKS
1950 Lawrence Rd, Havertown, PA 19083, USA
E-mail: Uspen-and-sword@casematepublishers.com
Website: www.penandswordbooks.com

For my family and their endless love and encouragement.

Contents

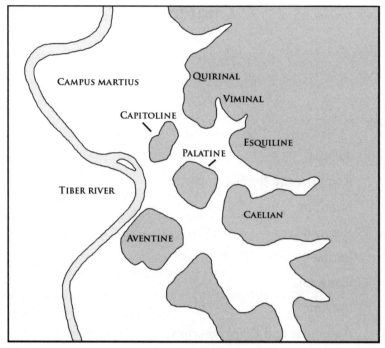

Seven Hills of Rome

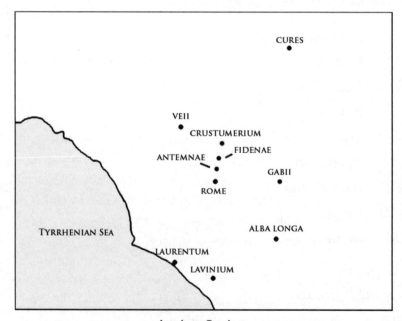

Ancient Latium

Preface

Fact, fiction, or somewhere in between, Rome's eponymous founder has long fascinated Western society and is a household name even to this day. Most learned about the Romulus myth in primary or secondary school and can recount some basic components of the legend: Romulus was the son of a god; he was left for dead until a she-wolf rescued him; sometime later, he murdered his brother Remus and ultimately established Rome.

Unfortunately, few people know much more about Rome's purported founding father than this because historians have, in large part, disregarded him. They generally only provide a cursory lesson on Romulus and quickly move on to later Roman times, which is understandable. Most historians doubt the veracity of the Romulus legend in its entirety and naturally prefer to spend their time chronicling better-attested histories, rather than what they consider to be little more than a fairy tale.

Admittedly, there is much to doubt in the Romulus myth. There are at least sixty different extant histories of Rome's founding (some don't even mention Romulus); even the canonical traditions presented by Livy, Plutarch, Dionysius of Halicarnassus and Cicero are inconsistent at times; and many accounts contain supernatural episodes, which cannot be true. All of this combined has evidently dissuaded writers from assembling a comprehensive biography detailing Romulus' supposed life. Indeed, no one has ever published an attempt in English until now.

The objective of this work is to rectify Romulus' long-term neglect. However, this is easier said than done, given that the extant sources often seem contradictory. To compensate for these deficiencies, this work required a little creativity.

I primarily relied on the canonical versions and frequently judged their variations as differing viewpoints of the same events. As such, when possible, I combined these accounts to provide a more comprehensive story.

Even so, sometimes the ancient authors presented chapters that were wholly incongruent with their fellow historians' versions. In these cases, I generally opted to give additional credence to the narratives that were more widely circulated, had the greatest amount of ancient agreement or provided a perspective that improved this work, while including many alternatives as endnotes.

My goal is not to present this as history, but as the myth that later Romans knew well. Still, there may be a kernel of truth within the Romulus legend, but that's for the reader to decide. True or false, this is the story that many Romans believed.

I

Aeneas

'We are natives of Troy, not the least famous city among the Greeks; but since this has been captured and taken from us by the Achaeans after a ten-years' war, we have been wanderers, roving about for want both of a city and a country where we may henceforth live, and are come hither in obedience to the commands of the gods; and this land alone, as the oracles tell us, is left for us as the haven of our wandering.'

– Aeneas

Mentions of ancient Rome conjure up images of mighty legions victoriously marching in unison across Europe, Africa and the Middle East as one of the world's greatest empires took form. Rome's name also inspires visions of grand monuments and architectural wonders that leave many men and women spellbound even to this day, but Rome wasn't always a magnificent cultural centre or a sprawling empire. It began as a rural, inconsequential backwater, and legend has it that kings ruled the Romans for over 200 years. As it turned out, they weren't a permanent fixture within the eternal city. Eventually, the Romans grew weary of their last king's contemptible behaviour, and they forcefully abrogated their monarchical system and resolved to govern themselves. As a result, the promising flower of Rome sprouted out of the filth of an overbearing and criminal kingship.

While Rome ultimately tasted unrivalled prosperity, without the people who made it what it became, Rome would be nothing more than a word with little meaning; but history turned out otherwise. Rome achieved astounding success thanks to a host of acclaimed individuals. The annals of history are peppered with many illustrious Romans' names, including Julius Caesar, Augustus, Hadrian and Constantine. These men and many others are deservedly remembered for their notable feats. Tales of their monumental triumphs have echoed for many centuries and remainied in the modern consciousness as constant reminders of the wonders that the ancients accomplished. Yet these men might have never reached their towering potential had it not been for fate, the gods' wills and the leaders who assiduously shepherded Rome during its humble foundation and infancy. Without distinguished men like Romulus, at least according to legend, the great civilization may have never been established, or it might have been nothing more than an unremarkable, historical footnote.

The Romans credited the fratricidal Romulus with founding Rome, but if the ancient texts are to be trusted, then he was clearly an unlikely leader. While he was a member of Alba Longa's royal household and supposedly the son of the god Mars, as a vulnerable infant, a villainous king's associate heartlessly left him for dead on the Tiber River's banks. Despite this, the gods had other plans for the youngling. After the Tiber swept Romulus away, he safely made landfall and a wild she-wolf astonishingly nursed the child until a shepherd rescued him and raised the hearty boy into manhood. As Romulus grew older, the fearless young man engaged in a series of perilous adventures that ultimately culminated in Rome's founding.

Romulus purportedly delineated Rome's borders, laid the settlement's primitive foundations and did much more. He formed a monarchy with different branches of government that all shared power, became Rome's fabled first king and promulgated laws and individual rights. He also dutifully built Rome into a respectable city as his subjects painstakingly erected walls, temples and other buildings. He instituted numerous beloved political, military, religious and social institutions that helped define Rome. However, establishing a new city had its price, and Romulus was frequently forced to defend the nascent community from dangerous foes. As he tirelessly safeguarded Rome, Romulus proved that he was a competent leader and talented general. Yet he also harboured a dark side, which reared its head in many ways and tainted his legacy, but despite all of his misdeeds, redemption and subsequent triumphs were usually within his grasp. Indeed, he is an example of how greatness is sometimes borne of disgrace.

Regardless of Romulus' many foreboding flaws, the burgeoning Roman kingdom allegedly existed because of him, and Rome mostly flourished for over a millennium after his death. Thanks, in part, to his endeavours, Rome became massively successful, and the Romans never forgot their celebrated founder or the essential foundations that he is said to have carefully designed.

More than 2,700 years after he purportedly died, Romulus is still a household name, which is an incredible achievement, even though many of today's historians regard him as an unhistorical myth. Possibly because of this prevailing opinion, modern writers and researchers have largely neglected and, in some cases, ignored his supposed history. Consequently, academics have spent much of their time discussing renowned Romans from later periods. However, if the ancient authors' accounts are even remotely credible, then Romulus' importance cannot be overlooked. To cast him aside is to disregard the man to whom the ancient Romans believed they owed everything, but Rome's long history doesn't begin or end with Romulus. Many ancient authors asserted that it actually started centuries before his time.

Romans from the Republican and Imperial periods, and perhaps earlier, traced their ancestral lineage to the legendary city-state of Troy, which was likely situated on the modern site of Hisarlik in Asia Minor. According to multiple timeworn traditions, Rome's birth was a direct consequence of the epic Trojan War and the protracted conflict's ultimate fallout. Rome's ascent into greatness wasn't due to Troy's unbounded success, but rather the Trojans' shameful actions and Troy's spectacular fall.[1]

At its zenith, Troy was a significant fortified settlement that rested on the far north-western corner of modern-day Turkey. It was well-placed for trade, given that it was not far from the Aegean Sea and the Dardanelles, known as the Hellespont to the ancients. Over time, Troy grew into a respected, wealthy and powerful city that exerted considerable influence throughout the region, but it seems that much of the Trojans' strength originated at home. While Troy may have been situated on

Asia Minor's open plains, it was far from defenceless. It boasted some of the ancient world's most intimidating and efficacious walls, which had repeatedly repelled their frustrated enemies. The fortifications were rumoured to be a supernatural marvel in Troy's heyday. Some even believed that the gods Poseidon and Apollo built them. As such, Troy's defences were largely considered impregnable by conventional means, and they loomed large in the eventual conflict with the Greeks.[2]

There is debate over when the Trojan War took place. Some ancients claimed that it specifically simmered from 1194–1184 BC, but this dating has generated scepticism among modern researchers.[3] Excavations at Hisarlik suggest that the war may have instead occurred around 1250 BC, but there is also doubt over whether it actually lasted ten years. It could have been a much shorter conflict, or actually a series of distinctly separate wars. Aside from the ongoing disagreement over the possible dates, by the Trojan War's era, a bold but sometimes incautious king known as Priam governed Troy. Because of Priam's limitations as a monarch, Troy fell, but one of his sons, Paris, also bears responsibility for its demise. He played an unmistakable role in the events that led up to the Trojan War and its lamentable conclusion.[4]

It all started when the ancient Casanova, Paris, set sail for the Greek city-state of Sparta. His trip was probably little more than a standard diplomatic mission meant to bring the powerful communities of Troy and Sparta closer together. At the time, Sparta's king was the vengeful Menelaus and his queen was Helen. She was known as a woman of astonishing beauty, and according to some traditions, her father was the god Zeus. Prior to her marriage, on account of her lineage, beauty and that she was a Spartan princess whose husband-to-be would become Sparta's king, a host of Greece's leading men understandably coveted her.[5] To their disappointment, she married Menelaus, who was a member of the Mycenaean royal family. Menelaus' brother, Agamemnon, was king of Mycenae, which was Greece's most dominant city at the time. Mycenae asserted hegemony throughout the Greek world, and considering Menelaus' close connection to the powerful Mycenaean military juggernaut, it is obvious why Helen chose Menelaus: his family offered Sparta greater protection. It is also clear why Menelaus agreed to the union: the marriage allowed him to become Sparta's king, while he wedded a woman of unrivalled beauty.[6]

During the supposed goodwill mission to Sparta, Paris and Helen fell in love with one another. In light of the era's realities, they couldn't have reasonably expected to live out their years together without serious consequences. While marital fidelity wasn't always expected in the ancient world, Paris and Helen certainly understood that Menelaus would be furious if he learned that his wife was disloyally involved in an affair. He would be even further incensed if she decided to secretly flee with Paris. Beyond these matters, there were also venerated codes of honour related to diplomacy in the ancient world. Engaging in carnal activities with another leader's wife, let alone trying to steal her away, was a clear violation of the unwritten rules of conduct.

Without a doubt, Paris and Helen's illicit affair was disgraceful, but they should have known that their ignominious activities could lead to irreparable harm between Sparta and Troy. Nevertheless, Paris and Helen conspired to elope together. Possibly when Menelaus was away in Crete for a funeral, the Trojan prince surreptitiously whisked away Helen and much of Sparta's treasures but left behind Helen's daughter, Hermione. Paris and Helen ultimately made landfall in the Trojans' homeland to hopefully live together in peace. Upon reaching Troy, Paris' father, King Priam, unwisely accepted the couple into his kingdom instead of attempting to rectify his son's egregious offence. This subsequently spawned a sequence of events far worse than Priam ever imagined.[7]

As could have easily been expected, Menelaus didn't take the shocking news lightly, and his seething anger was justified. Paris and Helen's immoral actions, and the inexcusable breach of conduct in foreign relations, infuriated him. As a result, Menelaus roused his power-hungry brother, Agamemnon, into action. Upon hearing his brother's impassioned entreaties, Agamemnon decided to invade Troy and began gathering together a reluctant but potent coalition of Greek forces with one goal in mind: the absolute destruction of Troy. One by one, numerous Greek cities joined with Agamemnon. They did so out of a desire to plunder the wealthy Trojan city, avenge Menelaus' dishonour and/or ensure that they appeased Agamemnon. Very quickly, Paris' flagrant actions and Priam's inexcusable refusal to appropriately address them threatened to spark a chain reaction with dire consequences.[8]

Even though Priam didn't take the situation as seriously as he should have, he still knew that he couldn't sit idly while Agamemnon diligently prepared the Greek forces. Once it appeared that war on a massive scale was inevitable, the Trojan king began readying his own troops, strengthening his city's defences and probably mobilizing his allies. Upon assessing their own capabilities, the Trojans must have felt confident that they could weather the coming Greek storm. The Trojans were a mighty people. They undoubtedly marshalled an impressive army, numbering as many as 50,000 men, according to Homer.[9] While the poet provided this estimation, it must have been an embellishment, given that some modern scholars believe that Troy could have supported a population of no more than 6,000 people. Aside from the presumably exaggerated troop estimate, Troy enjoyed other perceived advantages. Its walls seemed impenetrable, and Priam had his first-born son and warrior, Hector, by his side. If Priam suffered from any anxieties over the coming conflict, then having Hector's unshakeable loyalty and military prowess at his disposal provided a calming effect.[10]

Even in the face of Priam's laudable groundwork, Agamemnon had reason to be confident. His invasionary force was supposedly comprised of roughly 1,100 ships and an army of as many as 102,000 troops or more. Again, these numbers should be treated with extreme caution due to the ancient writers' tendencies to overstate the size of armies and navies. Nevertheless, like the Trojan king, Agamemnon mustered a colossal force and also had more than one celebrated hero, including Achilles, in his ranks.[11]

After raising this mighty force, Agamemnon loaded his troops onto his enormous fleet and set sail for Troy. As the massive coalition approached, the Greeks judiciously forwarded King Menelaus and King Odysseus of Ithaca to Troy in advance of the armada's arrival. After the two monarchs made landfall and reached Priam's kingdom, they admirably essayed to regain Helen through peaceful, diplomatic means. When they presented their complaints to Priam and asked for justice, the Trojan unwisely rejected their sensible overtures and may have even contemptibly threatened to execute them.[12] Yet these feelings weren't representative of all Trojans. At some point, there was dissension within the Trojan royal house. Priam's son-in-law, Aeneas, who claimed to be the son of the goddess Venus, apparently and very sagely sided with the Greeks. He advocated for surrendering the adulterous Helen to Menelaus and urged for peace with Sparta and its allies. Regardless of his endeavours, he was unable to persuade the short-sighted Priam to act with prudence. In fact, the Trojan king never seemed to give Aeneas the honour and respect that he was due.[13]

After shamefully rejecting the peace delegation's reasonable requests, war was imminent, but Priam felt safe from the Greeks behind his tall walls. The overconfident Priam felt that he had prepared well for the Greek invasion. Nevertheless, not long after, the Greek flotilla neared Troy, and the terrifying sight of over 1,000 Greek ships laden with enemy combatants surely sent shivers down the brazen king's spine.[14]

The Greeks soon landed in Priam's kingdom, and the easily avoidable diplomatic blunder officially transformed into full-blown war. Upon reaching the beaches not far from Troy, the Greeks quickly fought a battle with the Trojans, but Priam's soldiers were unable to forestall the invasion. The Greeks secured a beachhead and dug in for what they presumed would be a short, profitable war, but they were to be woefully disappointed. While the conflict was punctuated by periodic military engagements, according to legend, it simmered for about a decade without either side gaining a decisive advantage.[15]

During the waning days of the war, there was a considerable surge in action, including occasional instances of single combat. One such bout was the storied duel between Achilles and Hector, in which Achilles bested the Trojan prince and publicly abused his corpse, which left many Trojans offended and dejected. There were also many serious battles, but it seemed that no matter what the persistent Greeks tried, they couldn't vanquish their foes. Similarly, despite their valiant efforts, the Trojans couldn't permanently eject the Greeks from their homeland. The war appeared to be a stalemate, with no end in sight.[16]

Had the conflict continued indefinitely at this rate, the Greeks would have likely lost interest and eventually returned home without punishing the Trojans or retrieving Helen. If this alternative history had transpired, then the tale of the epic Trojan War could have been much different. It might instead be heralded as a great Trojan victory or simply lost to the modern world, but this is not the case. The war's concluding events were far different.

Agamemnon's ally, Odysseus, shrewdly recognized the Greeks' conundrum. He knew that his countrymen would never breach Troy's walls and take the city solely by brute force, but they needed to sack Troy to defeat the Trojans. Therefore, he devised an adroit strategy to gain admittance into the fortified settlement without the use of arms. At Odysseus' direction, the frustrated Greeks decided to try a new tactic to turn the war's tide: clever trickery.

While some ancient historians differed over the specific strategy that the Greeks adopted, the most popular accounts centred around an equine construction.[17] According to these traditions, Odysseus first ordered his troops to build a massive wooden horse. Then they placed an inscription on it that made it appear as though it was an offering to the goddess Athena in exchange for a safe voyage back home. Convincing the Trojans that the Greeks were retreating was central to Odysseus' plan. So, the Greeks torched their camps, climbed into their ships and feigned retreat by sailing away. Before they disappeared, the Greeks left behind the enormous wooden horse with soldiers secretly stowed inside.[18]

The sight of the Greeks seemingly fleeing overjoyed the Trojans. They believed that when the Greeks shuttled away from Troy's beaches and left the gift to Athena that it signalled the long war's end. They were wrong and subsequently made some unfortunate decisions. After the Greeks' departure, the Trojans decided to unwisely transport the horse inside of their city and dedicate it as their own offering to Athena, which was all part of the Greeks' designs. Trojans naively carted the wooden construction and troops concealed within it toward the once-beleaguered city, but due to the horse's size, the Trojans had to deconstruct part of their walls in order to haul it inside of Troy. Once the Trojan horse was within the city, the relieved Trojans spent the night heartily celebrating their supposed hard-fought victory over the Greek coalition. Hours later, their relief quickly turned to horror.[19]

Sometime during the night, the Greek armada, which was covertly stationed not far away, returned to Troy's beaches. The soldiers exited their boats and quietly waited to storm the city. Meanwhile, the troops quietly hiding within the wooden horse stealthily climbed out, killed the guards defending Troy's walls and threw open the city's gates for the Greek army to enter. Agamemnon's coalition forces then poured into Troy and began a ruthless attack. Once inside, the disorientated and disorganized Trojans were no match for the Greeks, and pandemonium quickly ensued. During the sacking, the Greeks torched houses, toppled great statues, pillaged valuables, ravaged women and a general massacred ensued; it appears many Trojans were killed as they slept in their beds. The persistent Greeks had finally defeated the Trojans, but Agamemnon's troops weren't gracious victors by any means. The Greeks razed the city and murdered or enslaved large swathes of its population, save for a lucky but sizeable cadre.[20]

The Trojan civilization was almost made extinct following the war, according to ancient accounts. If it had, then Rome may have never reached its potential and Romulus might have never been born, but this is not the case. One of Troy's skilled warriors managed to survive, Priam's son-in-law, Aeneas. When the chaotic melee within the city began, Aeneas lay sound asleep, and he experienced a vivid but troubling dream in which Hector warned Aeneas that the Greek forces were overrunning Troy. Upon receiving this startling and ominous vision, Aeneas awoke in a fearful frenzy, likely to the sound of roaring fires, screams and destruction. He rushed out to view the terrifying spectacle and comprehend the situation. He saw the once great Troy ablaze and brave Trojans vainly attempting to defend their countrymen. Without hesitation, Aeneas armed himself, gathered some of his trusted comrades and hurried to aid his fellow Trojans.[21]

Once in the thick of the fighting, Aeneas and his band of fighters slew a host of Greeks. While his heroic actions may have allowed many Trojans to safely escape the city, the battle was already lost. Aeneas recognized that his efforts were futile, and his thoughts turned to his family's safety. He consequently quit the hopeless battle and located his loved ones and their followers, and he instructed them to flee Troy with him. With wife Creusa and son Ascanius by his side and selflessly carrying his disabled father Anchises on his back, they frantically rushed to escape the carnage, but somehow Creusa perished during the flight. Even though she was unable to escape, Aeneas and many other Trojans were able to dodge the Greek intruders and safely desert Troy. After Aeneas and his surviving family were outside the walls, they apparently found countless other Trojans who had likewise abandoned the doomed city.[22]

Aeneas and his followers fled for the safety of the nearby Mount Ida. This was only a temporary stop, however, because sometime later, the Greeks surprisingly decided to spare Aeneas's life and his followers. The Greeks did so with the caveat that the remaining Trojans must abandon the Troad, a welcome but curious act of clemency. The Greeks may have exhibited compassion toward Aeneas because he was a man of upright character who had vocally advocated for peace with the Greeks and even suggested returning Helen to Sparta.[23] It is also possible that the Greeks simply felt that it wasn't worth the effort to capture the rest of the Trojans. For whatever reason, the Greeks opted to grant Aeneas mercy, but the Trojans needed to quickly withdraw from the region and safely settle elsewhere. Therefore, Aeneas led his fortunate exiles to the coast, where they busily prepared a makeshift fleet to transport them to their new home, wherever that may be. Little did the Greeks know that after they toppled Troy and pardoned Aeneas, they had sown the seeds of their own eventual subjugation. This was because Aeneas purportedly laid the foundation for the rise of Romulus and Rome, and many centuries later, Rome would conquer Greece.[24]

Long before this came to fruition, the exiled Trojans readied their fleet, and Aeneas and his homeless countrymen departed Asia Minor, wandering about desperately searching for a home on the Mediterranean. Their perilous journey purportedly brought them to many different ports, but they were initially unable to find a suitable place to live because the gods didn't approve of these locations. As their long and aimless journey continued, Aeneas reportedly encountered a number of mythical beasts and endured many hardships. After completing myriad labours, Aeneas and his people finally made landfall on the Italian peninsula's western coast, near the Tiber River.[25]

Once in Italy, or Saturnia as it was once called, the Trojans began to plunder the countryside, which drew attention to themselves. As a result, they quickly came face-to-face with the locals, known both as the aborigines and the Latins, whose king was Latinus. He was allegedly descended from the legendary Hercules, and his people claimed Greek ancestry. Supposedly, earlier migrations had left Italy inhabited by many Greeks, including Arcadians and Pelasgians, who may have mingled with Italy's Ligurians and Umbrians. Regardless of the Latins' ethnicity, Latinus was far from pleased by the Trojans' arrival in his domain, especially since he may have been at war with the nearby Rutulians at the time. Thus, he prepared his forces to forcibly eject the Trojans from his lands. He understandably didn't wish to meekly surrender any of his kingdom to these unwelcome newcomers, but the Trojans were determined to end their wandering and settle in the area once and for all. Consequently, both Aeneas and Latinus drew their men into battle array in advance of a potential clash of arms. However, some of the ancient sources differ over the following sequence of events. In one account, the opposing factions clashed in a fierce battle, but Aeneas soundly defeated Latinus. After being outmanoeuvred, the king begrudgingly formed a peace treaty with the Trojans, which permitted them to live in the area indefinitely.[26]

In another tradition, as the two armies anxiously stared at one another before the would-be battle, Latinus strode out in front of his men and called on Aeneas to confer with him. After the two greeted one another, Latinus demanded to know why the Trojans had encroached on his land. Aeneas explained that his people were displaced Trojans whose homes had been mercilessly razed and who had been driven from their ancestral homeland. Latinus listened intently and was moved by Aeneas' harrowing story. Latinus was also awestruck to be in the presence of the renowned Trojans. So, rather than expelling the weary refugees, he offered Aeneas an attractive deal. He proposed that they remain in the region and help defend his land when necessary. At some point, to solidify the compact, he even suggested that his daughter, Lavinia, should marry Aeneas.[27]

Upon hearing these favourable terms, the Trojans accepted, perhaps eagerly. This was a good deal for both the Latins and the Trojans. It provided Aeneas' followers with a permanent home and the Latins additional protection, which Latinus felt was desperately needed. After all, he was more worried about his kingdom's long-term survival than the loss of some of his domain to the refugees, and for good reason. There were many powerful, bellicose peoples nearby, including the Rutulians, who certainly worried Latinus. Realizing that he needed more manpower, the Trojans' arrival presented a great opportunity for him to supplement his forces.[28]

Following the formation of Aeneas' and Latinus' alliance, Aeneas' first order of business was to build a defensible city for his people. Luckily for him, there was ample room to do so because Latinus agreed to allow the Trojans to settle in a district around a wooded hill not far from the Tyrrhenian Sea. It probably corresponds to the modern village of Pratica di Mare, which rests less than 20 miles from the heart of Rome.

The Trojans were thrilled to finally have a permanent residence, which Aeneas officially founded around 1181 BC, according to ancient traditions. Once completed, while its defences weren't as impressive as Troy's once were, it seems plausible that Troy may have served as a model for their new home, but on a much smaller scale.

Sometime after the Trojans and Latins ratified the mutually beneficial terms, Aeneas married Lavinia. This helped strengthen the alliance and foster goodwill between the two peoples and must have pleased Latinus. He was, after all, linking his family with the son of a goddess and a member of the Trojan royal family. In time, Aeneas named his new home Lavinium, after his wife.[29]

Eventually, the Trojans and Latins grew closer to one another. The Trojans began calling themselves Latins too, and they certainly began intermarrying and procreating with the locals. Aeneas and Lavinia allegedly had a son together, who may have even been the first Trojan–Latin offspring. However, the ancient historians disagree over his name. According to Livy, the boy's name was Ascanius, like Aeneas' first born, but others called him Silvius.[30]

Regardless of these discrepancies, it wasn't long before the Trojans were called to arms because the nearby Rutulians felt that they had just cause for war. Regrettably, the subsequent events and the parties involved are unclear. Despite the sources' inconsistencies, it appears that there were several battles, with the first likely occurring before the Trojans had completed Lavinium's construction.[31]

During the course of the struggle, Aeneas' men performed ably against the Rutulians, but Latinus perished during the conflict. As a result, Aeneas inherited his father-in-law's kingdom and continued to defend his people from external threats. They needed his help because their enemies were persistent, but Aeneas proved to be a capable commander who tasted success on the battlefield. Even so, the Trojans' victories came at a cost.[32]

Once a subsequent hard-fought battle led by Aeneas concluded, the Trojans and Latins realized that Aeneas had inexplicably vanished. To the people who were present and to the later Romans, there were only two possible explanations: either Aeneas had been slain in the heat of battle and perhaps the river's current had ingloriously swept his body downstream never to be found, or at the gods' direction, he had ascended into the heavens. Without Aeneas' corpse or witnesses, it was impossible to prove one hypothesis over the other, which only helped his legend to grow.[33]

Despite his missing body, there likely was a sombre but elaborate funeral. Some time afterwards, the Trojans or Latins allegedly erected and dedicated a shrine to Aeneas on the banks of the Numicius River, possibly today's Rio Torto, near Lavinium. His epitaph supposedly read, 'To the father and god of this place, who presides over the waters of the river Numicius'.[34] Aeneas' many heroic acts didn't escape his adherents' notice, nor apparently that of the gods either. Indeed, he was posthumously deified, and from the point of his apotheosis onward, he became known as the god Jupiter Indiges.[35]

Legend has it that Aeneas' mysterious demise was only the beginning of Rome's great rise to power. If Aeneas was a historical character, then he probably never thought that his actions would ultimately lead to the formation of one of the greatest civilizations that the world has ever seen. Not only did he allegedly plant Rome's seeds by leading the Trojan exodus, but one of his descendants was purportedly none other than Romulus, Rome's legendary founder. Many ancient authors contended that Aeneas and Romulus laid the ancient, rudimentary foundations that contributed to Rome's greatness. Their hard work eventually resulted in an empire that stretched from modern-day Iraq to Scotland and had an incredibly lifespan. Before Rome achieved this greatness, however, its early progenitors faced many great struggles.

II

Romulus and Remus

'When they grew up, they were both of them courageous
and manly, with spirits which courted apparent danger, and a
daring which nothing could terrify. But Romulus seemed to
exercise his judgment more, and to have political sagacity, while
in his intercourse with their neighbours in matters pertaining
to herding and hunting, he gave them the impression that he
was born to command rather than to obey.'

– Plutarch

With the revered leader of the fabled Trojan exodus dead,
Aeneas' power ultimately fell to his oldest male heir, the first-
born Ascanius, whose posterity supposedly later obtained
great acclaim. Some even believed that the lauded Julian clan, from
which Julius Caesar descended, traced their ancestry to Ascanius.[1]

Aside from Ascanius' possible antecedents, at some point, he assumed
his role as king, and he eventually looked beyond his young city's borders.
It seems that Lavinium had not been constructed with an eye for the
long-term. Rather, the Trojans may have originally built it somewhat
hastily in order to quickly address Aeneas' immediate concerns, including
providing basic shelter for his people. Its population had presumably
since grown too large for the town's confines, and many of its inhabitants
clamoured for a newly built city that better fit the people's needs. It also
appears that Ascanius personally disliked Lavinium for whatever reason.
Therefore, Ascanius issued orders to begin erecting a new settlement,
but this was to be much more than a mere colony of Lavinium. Ascanius
decided to permanently relocate there and rule it as the city's monarch.[2]

Thirty years after his beloved predecessor had established Lavinium, Ascanius built a new town nearby. It rested near the Alban Hills, less than 15 miles south-east of the yet-to-be-founded city of Rome. It was named Alba Longa, which means 'long white'. Supposedly, its name was derived from a nearby river, which was called Alba or Albula, but the river bore another ancient alias: Rumon.[3] In time, the waterway became known as the Tiber River. It was allegedly renamed the Tiber after a subsequent Alban king named Tiberinus Silvius drowned in or died near the river. At any rate, after founding Alba Longa and enjoying a long, fruitful reign, Ascanius died, and as the centuries passed, a series of monarchs of relatively little note guided the Alban kingdom.[4]

Over time, the fledgling city of Alba Longa took form and gained local prominence. While many ancient writers presented it as a large city, in reality, even after several generations, it was probably little more than a humble settlement.[5] Regardless of its actual size, eventually one of Aeneas' descendants named Proca assumed the throne. Not much is known about his tenure, but following a twenty-three-year reign, he passed away. In his will, he bequeathed his ascendant kingdom to his eldest son, Numitor.[6] Proca didn't heartlessly neglect his other son, Amulius, though. Indeed, he came into possession of Alba Longa's ample treasures.[7]

In accordance with Proca's wishes, Numitor became Alba Longa's rightful king, but Amulius grew jealous of Numitor's power and authority. He began to treacherously scheme against his honourable sibling, and Amulius used Alba Longa's considerable wealth to his advantage, likely by bribing many of Numitor's subjects into serving as his own network of spies, thugs and traitors. When Numitor took an ill-advised trip far from Alba Longa, Amulius launched an insidious coup attempt. Perhaps through the use of perfidious agents and violence, Amulius somehow seized the throne and ultimately overpowered his older brother. However, it is a mystery exactly how he was able to overthrow Numitor's government. Nevertheless, he did, and he subdued his brother and his sibling's immediate family too.[8]

Oddly for a man with so few scruples, Amulius opted against ruthlessly executing his brother, which was often the case during such coups.[9] Instead, Amulius permitted Numitor to live what appears to have been a life of relative comfort and wealth. While Amulius stripped Numitor of his regal authority, Numitor continued to yield some sway in the kingdom. He apparently also retained ownership of lucrative livestock and possibly large tracts of land. This shouldn't be misconstrued as him living a life of independence, though. Every privilege that he enjoyed was because his younger brother permitted it.[10]

It isn't evident why Amulius allowed Numitor to live. Perhaps Amulius believed that his countrymen would revolt against his rule if he unnecessarily ordered his sibling's death. Alternatively, Amulius may have simply felt some sort of loyalty and love toward his brother, and if this was the case, then he simply didn't have the stomach to kill the person whom he grew up with. For one reason or another, Amulius chose to keep his brother alive, at least for the time being.

While Amulius had surprisingly exhibited a degree of clemency to his deposed sibling, he was quite clearly an insecure man. He keenly understood that Numitor's descendants would bear no affection toward him. In fact, they would most likely seek the first opportunity to place Numitor or one of his heirs on the throne and severely punish Amulius for his despicable behaviour. Thus, once Amulius was firmly in control, he planned to quickly extinguish his brother's hereditary line.

Amulius wanted to guarantee that his own reign would be long and fruitful and that none of Numitor's descendants could ever challenge his claim to the throne. To accomplish this end, he instructed his agents to keep close tabs on Numitor's son, Aegestus, so that they could seamlessly hatch a plot against his life. Yet Amulius wanted Aegestus' untimely death to appear as a random act of violence in order to avoid offending Alba Longa's subjects. Consequently, Amulius secretly instructed his loyal subordinates to execute Numitor's son in such a way that the usurper couldn't be blamed. As a result, one day, while Aegestus was hunting, Amulius' operatives lay in wait, and when the unsuspecting Aegestus momentarily let down his guard, they viciously slew him. Amulius took great pains to ensure that Aegestus' death appeared to be the result of an indiscriminate robbery gone awry, but rumours of what really transpired permeated Alba Longa. Like many of Amulius' perceptive subjects, Numitor wasn't fooled by Amulius' efforts to present Aegestus' murder as a random encounter with robbers. Nevertheless, Numitor was powerless to respond and simply acted as though he was unaware of Amulius' involvement.[11]

Aegestus may have been dead, but Amulius hadn't finished securing his firm grip on power. Numitor also had a daughter, Rhea Silvia, who threatened Amulius, but he curiously allowed her to remain alive. She was a female who couldn't realistically expect to rule as a monarch, and without any heirs, she was, for the most part, politically impotent. Given all of this, Amulius may have thought that killing her would be unnecessary and distasteful. Her death could additionally turn many of his people against him because it would have been abhorrent to slay an innocent, powerless girl, especially following Aegestus' death. Still, Amulius wanted to completely neutralize her as a threat and as a potential vessel for rival heirs.[12]

To achieve this, Amulius mandated that she become a priestess in the important cult of Vesta, the goddess of the hearth. Her priestesses, the Vestal Virgins, were held in high esteem and carried out important tasks. Their primary functions, at least in later Roman eras, was to maintain the sacred fire in Vesta's temple, perform the requisite duties to please Vesta and participate in her annual celebration, the Vestalia. At any rate, law dictated that all Vestal Virgins must remain chaste during their tenure in Vesta's service, under penalty of death. Amulius ostensibly believed that this would prevent Rhea from siring children who could ever challenge him. Amulius cleverly chose Rhea's sentence for another reason too. Being a Vestal Virgin was a venerable position that women of high birth held. Because of this, he assumed that many Albans would sincerely believe that he was rewarding her with a great honour. Numitor, on the other hand, wisely saw through Amulius' transparent ruse, but there was nothing that he could do about it.[13]

With Aegestus dead and Numitor and Rhea seemingly neutralized, Amulius presumably felt that his safety was assured. He further believed that his hereditary line would rule Alba Longa without any meddling from unwanted relatives. Yet fate had other plans. According to the ancient astrologer Tarutius, Rhea was impregnated on the morning of 24 June 772 BC, although the ancients didn't uniformly agree on this date.[14]

Regardless of this, the conception occurred a mere four years after Amulius had assumed dominion over Alba Longa.

If the Vestal pregnancy became public, then it would become a colossal scandal. When a Vestal Virgin broke her vow of celibacy, it was considered an egregious affront to Vesta. In most cases, it also offended Vesta's followers, who would be terribly worried that the gods might collectively punish the community for the priestess' immorality. Rhea understood that she could face a tortuous execution for her perceived improprieties, and her offspring would fare no better.[15]

When a select few, possibly including her fellow Vestals or her personal attendants, discovered the unexpected pregnancy, Rhea either concocted a clever explanation or revealed a supernatural experience. She steadfastly claimed that on 24 June, she went to a grove sacred to Mars to retrieve ceremonial water for a ritual. While she was there, the god of war himself, Mars, raped and impregnated her. Rhea asserted that, after the sexual encounter, Mars explained that she shouldn't mourn over their affair. She should rejoice because she was part of a heavenly union formed between her and a great deity. Nine months later, the god purportedly claimed, she would give birth to twins who would surpass all others in bravery and military prowess. Then the clouds dramatically enveloped Mars as he ascended into the heavens. According to legend, there was also a solar eclipse around this time, which the ancients thought announced a development of great importance. This, in turn, appeared to give credence to Rhea's suspicious claims. Indeed, some of Rhea's associates evidently believed her account when she shared it with them.[16]

Rhea was still in communication with her parents because, at some point, she relayed the miraculous experience to her mother. She must have been shocked by her daughter's announcement, but before long, Rhea's mother seemed to have accepted the story as genuine. She even instructed her child to act as though she was ill and remain out of the public eye to help conceal the illicit pregnancy from Amulius, his loyal agents and the general population, and for good reason.[17]

Promiscuous Vestals were treated with severity, but how could she be punished if her pregnancy was truly a divine conception? If Amulius' subordinates killed her and her offspring, then the people would be opposing Mars' will, and they obviously had no desire to risk the god's wrath. Alternatively, Rhea may have fabricated the story as a creative ruse. If she did, then it demonstrated her shrewd cunning because those who believed the alleged supernatural account would wish to avoid angering Mars by punishing the Vestal and her progeny. Therefore, her protection and her offspring's safety seemed more likely to be ensured, but other ancient historians claimed that there might have been a simpler cause of Rhea's situation. Some writers suggested that Amulius or one of Rhea's admirers may have raped her, leading to her unplanned pregnancy. Regardless of the conflicting reports, for the time being, she followed her mother's sound advice and claimed to be suffering from an ailment that kept her from fulfilling her Vestal obligations, which helped hide her growing stomach from prying eyes.[18]

For months, Rhea and her confidants kept the pregnancy a guarded secret from Amulius. Those who aided Rhea probably did so because they believed her supernatural account or were still loyal to Numitor, but the scandal was too large to conceal in perpetuity. As Rhea's pregnancy progressed, she continued to shirk her Vestal responsibilities and doubtlessly became more reclusive. As the weeks passed, rumours about her sudden seclusion must have circulated widely, but her precautions proved only temporarily sufficient.[19]

In time, Amulius noticed Rhea's conspicuous absences from solemn public sacrifices and her other Vestal tasks. He made many inquiries into her situation, but it seems that his questions about Rhea's whereabouts were repeatedly countered by inadequate answers that alluded to Rhea suffering from some vague ailment. These contrived excuses roused Amulius' suspicions, and he ordered doctors to visit her on more than one occasion to determine whether she was really ill or if there was a subversive scheme afoot. Rhea's fellow Vestals tried their hardest to protect her from Amulius' ire. Thus, once the physicians arrived, the Vestals instructed them that Rhea's ailment must be kept a secret. The doctors presumably transmitted this information back to Amulius, which surely generated further suspicion in the insecure king.[20]

Briefly stymied, Amulius asked his wife to visit Rhea until she knew why the priestess wasn't performing her Vestal duties. When and if she discovered the truth, he demanded that she report back to him. After Amulius' queen obediently observed Rhea, it didn't take long to realize that the Vestal wasn't suffering from an illness but was pregnant. When Amulius' wife transmitted this unwelcome news to the king, he was understandably furious. This could have spelled a swift demise for Rhea, but Amulius' only daughter, Antho, supposedly intervened on Rhea's behalf because she was fond of her or may have simply sympathized with her situation. For one reason or another, Amulius opted against executing the Vestal, at least for the time being. He did, however, place Rhea under house arrest and posted guards to ensure that she couldn't escape. In the meantime, Amulius deliberated over how he should deal with the scandal.[21]

Amulius felt confident that others within Alba Longa had abetted Rhea, and he assumed that his sibling was aware of the pregnancy and had kept the shocking news a guarded secret. He genuinely believed that Numitor also knew who had fathered Rhea's offspring and had been quietly harbouring him. Thus, with the pregnant Vestal Virgin under guard, Amulius summoned Numitor to testify before him and some of Alba Longa's elders. After Numitor reached the hearing, Amulius openly implicated Rhea's parents in the adulterous and criminal events, and he demanded answers from his brother. Amulius subsequently commanded Numitor to expose the father and surrender him without demur.[22]

During the probe, Numitor stood dignifiedly before the assembled men, ready to defend himself and his daughter. After Amulius barked questions and accusations at him, he clearly and earnestly recounted the incredible story that his wife had relayed to him about Rhea's rape by Mars. Numitor disclosed the prophecy that Rhea would give birth to magnificent twins, but it appears that Amulius rebuffed his testimony. Numitor pleaded with Amulius to patiently wait until Rhea gave birth. If she bore twins, then that would ostensibly prove the veracity of her claims. Upon which, Numitor continued, Rhea and her sacred children should be treated with the respect that they deserved. Numitor additionally asked Amulius to interrogate Rhea's fellow Vestal Virgins because they would corroborate the story.

Most of Amulius' advisors were inclined to accede to Numitor's proposal, but not Amulius. Even though Antho had acquired Rhea a temporary stay of execution, Amulius was most likely still considering ways of disposing of Rhea and her alleged profane offspring. As such, he scoffed at Numitor's suggestion to wait and see if Rhea gave birth to twins, and, if she did, use them as evidence confirming her claims.[23]

It appears that around this time, Rhea was well into the third trimester of her pregnancy, because during Numitor's inquiry, one of the guards tasked with watching Rhea rushed into the council with news that she had just given birth to twin boys. They were born, perhaps at sunrise, on 24 March 771 BC, at least according to Tarutius, and were eventually named Romulus and Remus.[24] In some of the earliest written accounts of Romulus' and Remus' births, historians listed Remus before Romulus, which implies that he was technically the first-born of the twins.[25] Regardless of the birthing order, even as newborns, they appeared almost superhuman due to their extraordinary physiques and handsome appearances. The fact that they were twins seemed to confirm Numitor and Rhea's story. Yet Amulius claimed this wasn't proof of divine intervention, but some crafty deception that Numitor's dishonest allies had orchestrated. Amulius suggested that another child was simply smuggled in and posed as the twin of Rhea's real infant.[26]

Before long, the existence of Rhea's newborn children became common knowledge, likely because the news of a Vestal Virgin bearing children was far too scandalous to conceal in perpetuity. This placed the rogue king in an uncomfortable position. He was probably furious that he had not been alerted to Rhea's pregnancy earlier, but the organized effort to withhold this information from him was incredibly disconcerting. After all, it appeared that many of his subjects had aided and abetted Rhea, even though she had apparently violated her Vestal oath. This may have led Amulius to anxiously wonder how firm his grasp on power really was, given the conspiracy to mislead him.

Once Rhea's children were born, Amulius acted swiftly. At the time, the statutory punishment for a Vestal's impropriety was to savagely beat her to death and drown her infant children. Amulius may have asked himself, should he punish a priestess for purportedly losing her virginity to a deity? Should he slay any rival heirs to the throne, despite their alleged relation to a god, or should he respect Mars' supposed involvement in the episode? It's certainly possible that he may have simply disregarded the supernatural tale and felt that he ought to execute Rhea and her offspring. Alternatively, if Amulius had fathered the children, as some ancient writers alleged, then he had reason to want the human evidence destroyed because they potentially linked him to the crime of deflowering a Vestal Virgin. Whatever the case, after considering his options, he decided to risk the gods' disfavour and secure his hold on power. He advocated for executing Rhea and her children, and the council overseeing the inquiry approved his request to punish the Vestal and the boys to the fullest extent of the law. They did so not because they necessarily believed that she deserved a harsh penalty, but because they feared Amulius and sensed his implacable anger.[27]

Regrettably, there is disagreement over what happened next. Some sources claim that Amulius' agents remorselessly executed Rhea following his orders, bludgeoning her to death with rods, as was the prescribed penalty at the time. Others state that the king instead placed her in what must have been solitary confinement. The ancient geographer Strabo specifically contended that Amulius spared her life out of deference to his brother, but given that he had already ordered the assassination of his brother's son, this seems like an implausible reason. If she was not executed, then it was, in all likelihood, because Amulius' daughter, Antho, once again passionately defended Rhea and ultimately persuaded him to spare Rhea's life. Rumours that the Vestal had been executed might have been purposefully circulated throughout Alba Longa in order for Amulius to save face and appear as though his judgment was resolute. He presumably wanted to seem as though he closely followed the letter of the law, while also appearing unforgiving of disobedience in order to maintain his position of authority.[28]

While Antho likely saved Rhea from death, her vulnerable infants were still at risk. Their existence threatened Amulius because they could one day challenge his claim to the throne and potentially assassinate the tyrant. To prevent this from transpiring, he instructed one of his agents to murder the infants.[29] Amulius' lackey obediently and promptly gathered the newborns and transported them to the nearby Tiber River at a place not far from the Palatine Hill, which Livy and Dionysius of Halicarnassus stated was originally named the Pallantium after an Arcadian city. Later renamed the Palatine Hill, it became one of the famed Seven Hills of Rome, and it was near there that Amulius' deputy planned on drowning the innocent boys.[30]

However, as he timidly approached the waterway, he began to fear his task. The Tiber's waters had risen, possibly as a result of a flash flood. He worried that he risked being swept away and drowning if he approached the river too closely. Consequently, he opted to execute his orders, while avoiding any real peril by letting nature complete his task. So, with tears in his eyes, he left the vulnerable children near the riverbank. He assumed that the Tiber would continue swelling and sweep the children to their deaths. If they didn't drown in the waterway, then he probably felt assured that they would certainly die from exposure or be devoured by a hungry wild animal. Either way, he felt that his charge would be fulfilled, and after he abandoned the boys, he evidently returned to his infanticidal king and dishonestly reported that he had dutifully completed the deed.[31]

As Amulius' servant had predicted, the water snatched the younglings, who were in some sort of a crib, and carried them downstream, but their brush with danger didn't last long. Their cradle struck a rock on the riverbank and capsized, tossing the children onto the ground. They came to rest at the foot of the north-western end of the Palatine Hill near an area that the ancients called Cermalus. It was on the swollen river's edge that the condemned children lay exposed under a fig tree's shade.[32]

Local wildlife apparently frequented Cermalus. The tree, which later Roman generations revered and called the Ficus Ruminalis – either for Romulus or because beasts ruminated near it – shielded the animals from the bright sunlight and provided them with fruit. It was also conveniently located near a life-sustaining water source, as well as a cave later named the Lupercal Cave, which doubtlessly housed wildlife. It was a sizeable cavern beneath the Palatine Hill with a natural spring, and thick copses and vegetation surrounded it. This cave later became closely associated with a Roman holiday called the Lupercalia.[33]

Ordinarily, being abandoned there as the twins were would have spelled doom for them. Vulnerable infants were easy prey for the hungry beasts that constantly stalked the countryside, but it appears that the gods compassionately intervened on the boys' behalf. As they lay defenceless in the elements, a she-wolf, later called Lupa, heard the abandoned infants' desperate cries. She observed the children from a distance, perhaps watched them squirming in the mud, and slowly crept near them. She could have mauled them to death, but the wolf had apparently given birth to a litter recently and was overwhelmed by her maternal instincts. She approached the infants, protected them and may have even lovingly nuzzled the newborns as she would her own pups, but the boys needed more than just affection. They were likely famished and dehydrated. So, Lupa exposed her distended teats to the infants, who suckled their guardian's milk. Meanwhile, she licked the riverbank's detritus off them.[34]

It is important to note that a few ancient authors recorded their doubts over whether a wolf named Lupa came to the boys' rescue. Instead, a prostitute may have nursed them. The justification for this seems to be the fact that *lupa* was an old slang term for whore. Notwithstanding this alternative account, according to the canonical legend, Lupa wasn't the only blessing that the gods allegedly provided.[35]

A woodpecker also purportedly came to the children's aid. The bird watched over them from its lofty vantage point and even delivered much-needed sustenance in the form of tiny bits of food to the infants, while they simultaneously consumed Lupa's milk and benefited from her protection. Unsurprisingly, the ancients believed that the twins' godly father, Mars, considered wolves and woodpeckers sacred. Thus, the later Romans probably thought that either Mars sent the animals or they may have been a manifestation of the deity. Regardless of the wildlife's origins and motives for assisting Romulus and Remus, the twins remained in the care of Lupa and the woodpecker for an untold amount of time. All the while, their guardians apparently kept them in good health.[36]

As the gods and nature diligently watched over the newborns, some of King Amulius' shepherds, including a man named Faustulus, were nearby. During the course of their work, one of them discovered the children as they were enjoying the she-wolf's milk and called on the others to observe the strange scene. The sight of newborns suckling a wild wolf shocked them, and they naturally worried for the boys' well-being.

It may have seemed that Lupa was maternally and selflessly caring for the children at the time. Even so, the astute shepherds knew that the wolf's carnivorous nature would ultimately emerge, possibly resulting in the boys being brutally consumed. To counter this potential outcome, the kind-hearted shepherds resolved to rescue the children and worked in concert to safely scare the wolf away, but she initially seemed fearless in the face of the sizeable body of men. Nevertheless, their persistence paid off, and after some time, she retreated. Once Lupa scampered off to the nearby Lupercal Cave, they promptly scooped up the children, but they weren't sure what to do with the babes at first.[37]

After some discussion, the group decided to give the twins to Faustulus to raise as if they were his own. Thereupon, he gathered them up and journeyed home, where he lamentably learned that his wife, Acca Larentia, had recently suffered a miscarriage. He subsequently attempted to use the twins to ease her great pain, which evidently worked. After introducing Larentia to the infants, Faustulus likely also told his wife that the boys were incredibly special. While most of the herdsmen hadn't the slightest idea of the infants' identities, it seems that Faustulus deduced that the boys were Rhea's offspring. First of all, their physiques were remarkable and wild animals had cared for them, which intimated divine intervention and implied the babes' importance. This may have suggested to Faustulus that they descended from noblemen. Secondly, some writers claimed that Faustulus was present in Alba Longa during the height of the Rhea Silvia scandal and knew of twins being born to a Vestal Virgin. This induced him to believe that they were Numitor's grandchildren.[38]

Because the boys had been condemned to die, Faustulus actively strove to keep their ancestry a secret. For some reason, though, he maintained possession of the basket that had transported them down the Tiber. It was unique, had a special inscription and its make seemed appropriate for royalty. Perhaps he felt that if he ever needed to prove who the boys were, then he could present the crib as confirmation. Aside from preserving this evidence, Faustulus was apparently capable of keeping the twins' identities confidential. As far as most within Alba Longa knew, the brothers had died. To keep their origins a secret, Faustulus even decided to rear the boys in complete ignorance of their noble lineage. They knew nothing about being the rightful King Numitor's grandchildren. They were likewise unaware that their true parents were supposedly a Vestal Virgin and Mars, but in time they learned about some of the strange circumstances surrounding their abandonment and rescue.[39]

Since Faustulus discovered the twins as they suckled a she-wolf, he and his wife named them Romulus and Remus, which were derivatives of the Latin word for teat: *Ruma*. For several years, Faustulus and Larentia fostered the boys in their humble hut, probably on or near the Palatine Hill, and provided them with a respectable upbringing. They must have taught the boys valuable life lessons, whereby they could combine their royal heritage with an appreciation for hard work, the understanding of the common people's plight and the benefits of modest, upright living. As their early years passed, Romulus and Remus may have received a very basic education, possibly including rudimentary reading, writing and arithmetic if they were lucky.[40] However, there is modern scholarly debate over whether people from this era in Latium were literate. After all, the region's earliest known writing dates to the sixth or seventh century BC, long after Romulus and Remus' fabled childhood, but it's possible that the Latins were literate at an earlier age. Indeed, Dionysius of Halicarnassus claimed that Italian literacy existed in Latium to some degree during the age of Aeneas.[41]

Regardless of when those in Latium learned how to read and write, Romulus and Remus may not have been educated alone. They apparently had many brothers. Faustulus and Larentia reportedly sired eleven other sons who survived to adulthood, although it isn't clear if they were older or younger than Romulus and Remus. The ancient writers didn't bother recording much about their history. In addition to this omission, it isn't evident whether Faustulus and Larentia conceived any daughters, but it's plausible.[42]

As the children aged, Romulus, Remus and their brothers probably aided their father and mother around the house and completed various chores. They must have hurriedly finished these so that they could run, play, compete with one another in physical contests and pester the livestock that their father assiduously watched. Once Romulus and Remus grew a little older, they conceivably followed their adopted father on a regular basis to learn his craft. He additionally imparted foundational knowledge with the twins to prepare them for life in the ancient world.[43] Faustulus and Larentia didn't rear and educate the young Romulus and Remus on their own, though. Apparently, Faustulus' brother, Pleistinus, also helped raise the boys, which lessened the burden on Faustulus and Larentia.[44] With so many children, they likely needed the assistance too.[45]

Being one of the king's humble shepherds probably was not a lucrative position, but Strabo contended that Faustulus was a figure of some significance. Faustulus' connections, thanks to his service to the monarch, may have provided him with some influence and many privileges, which might have included valuable contacts within the royal court. Possibly through Faustulus' relationships with Alba Longa's royal family, Romulus and Remus' foster parents might have arranged for the twins to receive formal schooling when they reached the appropriate ages.[46]

Some of Dionysius' sources believed that Numitor somehow knew of his grandsons' survival and that Faustulus was caring for the boys. Numitor may have even hoped that when they grew older, they would avenge the wrongs committed against him. In the meantime, Numitor decided to generously, albeit quietly, provide the youngsters with a proper education. He must have wisely kept the boys at a safe distance from himself to avoid alerting anyone to their existence. His precautions seem to have been adequate, and they received an excellent schooling funded by their grandfather.[47]

Formal education was an immense opportunity for the boys and a luxury that a scarce few enjoyed. If there is any truth to this account, which only a small minority of writers gave any credence to, then Numitor arranged for the twins to travel to the nearby Latium city of Gabii. The Albans had founded it, and it rested less than 15 miles east of the Palatine. Apparently, it was home to some sort of higher learning institution, and it was there that the boys supposedly honed their academic skills. Instructors taught them the Greek language, and Romulus and Remus learned about music and were even trained in Greek warfare. Romulus later used this valuable knowledge to his benefit on multiple occasions.

The brothers may have even been taught the art of public and persuasive speaking, skills that eventually served them well.[48]

As the boys matured, they grew into adolescents of magnificent stature and stunning beauty, with personalities that matched their physical attributes. The twins often acted especially nobly but modestly at the same time, and they were well known for their intelligence, bold nature and willingness to gratuitously participate in hazardous endeavours. Aside from their daring behaviour and physical features, as far as they knew, they were the sons of a humble herdsman. Therefore, once they completed their education, they continued their adopted father's shepherding business. They diligently tended to the animals and, as they did, the boys lived in meagre huts built from sticks and other vegetation.[49]

The youngsters were dedicated to their father's business, but they also found time to roam the countryside. Romulus was fond of exploring, and particularly loved spending time near the mountains and rivers.[50] The twins were avid hunters too, and they certainly displayed their courage while doing so. While Romulus and Remus had many secular interests, they were both religious men who sincerely respected the gods. They were even skilled at learning the deities' wills and opinions by employing the use of augury, a method of interpreting natural events, including flights of birds, as messages from the gods.

While Romulus and Remus scrupulously honoured the gods, they didn't exhibit the same devotion to all of their fellow Latins. Indeed, the brothers were far more discerning over which countrymen received their goodwill. The boys were not haughty or off-putting to their allied neighbours, though. Instead, they were mostly affable, but they were overtly contemptuous toward many of those who wielded authority, which must have ruffled a few feathers.[51]

Romulus and Remus' bravery and occasional rashness earned them acclaim among the local shepherds, and their eagerness to help their fellow herdsmen secured their companions' love and admiration. The boys were always willing to extend a helping hand to assist their fellow shepherds, but the adolescents never asked for anything in return, which their friends appreciated. In this way, they exhibited great character, but it seems that the favours that were asked of them progressively grew. Eventually, Romulus and Remus regularly found themselves defending their allied shepherds from rivals and even dangerous marauders, which undoubtedly turned bloody on more than one occasion.

Perhaps as they were safeguarding their friends, they realized that their extra-judicial actions could become fairly lucrative. So, while they were busily tending to their flocks, Romulus and Remus began robbing other thieves and herdsmen who weren't associated with them. This wasn't a get-rich-quick scheme. On the contrary, the twins generously shared the spoils with their poor, friendly shepherds. This endeared a large body of people to the boys and cemented their loyalties to them, which essentially placed the twins at the head of a growing gang. Yet others also noticed Romulus and Remus' activities and were irked by them. This ultimately created enemies who later impacted the twins' futures.[52]

III

Numitor

'[Romulus] decided to give up his plan for an immediate attack, but to get ready a larger force, in order to free his whole family from the lawlessness of Amulius, and he resolved to risk the direst peril for the sake of the greatest rewards, but to act in concert with his grandfather in whatever the other should see fit to do.'

– Dionysius of Halicarnassus

The hardheaded Romulus and Remus continued to exhibit their steadfast loyalty to their fellow herdsmen by aiding them in various ways. Meanwhile, the adolescents also seized many opportunities to rob unsuspecting men who passed through the region. Given how intelligent the brothers were, they certainly realized that these actions could, in time, prove hazardous. If they continued their violence and thievery, then a dangerous showdown with their adversaries was inevitable, but Romulus and Remus would at least have help warding off their enemies.

Nearby friendly shepherds had joined arms with the unruly twins, probably because promises of abundant plunder and safety in numbers were too tempting for them to pass up. While engaging in such banditry posed many dangers, Romulus and Remus presumably estimated that they had the necessary manpower to shield themselves and their allies from any reprisals. After all, they had recruited a potent and intimidating body of men on whom they could rely in the event that they were a target of a counter-attack. Despite their growing numbers, they still weren't impervious to this risk, and their enterprises' ultimate consequences had far-reaching implications and brought them face-to-face with their maternal grandfather, Numitor.[1]

Numitor's societal standing had been considerably curtailed ever since Amulius shamefully deposed him. Numitor had largely been relegated to political impotence, but he still maintained substantial wealth and was living well. He apparently possessed an impressive villa in Alba Longa. He additionally owned many head of valuable livestock and slaves who were centred on the Aventine Hill. The elevated ridge was immediately south-west of the Palatine Hill where Romulus and Remus primarily resided.[2] The Aventine eventually became one of the Seven Hills of Rome and was apparently named for a previous Alban king called Aventinus.[3]

Like his brother Amulius, Numitor employed shepherds and owned slaves who loyally tended his flock, and it seems that on occasions, his paid labourers and slaves perilously crossed paths with Amulius' herdsmen, including Romulus and Remus. Even though they were Numitor's kin, there was no reason why the brothers would treat Numitor's men well. The twins were wholly ignorant of their high births and relation to him. Similarly, the deposed king was likely unaware that they had survived, despite the questionable tale about him providing their education. Given his ignorance, he had no reason to respect Romulus and Remus or Amulius' other shepherds, and Numitor's employees likely felt the same about Amulius' servants. Numitor's herdsmen instead considered Romulus, Remus, and Amulius' various herdsmen as competitors who were fair game for plundering.[4]

It's probable that Numitor's and Amulius' employees regularly quarrelled for control of the most fertile pastures and sought to illegally commandeer some of their foes' cattle. These skirmishes happened an untold number of times without any major consequences, but that eventually changed. One day, Numitor's shepherds ejected Amulius' livestock and herdsmen from whatever pasture that they were grazing and may have stolen some of their possessions in the process. It's not entirely clear how it transpired, but Numitor's shepherds probably organized an ambush of sorts and caught their victims unawares. This probably permitted Numitor's men to abscond with much of their rivals' property and livestock, while Numitor's herdsmen expelled the rest from the fertile meadow.[5]

As the herd scattered, Amulius' employees, possibly including Romulus and Remus, frantically rushed to recapture their cattle. Afterwards, they likely struggled to find a suitable location to station them. Possibly during this process, Amulius' herdsmen learned that Numitor's men may have snatched some of their belongings and livestock.

Romulus and Remus decided to not only respond in kind, but to greatly escalate the simmering conflict between the competing herdsmen. The twins believed they were justified in doing so too. They felt as though they and their fellow shepherds had been wronged, and they were justifiably angry. Their cattle had previously been grazing on a certain fertile field, but Numitor's men had unfairly driven them off to make way for their own herd. This could cause serious problems for Romulus, Remus and Amulius' other shepherds. Their well-being largely depended on healthy and well-fed livestock, but Numitor's herdsmen had displaced them from their chosen pasture. Worse still, their herd's numbers may have dwindled to some extent because their opposition likely poached a few cows, goats, and/or pigs. Considering the severity of the offences, the combative twins determined that they must rectify the situation, and they decided to do so with unforgiving ferocity.[6]

Romulus and Remus assembled their fellow herdsmen and devised a plan to assault Numitor's men, but the details of their scheme are unknown. Nevertheless, it seems that once everything was in place, they attacked Numitor's servants at an unrecorded location. During the brawl, Romulus, Remus and their allies injured and may have even killed some of the opposing shepherds, forcing most of the remaining men to hastily retreat and abandon much of their master's property. Then the brothers and their adherents collected much of Numitor's livestock, and they even recruited some of Numitor's remaining labourers into joining their company of brigands.[7]

At first, Romulus and Remus' gamble seemed to have paid off handsomely. They had ejected their rival shepherds from their preferred meadow, stolen some of their livestock and even enrolled some of Numitor's slaves and employees into their gang. Romulus and Remus' counter-attack was a major escalation in the ongoing conflict between the shepherds, but the brothers probably felt that their actions were warranted. They presumably anticipated that this operation would allow them to assert their dominance over the area and teach their rivals the valuable lesson that they should avoid their pastures at all costs. Despite their hopes, Numitor's men refused to meekly stand by and permit this violent provocation to go unpunished.[8]

Numitor's servants were left smarting, but they were worried about more than just their injured pride, bruises and fallen comrades. Amulius' men had noticeably thinned Numitor's personal herd on their watch, which was cause for concern. The shepherds were accountable to Numitor since they acted as stewards of his flock. He charged them with protecting it, fattening up the livestock and ensuring its overall well-being. After all, a hearty herd that was great in numbers provided a healthy revenue stream. However, Romulus and Remus' activities threatened to considerably reduce Numitor's profits. This certainly worried Numitor's herdsmen. The past king employed and understandably expected them to properly manage his livestock. If they failed to satisfactorily carry out their functions, then they could expect serious repercussions, which they sought to avoid.

Upon fleeing from Romulus, Remus and their brigands, Numitor's men must have hurriedly gathered the remainder of their employer's valued cattle. They subsequently convened to determine how to respond to their rivals' escalation. They clearly couldn't idly allow the act of aggression to pass. If they failed to properly respond, then they would have to answer to Numitor and might face a stiff punishment. Inaction would also set a dangerous precedent and suggest that they could be bullied into passive compliance. Thus, they decided that they must recapture Numitor's stolen property, seize the ringleaders (Romulus and Remus), bring them to justice and leave a lasting impression on their rivals.[9]

To achieve these goals, they carefully designed and laid an ambuscade. The twins' foes chose to launch their offensive when the brothers were separated and preoccupied, but the ancient writers differed over what exactly transpired. According to one tradition, Romulus and Remus' enemies patiently waited until the Lupercalia festival, which was a strange but venerated holiday celebrated in February. Later Romans believed the holiday was intended to purify the city and guarantee good health and fertility among the inhabitants. During the Lupercalia of the Republican and Imperial Roman eras, some younger males disrobed, perhaps save for a loincloth, and ran about acting foolishly. They carried with them goatskin thongs, with which they smacked people. Strangely, participants even sacrificed a dog during the holiday, but there were also less outrageous parts to the festival, including a feast.[10]

It may have been during this outlandish festival that Romulus and Remus' enemies commenced their assault. Once the celebration was underway and the twins were happily engaged in the revelry, it appears that certain participants stripped off most of their clothes and jovially carried on with the festival. In the process, they split their group into three bodies, with Remus being in the first party, while Romulus was part of one of the latter ones. As the adolescents marched or possibly sprinted down a street, their enemies waited for them to arrive at a predetermined location. When Remus and his comrades in the first band reached that point, their adversaries raised a mighty shout, pelted them with missiles and then charged at them.

Unfortunately, Remus and his comrades probably didn't have clothes for the most part, let alone appropriate weapons. Despite their handicap, they strove to defend themselves from their assailants, but it was for naught. They were wholly unprepared, and Numitor's shepherds quickly and easily overpowered them. Before long, Numitor's men captured and bound Remus before making the trek to Alba Longa so that Remus could answer for his infractions.

It's not entirely apparent what happened to Romulus' party other than its members either weren't targeted or were able to defend themselves from their attackers. Romulus may have heard the commotion ahead and braced himself for the ensuing melee, successfully repulsed the attack and attempted to come to his brother's aid. Perhaps seeing that Romulus' band wouldn't be so easily captured, the attackers may have simply retreated back into the countryside or rushed to Alba Longa with Remus in tow. For the time being, Numitor's men were pleased with seizing Remus, but they wouldn't be fully satisfied until they captured Romulus too. Yet they apparently decided to prudently wait until they felt assured that they could handle Romulus and his men before they ventured to seize him.[11]

Another version of this episode presents a much different sequence of events, but with a similar conclusion. In this account, the twins' enemies concealed themselves in a roadside ditch and patiently waited for Amulius' shepherds to wander by them. However, at the time, Romulus and influential men from the Palatine settlement were in the nearby city of Caenina to conduct sacrifices to the gods. While Romulus was either slaughtering a sacrificial animal or preparing to do so, Remus was elsewhere on an unknown errand. As the twins were separated and busy with their respective business, their fellow herdsmen carelessly travelled the road where their rivals discreetly lay in wait. Then when the time was right, Numitor's employees successfully launched a vicious attack against them and easily overwhelmed Romulus and Remus' vulnerable friends.

Some shepherds managed to escape and inform Remus of the skirmish. Without notifying Romulus, who was still in Caenina, Remus hastily recruited a body of men and rashly set out to attack the ambushers. In response, Numitor's men withdrew and cleverly lured Remus further into the hinterland, and the adolescent obliviously walked directly into their trap. When he reached a location deep in the wilderness, Numitor's herdsmen sprung their surprise counter-attack and surrounded Remus. A violent skirmish arose as Remus and his loyal companions struggled to escape, but they were resoundingly defeated. As the dust settled, Numitor's shepherds had beaten their foes and seized Remus, and Numitor's servants took him into custody. Then they transported him to Alba Longa to stand trial and possibly face a death sentence.[12]

Aside from the differing accounts, it seems that Numitor's shepherds somehow captured Remus. Romulus later learned that Numitor's men had apprehended his brother and were taking him in chains to Alba Longa. Realizing the gravity of the situation, Romulus evidently rushed to share the terrible news with his adopted father, Faustulus, who was wracked with concern. Romulus told Faustulus that he intended on retaliating by leading his gang's strongest men in an immediate attack against those holding Remus. Faustulus seriously feared that Romulus may also be captured if he recklessly flew to Remus' defence. Given the dire situation and risks facing the twins, Faustulus determined that the time was right to inform Romulus of his noble lineage.[13]

Romulus had heard vague references about his infancy's strange circumstances, but Faustulus had done his best to shield the children from the bulk of that knowledge. However, because Remus was endangered and to forestall Romulus from immediately launching an attack, Faustulus disclosed the whole truth to Romulus. Faustulus' revelation likely astonished the teenager, even though Romulus had already sensed that there was much more to his origins than Faustulus had let on. Regardless of Faustulus' admission, Romulus' thoughts remained focused on his brother, who was still in danger. Yet Faustulus wisely calmed his inflamed foster child and urged him not to impulsively rush to Remus' aid. He advised him to act more judiciously and thoroughly prepare to lead a larger, organized assault to save Remus and possibly depose the usurper Amulius, but only when the moment was right and if there were no other options. Even at this juncture, Faustulus apparently still hoped that he could prevent Remus' execution without resorting to violence.[14]

Romulus bowed to Faustulus' will and began piecing together a sophisticated mission to rescue Remus and possibly confront Amulius if necessary. Romulus rapidly recruited a number of men who were ready to do his bidding, and asked many of them to gather weapons and quietly head toward Alba Longa. He instructed them to cautiously enter the city at different times and entrances so as not to arouse suspicion. Once inside, they were to remain undetected in the marketplace, blend in with the residents and patiently wait for his orders to attack. Meanwhile, Romulus raised another large group of combatants and kept them on alert outside Alba Longa's walls.[15]

Around the same time, Numitor's shepherds may have notified the former monarch that they had successfully captured Remus, one of the chief men responsible for harrying his flock and herdsmen. This unquestionably came as a relief to Numitor, who might have even eagerly awaited Remus' arrival. Soon enough, the restrained Remus was brought into Alba Longa and transferred to Numitor's custody. While the former king doubtlessly felt a sense of ease knowing that one of his many problems would soon be solved, he was in a quandary. Remus was one of King Amulius' shepherds, and Numitor had little official power in Alba Longa. As a result, once the shepherds had taken Remus to Numitor, he excoriated the adolescent for his lawlessness but didn't pay him much heed other than that. Afterwards, he directed his men to help him deliver Remus to Amulius to be judged. Numitor anticipated that the king would censure and maybe even punish his uncontrollable shepherd, which could help end Romulus and Remus' reign of terror.[16]

Upon handing Remus to Amulius, it appears that Numitor and his men produced a list of Remus' alleged crimes, and they humbly petitioned the king to act swiftly and justly. In response, members of the king's court berated Numitor and his requests, which didn't bode well for him. While Amulius' advisors didn't necessarily speak for the monarch, Amulius probably had no desire to accommodate Numitor and punish one of the royal shepherds, especially one who had stolen from his brother's flock. Yet the situation necessitated at least the appearance of a just response from the king. Amulius didn't want his subjects to view him as entirely prejudiced when confronted with his employee's crimes. Furthermore, it seems that many Albans agitated for Numitor to receive the justice that he deserved in this case. Despite their interest in the matter, Amulius didn't seem too interested in settling the issue himself. So, he simply instructed the petitioners to return Remus to Numitor's custody and let him decide how to punish the unruly shepherd. In this manner, Amulius laboured to seem impartial, while also washing his hands of the matter.[17]

Thereupon, Numitor and his servants began escorting Remus back to Numitor's Alban estate. During the trek, Numitor closely examined Remus. The lawless herdsman's impressive physique, along with the tales of his valour and daring, struck Numitor. The young man's conspicuous courage and boldness especially impressed him because these traits were, for the most part, allegedly only present in royalty, which piqued Numitor's curiosity. When they finally entered Numitor's home, the deposed monarch organized a thorough conference with his prisoner so that he could learn more about the disorderly teenager.[18]

As Numitor inquisitively gazed at the muscular young man, he calmly asked where Remus was born and who his parents were. Remus unhesitatingly responded:

> Indeed, I will hide nothing from thee; for thou seemest to be more like a king than Amulius; thou hearest and weighest before punishing, but he surrenders men without a trial. Formerly we believed ourselves (my twin brother and I) children of Faustulus and Larentia, servants of the king; but since being accused and slandered before thee and brought in peril of our lives, we hear great things concerning ourselves; whether they are true or not, our present danger is likely to decide. Our birth is said to have been secret, and our nursing and nurture as infants stranger still. We were cast out to birds of prey and wild beasts, only to be nourished by them — by the dugs [teats] of a she-wolf and the morsels of a woodpecker, as we lay in a little trough by the side of the great river. The trough still exists and is kept safe, and its bronze girdles are engraved with letters now almost effaced, which may perhaps hereafter prove unavailing tokens of recognition for our parents, when we are dead and gone.[19]

Numitor's old agile mind quickly absorbed the remarkable tale that Remus had relayed to him, as well as everything else that he had learned during the course of his investigation. Once he knew that Remus had a twin, and the brothers were both around the age of Rhea's children, he began to wonder if Remus could be his grandson. There may have been a family resemblance, and the gods even seemed to greatly bless Romulus and Remus. This might have intimated divine intervention on behalf of Alba Longa's rightful royal line. Beyond these matters, Numitor couldn't ignore Remus' many distinctly noble traits. All of this gave Numitor hope that his grandchildren were still alive and well.[20]

In time, Numitor privately concluded that Remus was his grandson, but he didn't immediately inform Remus of the revelation. Even so, he had evidently already decided to help the young man. He obviously wished to shield his grandson from danger, in part because he was one of his two surviving male heirs, but he also sensed a valuable opportunity. Numitor thought Remus could somehow help him regain his throne, and he consequently decided to pose a related question to Remus. The old former monarch said:

> I need not inform you, Remus, that you are in my power to be punished in whatever way I may see fit, and that those who brought you here, having suffered many grievous wrongs at your hands, would give much to have you put to death. All this you know. But if I should free you from death and every other punishment, would you show your gratitude and serve me when I desire your assistance in an affair that will conduce to the advantage of us both?

Remus emphatically agreed to aid Numitor, and upon hearing Remus' quick response, Numitor ordered his servants to remove the youngster's restraints. After they unbound Remus, Numitor asked everyone else to leave the room. Numitor then began to describe in detail the many ignominious dishonours that he and his family had received at Amulius' hands. At this point, he also informed Remus of their familial relation, and Numitor encouraged Remus to avenge him. All of this surely came to Remus as a great shock. He knew the details of his infancy were unique but, in all probability, he never considered that he might be Numitor's direct descendant.

Remus slowly digested everything that he had learned and greatly desired to requite the wrongs perpetrated against his grandfather. Numitor thanked Remus for his enthusiasm but strongly cautioned against impetuously rushing to attack Amulius. As Numitor calmed Remus, the deposed king explained, 'I myself will determine the proper time for the enterprise; … send a message privately to your brother, informing him that you are safe and asking him to come here in all haste.' Remus obediently complied and dispatched a missive summoning his brother to Alba Longa for a secret meeting with Numitor.

Shortly thereafter, Romulus received Remus' letter and was no doubt relieved to learn that he was alive, in good health and being treated well. It seems that Faustulus somehow learned of this information too, but he was disquieted by the invitation and the hazards involved with heading to Alba Longa. Faustulus worried that Numitor might not conclude that Romulus and Remus were his kin without physical proof. Despite Faustulus' reservations, after reading Remus' urgent message, Romulus decided to accept the invitation to Alba Longa even though it could potentially be a trap. Regardless of the risks, he travelled posthaste for Numitor's estate to greet his brother and come to his aid if necessary.

As Romulus arrived, he entered his grandfather's presence for the first time since his infancy. Thereupon, the aged former monarch probably disclosed to Romulus that they were relatives and why he had been left for dead on the Tiber as a vulnerable infant. Numitor and the twins shared a brief moment of joy and thanks as they held one another and discussed their true royal lineage. As their enthusiastic emotions slowly subsided, the trio began devising a daring strategy to remove the rogue king, Amulius, from the throne. Romulus had already dispatched men to Alba Longa's marketplace, and he had also been busily rousing the rural population to rise up. He shared this information with Numitor and Remus, which they incorporated into their plan. When they finalized their strategy, Romulus departed for the countryside to finish his preparations for their coup attempt. Meanwhile, Remus remained in Alba Longa to lead a portion of the coming revolt.[21]

At some point after Romulus left for Numitor's estate, Faustulus grew increasingly worried that perhaps Numitor wouldn't believe that Romulus and Remus were his grandsons. He was unaware that the deposed king had recently recognized them as his kin and opted against punishing Remus. So, in order to prove that the boys were Numitor's grandsons and possibly resolve the situation without violence, Faustulus decided to try to meet with Numitor and present evidence of his grandsons' survival. As such, Faustulus gathered the crib that had once ferried the boys down the Tiber River. Faustulus and his wife, Larentia, had kept the trough hidden for many years. He now believed that it would somehow save the twins' lives if he could use it to prove to Numitor that they were members of the royal family. The cradle had a special inscription and its make was unique, which induced Faustulus to believe that it was meant for royalty. Thus, he hoped that Numitor might recognize it and it would persuade him to accept the boys as his descendants.

Upon collecting the basket and everything Faustulus needed for his trek, he set out for Numitor's Alban estate. When he arrived at the city's gates, Alban guards greeted him, and Faustulus begged for admittance into the town. Yet every time the guards questioned him about where within Alba Longa he wanted to go and why, Faustulus' answers were confused and vague. He purposefully did this to keep from exposing Romulus and Remus, but it made the sentries suspicious. Making matters worse, he clumsily carried the crib under his robe because he feared that an enemy agent might recognize it, which could in turn alert Amulius of the boys' survival. Indeed, the attentive guards easily detected the cradle and seized it from him.[22]

At first, some of the guards were puzzled over why Faustulus strove to hide something as mundane as a cradle. Unfortunately for Faustulus, among the sentries was one of the men who had either originally carried the babes to the Tiber or had intimate knowledge of the deed. He quickly recognized the crib and feared that the boys had lived, and he probably worried that he might be held responsible for this failure unless he attempted to rectify the situation. In response, he immediately detained Faustulus, informed Amulius about the discovery and delivered Faustulus to the king for questioning.

As soon as Faustulus arrived before Amulius, the king and his subordinates interrogated Faustulus under threat of physical injury. Amulius was concerned that his deputies had disobeyed his commands to drown the infants years before, and now he feared that Numitor's heirs – and rivals to his throne – were alive and likely roaming the countryside. This meant that one of his subordinates had violated his direct orders and lied about the result.

During the protracted interview, Faustulus did his best to protect his adopted sons. He nervously mixed half-truths, lies and a few valid claims to confuse Amulius and throw him off Romulus and Remus' trail. He freely admitted that the twins had indeed survived and were living as humble shepherds in the monarch's service. Faustulus also falsely informed the king that at that very moment, they were off tending to the herd. Faustulus didn't wish to let Amulius know that Remus was in Numitor's custody, lest Remus risked being executed. Faustulus also struggled to conceal the fact that, as far as he knew, Romulus was either with Numitor or preparing for a possible rescue mission and coup attempt.

Amulius seems to have accepted Faustulus' tale as genuine, but he didn't understand why the shepherd was in possession of the boys' cradle. The quick-witted Faustulus had an answer for this. He claimed that, at the adolescents' direction, he was trying to deliver the crib to Rhea. He asserted that this was a well-intentioned act of goodwill meant to prove to her that the twins had survived and were living wholesome, albeit quiet, lives. He stated that his motives were pure, not sinister, and there was nothing more to it than this.[23]

Amulius was quite pleased with how easily Faustulus was surrendering information, which he presumed was reliable. After considering Faustulus' testimony, Amulius responded, stating, 'Well then, since you have spoken the truth about these matters, say where they may now be found; for it is not right that they who are my relations should any longer live ingloriously among herdsmen, particularly since it is due to the providence of the gods that they have been preserved.' Amulius clearly intended on dispatching a search party to locate the twins, apprehend and kill them. Yet he tried to present himself as an altruistic king who wanted nothing more than to meet his family members and shower them with gifts. Faustulus understood the king's duplicity and replied, 'Now, therefore, since you have decided to have the youths brought here, not only am I glad, but I ask you to send such persons with me as you wish. I will point out to them the youths and they shall acquaint them with your commands.'[24]

Amulius took great pains to hide his fury. One of his subordinates had disobeyed his simple orders to murder two defenceless infants, and now Numitor's heirs were healthy adolescents. Amulius needed to ascertain whether Faustulus' testimony was, in fact, true, and Amulius felt that he must find the boys as quickly as possible in order to execute them. Amulius figured that Numitor must have some knowledge of the conspiracy. So, he ordered Numitor to be kept under guard, and Amulius forwarded one of Numitor's confidants to visit the deposed king. Amulius tasked him with investigating the veracity of Faustulus' claims, asking Numitor about the unfolding scandal and reporting back.[25]

Meanwhile, Amulius dispatched a host of men, presumably guided by Faustulus, to track down and execute Romulus and Remus. Faustulus obviously led them harmlessly away from the brothers, though. Unfortunately for Amulius, he didn't realize that to ward off the coup attempt, he would desperately need the troops that he had just tasked with locating and seizing the boys.[26]

Around this time, the supposed double-agent whom Amulius had dispatched neared Numitor's home. When he arrived, Numitor had already visited Romulus and Remus, concluded that they were his genuine heirs, and had been conspiring with them to overthrow Amulius. Given all of this, the timing should have been perfect to send a spy to learn more about Numitor's involvement in the controversy.

When the man sent by Amulius walked in, he witnessed Numitor and Remus warmly embracing one another. Despite being charged to collect intelligence for Amulius, the would-be-agent appears to have been Numitor's dedicated friend. Consequently, he aided Numitor and informed him that Amulius knew that Rhea's children had survived and that the king intended on capturing and killing the twins. This was unwelcome news, but it likely didn't matter. The brothers' plans were developing quickly, and they were intent on deposing Amulius.[27]

Romulus had an advanced military mind even at this early point in his life, possibly because of his education in Gabii and his experiences as a gang leader. He had pieced together a 'rag tag' army of misfits and shepherds for a special operation and somehow developed a sound stratagem to march the remainder of his men on Alba Longa. Many of them entered the city by stealth. They quietly filed into the town with their swords hidden under their clothes, and once they were inside, they evidently united with their allies who were anxiously waiting in the busy marketplace. Then Romulus divided the troops who still lingered outside Alba Longa into groups of 100 men. A junior officer of sorts led them, and each of the companies carried a crude pole topped with a bundle of hay. These were used to identify the different military units, but they could also be employed to communicate during the coming battle and serve as rallying points if necessary. These were the predecessors of Rome's famous legionary standards, which were eventually adorned with a silver eagle in the mighty legions well into the Imperial period. Interestingly, the Latin term for 'handful,' as in a handful of hay, was *manipulus*, and a derivative of this word, maniple, was the name of the Roman legions' most basic tactical units for centuries.[28]

While Romulus and his makeshift militia were marching full-speed for Alba Longa, Remus and Numitor were likewise busy. While under house arrest, Numitor somehow managed to speak with some of Amulius' loyal soldiers, perhaps those securing his incarceration, in order to share supposedly critical intelligence with them. He warned of an impending attack within the city. He even explained that the invaders were within Alba Longa and advancing toward a specific target, but Numitor gave a false location for the assault. He did this so that many of Amulius' soldiers would be transferred from the fortified citadel to the supposed problem location, weakening the stronghold where Romulus was heading. Numitor, who somehow escaped his house arrest, and Remus then incited discontent among the citizenry and began rallying their allies and the city's malcontents into joining an uprising to overthrow Amulius. This shouldn't have been too difficult, given that Amulius was evidently an unpopular king.[29]

Amulius must have heard about the rebellious commotion. Yet he failed to recognize the gravity of the situation until it was too late to stamp out the revolt rapidly spreading through his city. Little did he know that he was facing a growing force of disgruntled citizens and Romulus' men within Alba Longa. Moreover, there was a modest army commanded by Romulus beyond the city marching toward him with haste. Within a short period of time, Romulus and his militia reached Alba Longa and forced their way in. They united with the groups Romulus stationed in the marketplace and Alba Longa's mutinous citizens as they converged in a coordinated attack. They subsequently focused their efforts on the fortified citadel.

Their sudden appearance surprised Amulius and paralysed him with fear. His concerns quickly grew too because his agitated subjects and Romulus and Remus' followers surrounded the fortress, demanded Amulius' head and fought to breach the stronghold. Meanwhile, the rebels began cutting down many of the king's troops. Unfortunately for Amulius, he apparently didn't have the bulk of his armed guard mobilized or at least in the right place. Some were busily hunting for Romulus and Remus in the countryside along with Faustulus, while others were ignorantly seeking the alleged threat that Numitor had falsely warned them about. Without his loyal troops, no amount of treachery or persuasive speaking could save Amulius. His only hope was that his disgruntled subjects would eventually lose interest, but he had no way of holding out for long against the onslaught.[30]

In short order, Romulus and Remus' insurgents, along with many of Alba Longa's armed and inflamed citizens, forced their way into the fortress. Once inside, they clashed with the remaining royal guards, who were no match for the large number of combatants. The rebels swiftly killed many of Amulius' loyalists, and the stronghold fell to Romulus and Remus without much difficulty. As they penetrated the fortress and discovered Amulius, his worst fears were fulfilled: according to the ancient poet Ovid, Romulus personally ran him through with his sword. Amulius' sons apparently fared no better and also met grisly ends. Regardless of Amulius' efforts to end his brother's hereditary line, Numitor's descendants had survived, killed Amulius and ensured that the usurper's children would not rule Alba Longa.[31]

Feelings of relief and excitement spread throughout much of the city as Alba Longa was finally rid of its tyrannical king. Romulus, Remus and Faustulus, who had since returned from leading Amulius' search party on a fool's errand, were overjoyed to find each other alive and well. When they reunited, they must have warmly embraced one another and been filled with great cheer. As the excitement waned to some degree, one of their first actions was to rescue and release their mother, Rhea, from her incarceration. They had not been in her presence since they were infants, but after many years, they were rejoined at last and paid her the proper respects. Rhea was undoubtedly overwhelmed with delight and erupted into tears. She was finally freed from her life imprisonment and able to meet her adolescent sons, who had been snatched from her as newborns and left for dead.[32]

Many of the city's residents must have been confused over what had transpired and why. So, once Numitor and his grandchildren were firmly in control of Alba Longa, Numitor called an assembly of the town's citizens and delivered a speech explaining events. He sombrely described Amulius' many crimes against him and his family. He relayed Romulus' and Remus' harrowing tales to the gathered people, and he steadfastly defended his coup as a just act, which most of the people evidently supported. At the end of his oration, Romulus and Remus marched through the masses and respectfully saluted Numitor as the king of Alba Longa, and the crowd roared in approval. By what appears to be an acclamation of the people, the Albans officially placed the gentle old Numitor back on Alba Longa's throne in 754 or 753 BC, according to the orthodox dating of Rome's foundation. Afterwards, he probably enjoyed a grand coronation with great fanfare.[33]

Magnificent feasts and long nights of heavy drinking likely followed, but there were also religious rites that the Albans needed to observe. They surely conducted an impressive number of sacrifices to thank the gods for instituting proper order. While the succeeding days were mostly celebratory in nature, there may have been darker moments as well. Many years before, Amulius and his partisans had treacherously committed myriad crimes. They had deposed the rightful king, murdered Aegestus, attempted to kill Romulus and Remus, and wrongly imprisoned Rhea. There's no telling what other unfathomable transgressions had been perpetrated against Alba Longa's people, and as a result, those guilty of the offenses needed to be judged. There's no record of what happened to all of Numitor's bitter enemies, but he was a forgiving old soul who may have offered clemency to those who deserved it. However, it is possible that many others were either executed or exiled from their homeland.[34]

As the exuberance following the coup died down and Numitor resumed his kingship, Romulus and Remus pondered their own future. They had learned of their noble lineage and proven themselves as able leaders during the revolt and previously with their band of disorderly shepherds. Still, they desired to be more than just respected princes, but the city belonged to their kindly grandfather whose authority they had no plans to challenge. Instead, they resolved to look elsewhere for their destiny and they settled on founding their own kingdom. The brothers believed that they were ready to lead an entire people and establish their own city, and, upon bringing this to Numitor's attention, he readily gave the twins his blessing.[35]

Numitor clearly would have permitted Romulus and Remus to live in Alba Longa, but their decision to leave might have relieved him to some extent. He was genuinely thankful that they had restored the crown to him, and he was certainly pleased that his royal line would continue following his death. Yet he may have hinted that they should consider permanently settling outside of Alba Longa, given that their gang of lawless followers accompanied them. Numitor's subjects weren't happy to cohabit with these rustics. In fact, they refused to recognize them as Alban citizens or allow their families to intermarry with many of these lowly people. As such, it is plausible that the Albans asked Numitor to discreetly eject the rabble from the city.[36]

Numitor may have had other concerns too. He recognized that Romulus and Remus were highly ambitious and sometimes uncontrollable young men. What's more, there was no longstanding bond of love or mutual respect between Numitor and the twins. Considering this, the king might have been a little worried that in due time, Romulus and Remus could become dissatisfied with patiently waiting for one of them to become Alba Longa's king. Consequently, he may have feared that they might seek to seize the throne by force one day.[37]

Regardless of Numitor's feelings, he made good use of the boys' intention to create a colony. Alba Longa was overcrowded and another city was needed to house its growing numbers, which could be accomplished by Romulus and Remus' plan. There was also a large number of Amulius' partisans still residing within Alba Longa, and Numitor may have still considered some of those who weren't immediately executed or exiled potentially dangerous. Not surprisingly, Numitor preferred to see them live elsewhere. So, he essentially cleansed Alba Longa of malcontents by transferring them to Romulus and Remus' rule while at the same time easing Alba Longa's overcrowding dilemma.[38]

Numitor actively helped his grandsons in their endeavours too. He provided them with weapons, money, slaves and food to sustain their followers until they were capable of providing for themselves. As the boys prepared to leave Alba Longa, they drew up plans to form their own city in a region Numitor had approved. It was near where the twins had been abandoned eighteen years before as infants. The civilization that sprung from this decision became one of the greatest to ever exist, but its early days were marred by acts of ignominy.[39]

IV

Remoria

'These pleasant anticipations were disturbed by the ancestral curse – ambition – which led to a deplorable quarrel over what was at first a trivial matter.'

– Livy

As Romulus and Remus prepared to depart from Alba Longa and form their own colony, they may have dispatched advanced parties to scout and ready the foundations for temporary campsites to house their followers. Once this was completed and the twins had collected their supplies, they mobilized their followers within Alba Longa and together, they marched out of the city gates and slowly walked toward a grouping of hills adjacent to the Tiber River. It was the same region where Faustulus and Larentia had reared the twins, less than 15 miles from Alba Longa.[1]

Romulus and Remus' adherents were a motley bunch, many of whom weren't obvious allies. Within the rabble were lowly shepherds, Amulius' partisans and more than a few loyal residents of Alba Longa who simply wished for a new start. What most of the brothers' adherents had in common was that they were predominantly impoverished males. Indeed, there were hardly any women and only a small number of aristocrats who were willing to join the exodus. Only about fifty highborn families claiming Trojan lineage joined Romulus and Remus. Largely being people of little means, the twins' followers must have felt a great sense of opportunity. Many of them were leaving their ancestral domain as poor misfits, but they hoped to become wealthy, influential landowners in the city that they planned to build.[2]

Romulus and Remus also had great aspirations and desired individual distinction, and they naturally began pondering matters related to the colony's governance and leadership. Yet Numitor chose not to appoint a single leader of the new settlement. Rather, it appears that he resolved to allow the brothers to either govern jointly, come to an agreement among themselves over who should rule or allow the colonists to decide. Numitor also left other matters up to the twins. While he approved the colony's general location with his grandsons' support, he didn't identify the specific hill on which the boys should settle. He apparently permitted Romulus and Remus to pick the exact location themselves.[3]

Supposedly, Romulus and Remus had more than enough men at arms and provisions to have easily taken a brief jaunt toward the coast and form a colony on the Tyrrhenian Sea. Instead, they were pleased to settle amidst the hills around the Tiber, and Romulus, Remus and Numitor may have had very prescient reasons for selecting the district. At first, a seaside settlement may have sounded promising. Many celebrated empires and trading centres were close to the ocean, but access to the sea came with risks. For much of antiquity, it was much easier for attackers to ambush communities near the coast than those that were inland. Maritime travel was the quickest form of transport and the stealthiest, which posed a danger to new coastal communities. Conversely, cities built further from the sea often benefited from advanced warning of enemy attacks. This was because overland travel was slower and many could witness an enemy's conspicuous advance.[4]

Even though Strabo considered where Romulus and Remus settled less than desirable, others disagreed. In fact, the famed Roman jurist, Cicero, praised the region. After all, it evidently had great strategic advantages that served Romulus and his descendants well. Cicero felt that great maritime trading centres tended to lose their own culture because they were in constant contact with foreigners who had no respect for their religion or social norms. Therefore, through attrition, such communities' inhabitants lost touch with their own culture and slowly became corrupted and immoral. While a degree of xenophobia underlies this premise, Romulus and Remus had no reason to fret over such issues because their colony was landlocked and wouldn't immediately face these drawbacks.[5]

Cicero felt there were other positives to Rome's location. People who lived in cities with great harbours increasingly relied on trade rather than farming to sustain themselves, which left them less self-sufficient, subsequently weakening them. Moreover, increased travel and contact with foreigners associated with shipping could lead to conflict, endangering such communities. Romulus and Remus' chosen district didn't suffer from either of these disadvantages. From Cicero's perspective, the region where Romulus planned to settle was ideal for a burgeoning community. It was near the Tiber River and close enough to the sea that it was well-placed for trade, without the shortcomings of coastal cities. Another benefit was that it was in an area that could control communication lines throughout much of Italy, while still remaining relatively defensible.[6]

Regardless of the motivations for choosing the colony's site, when the would-be colonials arrived at the approved precinct, Romulus and Remus' followers joined with the locals. The brothers then split the whole population into two large bodies, each led by one of the twins. They did this because there was extensive work that they needed to accomplish in order to build a new fortified city. Romulus and Remus believed that with one of them managing each group, they could focus their efforts on specific duties and the brothers' competitive spirits would inspire them to strive to outdo the other. This, they believed, would help them quickly finish their assignments. While they may have split their followers into two, in part, for this reason, there were probably more obvious motivations.

Romulus and Remus had seamlessly worked in tandem with each other for their entire lives, and their ambitions had never caused serious strife between them. Yet with their foes mostly neutralized and a great honour hanging in the balance – that of being the leader of a colony – their relationship evolved. It seems highly probable that the hunger for singular distinction and unrivalled authority caused a degree of enmity between the brothers. Without a common enemy, they had no real reason to coordinate closely as a team, and in all likelihood, they must have secretly yearned to become the colony's sole ruler. Thus, their own ambition, desire for individual command and maybe even a degree of greed drove them apart.

Beyond this, a fair number of their followers preferred to see their chosen candidate become the colony's leader, and they likely confirmed and inflated the twins' aspirations. All of which may explain why Romulus and Remus divided the colonists into two distinct parties with different chiefs. This temporarily extended the peace, kept the twins largely apart and permitted them to hold sole leadership roles.[7]

At first, there were no major problems between Romulus, Remus and the other settlers, but that changed before long as they became more isolated. Both bands probably camped separately, possibly with Romulus' faction preparing a bivouac in the vicinity of the Palatine Hill and Remus raising one near the Aventine Hill or the Sacred Mount. The latter was a hilltop a few miles from the Palatine. Once on their respective hills, Romulus and Remus' followers continued to lay the groundwork for their eventual city. There was much to do too. Several thousand people were under their care, and even though Numitor had provided money, weapons and sustenance, the twins still needed to collect additional food to maintain their people's health. There were undoubtedly multiple hunting parties constantly stalking the countryside to provide meat and shepherds who were busily caring for their herds. Meanwhile, Romulus and Remus' other subjects may have even planted wheat and vegetables to ensure that they would have ample provisions in the seasons to come. All of this took considerable manpower and time to accomplish but it didn't put them any closer to having permanent homes.[8]

Upon arriving at their respective hills, the colonists presumably pitched tents or constructed makeshift huts to live in, but such housing could only temporarily suffice. They needed permanent dwellings, but they couldn't begin building them just yet. First, they likely had to dig defensive ditches and raise ramparts to protect their camps from incursions, robbers and hungry carnivores. Once they were secured by their protective bulwarks, had interim quarters and stockpiled the necessary foodstuffs, they could finally begin the laborious process of constructing the town for which they were dispatched.

They needed to begin raising permanent houses and quickly, but that wasn't an easy task. Building a city required a wealth of lumber and thatch. To obtain the proper materials, Romulus and Remus needed to put their followers to work raiding the countryside's seemingly endless supply of timber. They conceivably started by claiming the trees and reeds nearest to their campsites, but upon ravaging the nearby plant life, they certainly expanded further out as parties of lumberjacks laid waste to large, ancient groves. After they felled the lumber, they grappled with the difficult task of transporting the wood to their newly established lumberyards and construction sites. They must have relied on beasts of burden to help accomplish these tasks, but even with their aid, the entire process was tedious and time-consuming.

While all of this occurred, discord between the brothers was quietly growing. A rift, which was partly due to very important matters, sparked a sequence of events that changed Romulus and Remus' lives forever. Even though King Numitor had approved the colony and assigned the general region for its construction, he didn't identify the settlement's exact location within the district. As a result, he fatefully left that decision up to his grandsons, but they were in fierce disagreement over where to build the city.[9]

Romulus preferred the Palatine Hill, which was hardly an unpopulated wilderness. Romulus and Remus had been raised around there, and archaeological evidence suggests that it was inhabited since at least 1000 BC. While Romulus favoured the Palatine, Remus preferred another not-too-distant hill that he wanted to name Remoria. Ancient writers and modern academics have attempted to identify Remoria's location. Some have theorized that it was actually the Sacred Mount, but others believed that it was the Aventine Hill. Regardless of the location of Remus' preferred site, each of the brothers probably believed that their chosen position provided a bevy of benefits that the other did not.[10]

It seems that both choices were very promising. They were apparently defensible, relatively close to a water source and could support their agricultural and pastoral needs, but unfortunately, the dispute over the chosen site appeared to be at an impasse. Despite their steadfast refusal to settle on a location, Romulus proceeded to build the *Roma Quadrata* on the Palatine Hill, but there is confusion over what this actually was. Some modern scholars have assumed that it was a monument of sorts. Whatever it was, Romulus hoped that it would become part of the city that he wanted to build, even though he and Remus hadn't agreed on the city's location. Around the same time, Remus also began constructing the town of Remoria, or at least preparing to do so, on a different hilltop.[11]

This wasn't the only disputed matter facing the twins. There was the critical problem of leadership. A single monarch governed Alba Longa, and it seemed natural to expect one to lead the yet-to-be-built colony as well. However, Numitor hadn't addressed this matter, which caused problems. Each of the brothers yearned to be king, but since the boys were twins, neither could claim leadership based upon seniority. Nevertheless, Romulus clearly thought that he was best suited to be king, but Remus understandably disagreed. Meanwhile, their followers clamoured for their chosen candidate to be crowned as the city's sole leader. They encouraged the brothers to stake their claim to the throne, which generated even more discord between Romulus and Remus.[12]

The final controversy between the twins was the most trivial. It related to naming the settlement, which Numitor had likewise left up to the quarrelling adolescents. Romulus preferred to call it Rome, after himself, but Remus advocated for naming the city Remoria, a derivative of his name. All of these issues created a deep and growing divide between the twins, which their grandfather should have foreseen and addressed. On the contrary, Numitor's deference to his grandchildren and his *laissez-faire* method of ruling in this case failed to resolve these predictable matters in advance.[13]

After a number of impassioned debates and demonstrations, the twins exasperatedly admitted that they simply could not come to an agreement on these topics. While their discussions may have begun somewhat civilly, they quickly turned heated as the stubborn brothers drifted further apart. The antipathy must have swiftly grown among their followers too as the factions became more scornful of each other, which was a dangerous development. The groups gradually appeared less like friendly competitors from the same colony and more like potential enemies. Eventually, Romulus and Remus recognized that their dispute threatened to escalate to the point of violence. So, they sought to address the squabble without resorting to bloodshed.[14]

The brothers deliberated over possible solutions, but in the end, they agreed that they should leave the final determination regarding their city's location, leader and name to their grandfather. Numitor was their senior, wielded considerable power and had granted them the right to form the colony. Given all of this, appealing to him was a natural choice, and it was a commendable decision on their behalf. They obviously realized that they were at inexorable odds and were growing increasingly hostile. Thus, in one last effort to save their brotherly union, they deferred to Numitor.

Romulus and Remus must have eloquently presented their cases before their grandfather who probably listened attentively, while at the same time feeling rather disappointed. They were asking Numitor to make a major decision, but he preferred his grandchildren to resolve such disagreements without his input. Despite his wishes, his grandsons placed him in a difficult position in which he was essentially asked to choose one of his descendants over the other, a decision that vexed him. Not only were they his grandchildren, but he largely owed his crown to the boys. Without them, he would still be living under Amulius' heavy-handed rule. It's plausible that Numitor carefully considered his options and weighed the pros and cons of each grandson. Romulus and Remus were both excellent leaders who had proven themselves as able military men. However, Romulus had exhibited his ability to more calmly process complex situations before rushing into action than the more impetuous Remus. Conversely, Numitor might have enjoyed a closer relationship with Remus, since he had met him prior to Romulus, and it was Remus who had first agreed to aid Numitor in his bid to retake the throne.

Numitor was likely at a loss. Romulus and Remus both seemed as though they would be competent rulers, but they had asked him to make a choice to settle their squabble. Yet Numitor was too indecisive to resolve the situation on his own. He may have had no desire to hurt one of his grandsons by choosing one over the other, and he additionally didn't want to offend the followers of the grandson whom he didn't favour. Therefore, it appears that he preferred to relieve himself of the responsibility of endorsing one of the twins, and he instead instructed them to consult the gods. It seemed like the perfect response to such an important question. After all, who could argue with the gods? Numitor might have also conveniently and cleverly chosen this route in order to insulate himself from potential malcontents. If he had ruled in favour of one of his grandchildren, then the other would be insulted, as would his adherents. This could create an explosive situation, which might lead to reprisals. On the other hand, no matter who rose to power and chose the settlement's location, Numitor couldn't be held responsible if the decision was left up to the principal deities.[15]

Regardless of Numitor's motives, he instructed Romulus and Remus to defer to the gods over these contentious topics, and there was just the way to do it. The ancients had an affinity for birds, and they believed that the gods' wills and opinions could be relayed through signs delivered by different fowl. In Romulus and Remus' case, they agreed to seek the gods' guidance by observing vultures. This decision made sense for them, considering that the twins were both talented augurs, and they may have specifically chosen vultures because they appeared far less frequently than other birds. Therefore, their appearance was ostensibly more likely to be a divine sign. Furthermore, the ancients believed that vultures were purer birds because they don't eat their own species and cause no disservice since they only consume the deceased. Allegedly, the twins' resulting act of augury was the genesis of ancient Rome's long-lasting policy of practicing the ritual before many important decisions. [16]

After selecting vultures for their contest, Numitor and/or the twins hashed out the details of their contest, and their plan seemed quite simple. The brother who witnessed the more favourable sign would be declared the winner, proclaimed the colony's ruler and would determine the city's specific location and name. In a laudable effort, a referee was even assigned to each of the brothers to ensure the process was free of treachery.[17]

When everything was set, early one morning, Romulus and Remus set out for their chosen viewing stations. Remus marched to the Aventine Hill, where he intended on conducting a sacrifice and lingering until he observed a propitious omen from the deities. Meanwhile, Romulus was to head to the Palatine Hill, make an offering to the gods and patiently wait for a sign in the form of vultures.[18]

In all likelihood, Romulus took with him his *lituus*, which was a serpentine-shaped wooden staff that he used in augury throughout much of his life. His *lituus* reportedly had some sort of power eventually vested in it, which the Romans noted many years later. Around 390 BC, long after Romulus' death, an invading Gallic tribe sacked Rome and torched the building that housed his *lituus*. After the celebrated Roman commander Marcus Furius Camillus ejected the Gauls from Rome and the Romans examined the building's charred remains, they found that the conflagration remarkably hadn't harmed the staff. This seemed to prove its supernatural powers.[19]

Long before the Romans discovered the staff's alleged attributes, Romulus and Remus anxiously stood on their respective hills, scanning the sky for vultures. They remained in their positions for an undisclosed length of time without observing a single sign. As the hours passed, Romulus began to fear that Remus may be the first to witness an omen and thus become the settlement's ruler. Consequently, Romulus chose to better his odds by cheating.[20]

To achieve this end, the calculating Romulus somehow hoodwinked or corrupted his appointed witness and managed to have a deceptive missive delivered to Remus, summoning him to the Palatine Hill. Within the message, Romulus falsely claimed that he had already witnessed a sign from the gods, possibly in the form of twelve vultures, and wished to discuss it with Remus. It's quite clear that Romulus was lying, but he believed that his dishonesty would pay off. He hoped that as long as Remus was marching towards him, he wouldn't be able to view any birds from his observation post. In the meantime, Romulus would gain a distinct advantage because he would have more time than his brother to search the sky for birds. Even though the plan could benefit Romulus, he and his accomplices ultimately felt ashamed of their actions.[21]

Unfortunately for Romulus, the messenger travelled slowly and reached Remus' station a little too late. A little before the letter's delivery, Remus astonishingly observed six vultures flying over his position, which filled him with invigorating hope and excitement. He felt that the gods obviously favoured him, and he believed that this was undeniable proof. Shortly thereafter, the elated Remus received Romulus' missive. He subsequently learned that his brother likewise claimed to have witnessed a bird sign, and Remus obediently departed for the Palatine Hill to ascertain what had transpired.

By the time Remus reached his twin's post, Romulus hadn't seen any vultures, which didn't bode well for him. Romulus was still hoping for a sign anyway, but he was likely feeling increasingly nervous as Remus approached. In time, Remus climbed atop the Palatine Hill, and he somehow learned of his twin's lie. Romulus' dishonesty understandably upset Remus, but not long after Remus arrived and began excoriating his brother, twelve vultures soared over the Palatine Hill. Romulus believed that this was confirmation that the gods had anointed him the colony's ruler.[22]

Remus, on the other hand, wasn't convinced that this represented the gods' blessing. Rather, he protested his brother's treachery. He kept reminding Romulus of who had first observed the auspicious birds and that only afterwards did Romulus witness the vultures. This was following his deceit, which Remus pointed out repeatedly. Romulus would not yield, though, and he shrugged off Remus and responded to his questions and complaints by saying, 'Why do you demand to know what happened a long time ago? For surely you see these birds yourself.' They continued bickering as Remus reasserted that he had witnessed the vultures first, but Romulus declared that he had observed twice as many as Remus.[23]

Once again, the twins were at an impasse. They couldn't decide what proved the gods' favour. Was it the sign that was observed first or the greatest number of vultures witnessed? Romulus and Remus each disagreed and, by some accounts, obstinately refused to concede to the other. This left the twins at loggerheads, and the situation escalated as their followers similarly had no intention of capitulating to the opposing brother. Rather, the twins' adherents recognized their preferred leader as king and secretly began arming themselves for a possible conflict.[24]

Both Romulus and Remus were incredibly proud and ambitious young men. They genuinely felt that the gods had ordained them to lead their people, or at least they believed that they were the best equipped to rule. Their differing opinions and refusal to compromise created a dangerous wedge between them. This caused the brothers to continue growing apart, and Romulus' deceit regarding the omens further damaged their faltering relationship. Yet if there was any chance that they could somehow reconcile and coexist, then their subordinates probably ensured that rapprochement was unlikely. They presumably incited their commanders to firmly oppose the other and inflated their egos with overt flatteries. This only exacerbated Romulus and Remus' problems.[25]

Regrettably, what happened next is uncertain, given that there are various different versions, but combined, the ancient sources appear to provide a comprehensive account. Following the augury contest, Remus was still furious with his duplicitous brother. Despite his disgust, Dionysius of Halicarnassus claimed that Remus may have eventually swallowed his pride for their collective people's well-being and recognized Romulus as the settlement's lone ruler. This granted Romulus what he had long craved, being the settlement's uncontested leader and empowered to choose the colony's location. Simply because Remus had ventured to act selflessly didn't signify that he had accepted the turn of events with grace. In fact, it seems that he grew ever more spiteful and let his feelings show on at least one subsequent occasion.[26]

One day, as Romulus and his men were busily digging ditches or erecting walls on or around the Palatine Hill, Remus decided to personally observe their workings. It's not entirely clear what Romulus' followers were doing. They could have been working on defensive fortifications for his makeshift camp or possibly the rudimentary foundations for his city. What does seem apparent at this point is that Romulus hadn't officially founded Rome using the ceremonial rites later employed.[27]

Regardless of what Romulus was building, Remus, along with some of his supporters, eyed the fortification and likely exchanged a number of barbs at Romulus' expense. Finally, Remus decided to make his negative opinions of his brother's defences more publicly known. He loudly exclaimed that they were pitiful, cause for embarrassment and would be wholly ineffective. In response, Romulus quipped, 'I give orders to all citizens to exact vengeance of any man who attempts to get over.' Remus replied, 'Well, as for this wall, one of your enemies could as easily cross it as I do', as he crept closer to the barricade, intent on breaching it.[28]

Ignoring the threat, Remus vaulted over the barrier and landed within the inner perimeter, which proved his point that the defences were insufficient. Unsurprisingly, his actions were met with anger and hostility. He had belittled the wall or ditch created by those behind it, and Romulus' men didn't take kindly to his stinging criticisms. Indeed, one of Romulus' subordinates, named Celer, scoffed at Remus' gesture and declared, 'Well, as for this enemy, one of us could easily punish him.' Celer was not one for empty threats, and he obeyed Romulus' directive to discipline those who attempted to penetrate his defences. Thus, he tightly grasped his pickaxe and thrust it towards Remus, who was doubtless surprised by the immediate, violent response. Celer struck his target and mortally wounded Remus in the head, and he died shortly thereafter over this petty dispute. However, many sources claimed that Romulus was actually the one who personally killed Remus. Aside from these inconsistencies, upon gazing at the spectacle, Romulus choked back his tears and stoically declared, 'So shall it be henceforth with [everyone] who leaps over my walls.'[29]

There is no record of how the onlookers reacted, but the turn of events certainly shocked them. Celer had obeyed Romulus' decree and struck down his leader's brother. It was a stunning act, which conceivably caused a pall to come over the witnesses. The factions had needlessly turned on one another, but the end result neatly solved any lingering issues regarding leadership. Either Romulus or Celer had removed the only possible competition, Remus, who became the first person to die at Rome's walls.[30]

Because he killed Remus, by some accounts, Celer apparently feared for his life, and he withdrew posthaste to Etruria, a region in central Italy, to escape potential punishment for his actions. Perhaps due to the speed by which he fled, his name became the Latin word for swift (in English, 'celerity').[31] Fortunately for Celer, Romulus' fury may have soon passed – or never existed – because Romulus later rewarded a man named Celer with a senior position – possibly the very same Celer who killed Remus.[32]

Notwithstanding Celer's standing with Romulus, it probably didn't take long for the initial, paralysing shock of Remus' death to dissipate as his followers quickly became furious. They had previously laid the groundwork for an armed conflict, without their leaders' permission, and now their emotions were boiling over, which was a dangerous combination.

Ultimately, fighting erupted, and the factions became entangled with one another in a bloody battle. Yet it isn't clear how the conflict commenced.[33]

One way or another, the two contingents, each numbering thousands of men, fought somewhere in the vicinity of the low land around the Palatine Hill. It was apparently a fierce but chaotic event, but details of the battle are mostly scarce other than that a host of men died in a completely avoidable conflict. The dead littering the battlefield were more than just lowly, expendable followers. At some point during the disorganized confrontation, Romulus and Remus' adopted father, Faustulus, entered the fray. He had surely striven to facilitate some sort of peaceful agreement, but to no avail as the twins were headstrong and steadfastly refused to cooperate with each other. When the two groups finally met in battle, Faustulus probably watched with dread and disbelief. He couldn't halt the carnage no matter how hard he tried, and he preferred to die instead of living and witnessing the looming destruction.

As a result, Faustulus rushed into the battlefield without any weapons or armour. His purported goal was to be struck down, but it seems that he may have endeavoured one last time to stop the battle by walking between the armed combatants and trying to reason with them. But it was all done in vain. Regardless of whether he sought a quick death or was slain in the heat of battle as he tried to find a peaceful resolution, he was unceremoniously killed. The twins' petty dispute had claimed an undeserving casualty, but Faustulus and Remus weren't Romulus' only kin to die. Also among the battle's dead was Pleistinus, who had helped raise the boys.

By the end of the day, as the armies parted, Romulus could technically claim victory given that his only viable competition had died, but there was little cause for celebration because it came at a cost. Both factions suffered terrible losses. Supposedly, only 3,000 survived the conflict out of an unknown number of combatants. Even more devastating for Romulus was the fact that perhaps three of his family members had been slain, and Romulus may have even personally struck down his brother. When the battle's heated passion dissipated, Romulus probably began thinking rationally again. He was overtaken by the stinging pain of the unnecessary deaths of Faustulus, Remus and Pleistinus. Romulus had played an unmistakable role in the events that led to their demise, which could have been easily avoided, but it was too late to bring back his loved ones.[34]

Nostalgic memories certainly flooded Romulus' tormented brain. Cherished thoughts of his time with Remus, including playing together as children, learning letters in Gabii, hunting and engaging in daring enterprises, replayed in his mind. Memories of the selfless Faustulus must have additionally haunted Romulus. His adopted father had risked great peril to protect the twins, while expecting nothing in return. He had lovingly raised them as his own and provided for their well-being. Treasured memories of the twins walking through the herd's pastures, while tightly holding onto Faustulus' calloused hands as he shared life lessons, undoubtedly rushed through Romulus' troubled mind. However, the visions were of no consolation to Romulus. Remus, Faustulus, and Pleistinus were gone, and the only emotions Romulus felt were raw pain, sadness and regret.[35]

Even though crippling depression overwhelmed Romulus, he knew that he needed to pay the proper, final respects to his slain relatives. In all likelihood, he wished to show them the love and dignity in death that they were denied in their final moments. So, a funeral was organized to honour the recently deceased and bid them farewell. Unfortunately, this era's funerary practices aren't as well-known as those of later Roman periods, but it is likely that the early Romans and their descendants shared some basic components. If so, then friends or relatives bathed the bodies of Remus, Faustulus and Pleistinus to wash the dried blood, battlefield dirt and death's detritus from their corpses. Once clean, they were carefully dressed and dignifiedly arranged so that their bodies could be viewed one last time by their loved ones. Thereupon, many of the funeral attendees may have given the deceased one last heartfelt embrace goodbye. Indeed, Romulus kissed his brother and sadly said, 'Goodbye my brother; you were taken against my will', even though he had played a direct role in Remus' death.

Either before or after this juncture, a sombre cavalcade surely escorted the dead's funerary carriages, which transported them to Remoria. It appears that Romulus or some of Remus' supporters had decided that

Remus should be laid to rest where he had planned to build a home for their people, Remoria, but this may have been more than just a symbolic gesture. Later Roman generations believed that no person should be interred within the city's sacred boundary, eventually known as the *pomerium*, because the remains would pollute the settlement. If Romulus held strong to this notion, then he was still stubbornly married to the idea of building the colony on the Palatine Hill, which meant that no person could be laid to rest there. As a result, tradition may have compelled the colonists to bury the remains elsewhere, and Remoria fit the bill.

Once everyone arrived at Remoria, a grand funeral oration was probably delivered to the mostly muted masses that huddled around the lifeless bodies. Romulus, however, could no longer subdue his grief. He erupted into tears, perhaps as he listened to the solemn eulogies, which must have served as much as a celebration of the recently deceased as they were an apology to the gods and the dead for their senseless deaths.[36]

Following this emotional moment, Remus, Faustulus and Pleistinus were either ritually ignited on a funeral pyre and interred in a tomb, as Ovid suggested, or their bodies may have been buried. Unfortunately, it is impossible to know with confidence which method the colonists employed, but either form was certainly possible. Archaeological evidence has revealed that inhumation and cremation were both used during the Italian Iron Age.[37] Regardless of how they were disposed, Plutarch stated that their remains were buried in Remoria, where Remus, Faustulus and Pleistinus could remain in each other's presence for eternity on the site where Remus had intended to build a great city. However, Dionysius asserted that Faustulus was specifically buried elsewhere. The ancient historian claimed that Faustulus was laid to rest where he fell in battle, near the site of the speaker's rostra, within the area where the Roman Forum was eventually built.[38]

Ovid, who was more of a poet than a historian, recorded a colourful vignette about the events following the funeral. According to his *Fasti*, Faustulus wasn't killed during Romulus and Remus' senseless dispute. He somehow survived, and after Remus' funeral, Faustulus and Larentia despondently returned home. As they laid down to rest, memories of their beloved son haunted them, and Remus' ghost purportedly appeared and woefully declared:

> Look on me, who shared the half, the full half of your tender care, behold what I am come to, and what I was of late! A little while ago I might have been the foremost of my people, if but the birds had assigned the throne to me. Now I am an empty [wraith], escaped from the flames of the pyre; that is all that remains of the once great Remus. Alas, where is my father Mars? If only you spoke the truth, and it was he who sent the wild beast's dugs to suckle the abandoned babes. A citizen's rash hand undid him whom the she-wolf saved; O how far more merciful was she! Ferocious Celer, mayest thou yield up thy cruel soul through wounds, and pass like me all bloody underneath the earth! My brother willed not this: his love's a match for mine: he let fall upon my death – 'twas all he could – his tears. Pray him by your tears, by your fosterage, that he would celebrate a day by signal honour done to me.

According to Ovid, a shocked Faustulus and Larentia listened as Remus pleaded with them to implore Romulus to establish a holiday commemorating his life. Following Remus' entreaty, his foster parents, doubtlessly in disbelief, reached out to touch their deceased son, but they couldn't grasp the apparition. Remus subsequently disappeared, and the couple fell asleep. Once they awoke, they rushed to relay their supernatural experience with Romulus and begged him to grant Remus' request. Romulus acquiesced and created a festival dedicated to honouring – or more accurately exorcising – restless dead ancestors. He reportedly named the event after his brother, calling it Remuria.[39]

The festival became a lasting mainstay in ancient Rome. As years passed, the holiday became known as Lemuria and was held on 9, 11 and 13 May. It consisted of a modest feast, but a strange rite also accompanied it. The head of each Roman household walked throughout his home at midnight, and without looking behind him, he threw black beans over his shoulder as restive spirits allegedly followed the man of the house. As this transpired, nine times he said, 'By the beans, I redeem myself and my family.' Then he loudly banged some pots, making a terrible clamour. Finally, he commanded the spirits of his family to leave, exclaiming nine times, 'Ghost[s] of my fathers, go forth!'[40]

Regardless of whether there is any truth to Ovid's tale and whether Faustulus survived, after the funerals, Romulus and Remus' mourning followers returned to their makeshift homes. Soon enough, they eased back into their routines, but not Romulus. He was inconsolable. His heart ached for Remus, Pleistinus and possibly also Faustulus, but the pain was magnified because of his regrettable role in the affair. Romulus lived in constant grief and was numb to the outside world. He was not interested in any other aspect of his life, and he had no stomach for governing. His adopted mother, Larentia, felt the same misery but knew that despite their anguish, they must try to proceed with their lives, for themselves and others. Romulus and Remus' adherents needed a ruler, and she realized this.

She subsequently displayed her resolve and lovingly consoled Romulus, while simultaneously urging him to continue his role as the settlement's governing head. This mustn't have been an easy task for Larentia, given her grief. Romulus was likewise in agony, but his foster mother probably discussed his followers' needs with him in order to encourage Romulus to rise up from his sorrow and resume the mantle of leader. She likely also reminded Romulus of his divine and royal lineage, and how the gods had watched over him so that he could become one of the greatest men in history.[41]

It seems that Larentia may have eventually forgiven Romulus for his involvement in the tumult. The ancient author Aulus Gellius even claimed that upon Larentia's later death, she willed Romulus all of her wealth. Considering this, not only did she likely pardon him, but the two may have enjoyed a relatively close relationship even following Remus' demise. Romulus loved Larentia, and so did his people and their descendants, given that according to some traditions, the Romans ultimately founded and celebrated a holiday in her honour, the Larentalia. It's not apparent whether Romulus was involved in establishing the Larentalia. Nevertheless, Romulus greatly coveted Larentia's grace and received it. However, more was required of Romulus. He still needed to atone for his offences and regain the gods' favour before he could invest his energies into building his city.[42]

V

Parilia

'I am ready to comply with your desire, for I neither consider myself unworthy to command nor refuse to obey. So far as honours are concerned, I am satisfied with those you have conferred on me, first, by appointing me leader of the colony, and, again, by giving my name to the city.'

– *Romulus*

F ollowing Remus' death, Romulus struggled mightily with depression, but he eventually decided to assume his role as the colony's leader, thanks in part to his adopted mother's entreaties. While Larentia's words to Romulus were impactful, there may have been other contributing factors at play. According to the ancient grammarian Maurus Servius Honoratus, following Remus' death, a debilitating plague afflicted the colonists. This was almost certainly interpreted as divine displeasure for their involvement in the twins' quarrel and the fact that they had not collectively sought absolution for their actions. Someone needed to address this issue, and ultimately, the combination of the plague and his adopted mother's entreaties was enough to motivate Romulus to rise from his melancholy.[1]

Once Romulus' resolve returned, he resumed his position of power and decided that he needed to look after his people's well-being and finish constructing his fortified city. Much of the groundwork had occurred before Remus' death, and presumably some following it. Still, the bulk of the construction either hadn't started or been completed, but Romulus didn't feel as though he could immediately restart the building project. He believed that there were more important matters that he must address before concentrating on founding his city.[2]

It seems that the epidemic was still in full force at this time. So, Romulus consulted an oracle in order to learn how to appease the angry gods and end the crippling plague. The seer advised him, among other things, to govern as though he was a co-ruler with his absent brother and duplicate many kingly activities and forms to give the impression that he and Remus were serving as co-kings. While the instructions may have sounded bizarre, Romulus acquiesced, and afterwards, the plague apparently lifted. It should be noted, however, that this tale doesn't appear to have been included in the earlier biographies and accounts of Romulus' life. In fact, Dionysius of Halicarnassus claimed that Romulus' followers hadn't officially even appointed a king yet.[3]

Regardless of whether anyone directed Romulus to symbolically co-rule with his deceased brother, he felt a deep conviction to appease the gods in other ways. He wanted favourable signs directly from the deities regarding his planned city, and he aspired to make amends for his transgressions as well as those of his people. Therefore, Romulus first prepared to offer a sacrifice and asked his fellow countrymen to do the same. Romulus' religion was communal in nature and required action from all of his followers. If they had the resources to do so, then he required that they conduct sacrifices to propitiate the gods, ask for their blessing to build the city and ensure the settlement's success.[4]

Romulus' adherents complied, and after the massive sacrifice, he claimed to have learned that the gods favoured his vision for the city. He probably came to this conclusion by dissecting and examining the organs of an untold number of sacrificial beasts. When he didn't observe any physical abnormalities, he believed this was evidence that his chosen location for the city's construction didn't displease the gods. Upon completing this, Romulus felt that one critical step of the divine process had been concluded, but more was required.[5]

Romulus and his fellow colonists next sought absolution for their offences, including the unnecessary slaying of Remus and countless others. To achieve this goal, Romulus tasked his followers with building fires outside their tents. Thereupon, they methodically created a host of them, and as flames rose from the crackling firewood, Romulus ordered his people to leap over the fires in order to be pardoned for their misbehaviour.

It seems that Romulus believed, or at least wanted his followers to believe, that this symbolic gesture would cleanse them of their involvement in their comrades' deaths. His subjects obeyed, and after conducting what was quite literally viewed as a baptism by fire, Romulus and his subjects felt as though they had conducted the necessary rites and rituals to return to the gods' good graces.[6]

A relieved Romulus concluded that they could now refocus their full attention on erecting their city. He was eager to ritually begin laying his city's foundations too. As a result, Romulus first courteously summoned to the Palatine Etrurian priests who were knowledgeable in the appropriate rites that should be performed before establishing a new city. Following his invitation, they duly arrived and imparted the ancient, sacred customs to him. Subsequently, on either 21 April 753 BC – according to the most widely circulated tradition – or maybe the morning of 4 October 754 BC, *per* Tarutius, Romulus marched his followers to a designated location on or near the Palatine Hill. This was possibly near where construction had already begun and where Remus had fallen. Once there, Romulus' people must have quietly watched their leader with great anticipation. Then, in accordance with the Etruscan priests' directions, Romulus directed workers to excavate a trench. It received the name *mundus* and was likely on or near the Palatine Hill. During the process, participants deposited into the ditch sacred offerings, as well as soil samples taken from each of the regions from which his subjects hailed.[7]

Then, outside of this trench, Romulus painstakingly outlined another perimeter. It was marked with a plough drawn by both a white bull and a cow. As the beasts of burden and Romulus struggled to create the furrow, priests followed along and ceremonially arranged all of the larger pieces of dirt thrown up by the plough toward the city. If the clods remained facing outward, then it was considered unfavourable to the settlement. When the bull and the cow reached where the Romans would place the gate, the plough was lifted over the area because Romulus and his followers believed that cities' gates, unlike the walls, weren't hallowed boundaries. It was at this delineated border where boundary stones were laid and Rome's walls were subsequently built, which represented Rome's earliest sacred perimeter, or *pomerium*. Rome's first border might have been atop the Palatine Hill, wrapped around the foot of it or may have even extended far enough to include the *Comitium*. In later Roman times, the *Comitium* was a place of assembly within the Forum, whose name was supposedly derived from the Latin word for 'to come together'.[8]

Upon concluding this ritualistic process, Romulus and his subjects looked out over the ploughed area with relief and excitement. At long last, they were finally building their new home in earnest. In time, the moment of elation died down, and Romulus solemnly sacrificed the bull and cow that had obediently drawn the plough. Following the oblation, Romulus' first directive was to build – or finish building – the Palatine fortifications. The later Romans considered the day that they ceremonially broke ground to be Rome's founding. As such, many of them held 21 April in high regard, but there was also a pastoral holiday that predated Rome on that same date. It was named the Parilia. Thus, at least by the Imperial era, every 21 April, Romans simultaneously celebrated the Parilia as well as their city's founding.[9]

After officially establishing the city, Romulus once again resumed managing the construction project, and labourers slowly and tediously erected sturdy walls and built homes. Under Romulus' leadership, his city, which became known as Rome, eventually reached the stage where it could finally provide protection and shelter for its inhabitants. When the first phase of the building project neared completion, people flocked to live in Romulus' city. He had previously made a policy of offering sanctuary to all individuals who wished to live in the colony, which was a well-known ancient method of growing young settlements' populations. Romulus knew that his city's future and security depended on a large population that could defend its borders. For this reason, he even constructed an asylum. It rested between two copses on a nearby hill called Mons Saturnius, which later became known as the Capitoline Hill. The asylum's primary purpose was to help increase the Romans' numbers by providing immigrants with shelter. However, Romulus may have constructed it and instituted the unique immigration policy in compliance with the famed oracle at Delphi's instructions. Unfortunately, the ancient historians recorded little regarding Romulus' possible interaction with the oracle.[10]

It was within the asylum that practically anyone, regardless of their debts and crimes, could seek sanctuary, although Dionysius stated that the only precondition was that they must be free men. Once individuals took refuge there, the Romans likely vetted them, and if there were no serious objections, then Romulus permitted them to enter Rome as newly enfranchised citizens. Romulus' followers were already an odd combination of Amulius' partisans, shepherds, former gang members and Alba Longa's poor, but the citizenry grew even more diverse. Because of Romulus' new immigration policy, Rome's numbers continued to swell as other outcasts – including criminals and debtors – fled from the authorities and came to Rome's asylum seeking a new beginning.[11]

Perhaps as Rome's initial construction neared completion and the city's population was growing modestly, Romulus diverted his attention to other matters. He must have been serving as the building project's executive and maybe even its day-to-day manager, and he had also assumed the mantle of his people's religious leader. Yet with the latest phase of construction winding down, Romulus needed to focus on governing, laying down laws, conducting a census and perhaps even outlining religious edicts for his young city. There was more to founding a city than simply erecting walls and homes. Romulus wanted to form a lasting and cohesive sense of community, create permanent order out of chaos and enact a moral code to protect his people.[12]

According to Dionysius, following Numitor's astute advice to achieve these ends, Romulus assembled the colonists and empowered them to make a critical decision. He offered to let them choose which form of government they'd like to institute: monarchy, democracy or oligarchy. It's not clear why Numitor recommended this or why Romulus complied. It seems clear in most of the other sources that it was a foregone conclusion that Romulus and/or Remus would be the colony's monarch(s). It's conceivable that Numitor suggested taking this approach so that Romulus could formally gain the colonists' support. Numitor and Romulus may have felt that this extra step was needed following Remus' death and the subsequent battle.[13]

For one reason or another, Romulus supposedly placed the decision in his followers' hands and implored them to take their time as they carefully decided. He even declared:

> I am ready to comply with your desire, for I neither consider myself unworthy to command nor refuse to obey. So far as honours are concerned, I am satisfied with those you have conferred on me, first, by appointing me leader of the colony, and, again, by giving my name to the city. For of these neither a foreign war nor civil dissension nor time, that destroyer of all that is excellent, nor any other stroke of hostile fortune can deprive me; but both in life and in death these honours will be mine to enjoy for all time to come.[14]

Romulus' piety moved the people, and his leadership qualities had already impressed them, despite the dispute with Remus and his followers. Consequently, the colonists responded:

> We have no need of a new form of government and we are not going to change the one which our ancestors approved of as the best and handed down to us. In this we show both a deference for the judgment of our elders, whose superior wisdom we recognize in establishing it, and our own satisfaction with our present condition. For we could not reasonably complain of this form of government, which has afforded us under our kings the greatest of human blessings – liberty and the rule over others. Concerning the form of government, then, this is our decision; and to this honour we conceive none has so good a title as you yourself by reason both of your royal birth and of your merit, but above all because we have had you as the leader of our colony and recognize in you great ability and great wisdom, which we have seen displayed quite as much in your actions as in your words.

Thus, the people accepted monarchy as their form of government and confirmed Romulus as their king. Given Romulus' leadership role throughout the colonization process and that he was Numitor's only surviving male heir, this was a predictable result.[15]

Sometime after the people had proposed that Romulus should be king, he sought the gods' blessings for these matters as well. In the early morning, he marched out into the open and humbly prayed to a host of deities, including Jupiter, a powerful god associated with lightning. Romulus asked them to deliver a clear sign to inform him whether or not they had ordained him to serve as the settlement's monarch. Shortly thereafter, a lightning bolt darted across the sky from left to right. This seemed to confirm the gods' approval, because many ancients believed that lightning flashes from left to right represented the deities' favour, while those appearing right to left suggested the gods' displeasure. Purportedly because of this episode, it became a longstanding requirement to take the auspices before any Roman assumed a public office of importance. Unfortunately for some later Romans, unfavourable signs were observed following their elections, which nullified their appointments altogether, but that wasn't the case with Romulus.[16]

Upon taking the auspices, Romulus reconvened his people and informed them that the gods had approved their decision to institute a monarchy led by himself. His announcement was probably met by a roar of cheers and thunderous applause. As king, he assumed several different powers. He was the city's chief executive, religious leader and general. Yet he ultimately shared a degree of power with other governing bodies that he eventually created. They essentially represented an oligarchic function, headed up by the aristocrats, and a democratic component that gave voice to the masses.[17]

One of Romulus' first acts as Rome's king was instituting a new calendar. He undoubtedly did so for several reasons. First, he believed that it would aid his people in their efforts to cultivate the land. Second, it would ensure that they faithfully observed holidays and conducted the proper sacrifices on the appropriate dates, in accordance with the rites and gods associated with Alba Longa and in Greece. Romulus decided to name the calendar's first month after his godly father, Mars. He called it Martius, which today is known as March. Romulus' calendar was strikingly different from the Gregorian Calendar in that there were only ten months: Martius (thirty-one days), Aprilis (thirty days), Maius (thirty-one days), Iunius (thirty days), Quintilis (thirty-one days) Sextilis (thirty days), September (thirty days), October (thirty-one days), November (thirty days) and December (thirty days). Moreover, the Romulean calendar consisted of only 304 days, which again stands in stark contrast to today's Gregorian Calendar. Supposedly, Romulus chose the Roman year's length because he felt that it roughly correlated to human gestation. Regardless of Romulus' reasoning, it's possible that when he created the calendar he also set festival dates and days of rest for his people.[18]

Perhaps following his calendar's unveiling, he turned his attention toward conducting a very rough census, arranging his subjects into classes, organizing a militia and designing a system of government. Using the Lacedaemonians' constitution and maybe also Alba Longa's as a model, he announced rights and expectations, including military duties, for each class of people. Once he had documented all of the males who were the appropriate age and maintained sufficient means to qualify for service, he assigned them to military bodies called legions. He may have stipulated a minimum wealth requirement for service because many governments in antiquity expected warriors to provide their own equipment, and, in Rome's case, the poorest Romans simply couldn't afford such implements.[19]

Legion was the term for Rome's largest military unit, and the Romans used it throughout their history until its fall over a thousand years later. Early in Romulus' tenure, 3,000 foot soldiers and 300 cavalrymen comprised each legion, which was smaller than later Roman legions. The horsemen were almost certainly from Rome's most prosperous classes, as they were the only ones who hailed from families rich enough to own horses. Even though Romulus had admitted fugitives and additional locals into Rome, his earliest militia couldn't have been very large. Indeed, only 3,000 of the men who had initially left Alba Longa survived the battle with Remus, and Plutarch asserted that during Rome's earliest days there were no more than 1,000 houses. Therefore, it seems more than likely that few legions were raised at this point. Rather, there was probably only one.[20]

The remainder of Romulus' subjects who didn't qualify for military service were mostly either too young or old to fight. According to Plutarch, Romulus selected 100 wealthy men from this body for special service. It's unclear why Romulus specifically chose 100. Livy believed that Romulus either felt that the number was sufficient or there were only 100 heads of household within Rome – at least reputable heads of household – which may have been the case. Rome wasn't comprised of many rich people. Only around fifty highly esteemed families had originally departed from Alba Longa to lay down roots with Romulus and Remus. They must have composed Rome's relatively affluent classes, and Romulus and/or his people chose some of these prosperous older men to serve in his counselling body, which he named the Senate. This represented the oligarchic component in Romulus' government.[21]

While Romulus' Senate varied greatly from the later Senate of the Roman Republic and Empire, the governing body he created continued to exist in one form or another until Rome's collapse. Romulus' Senate, more specifically, essentially served as his advisory board and considered matters that he delegated to its members. Romulus called the fortunate 100 who comprised the Senate *Patres*, which is the Latin word for father. The ancient writers weren't entirely in agreement over why Romulus chose to name them *Patres*, but there are a few possibilities. They may have been some of the select few within Rome who either knew who their fathers were or who sired legitimate children, which demonstrates the largely unsavoury character of Romulus' subjects. Many were either bastards or had children out of wedlock. The other possible reason that Romulus dubbed the 100 *Patres* is because he wanted them to graciously act as fathers to their fellow, less fortunate countrymen. The *Patres'* descendants became the celebrated patricians who were the ruling elite during later Roman periods. Long before this time came to fruition, Romulus tasked the 100 *Patres* and the subsequent patricians with serving as priests, judges and administrators, but the majority of the Romans were of lesser eminence. Romulus supposedly called people from this class the plebeians, and they enjoyed fewer privileges. Indeed, he prohibited them from holding offices reserved for the patricians.[22]

In Romulus' youth, he had been unabashedly disdainful of some of his superiors and overseers, but he had been quick to help his fellow shepherds. While this was his inborn nature, he knew that in order for his vision of a functioning society to come to fruition, his people needed to follow a different path. He didn't wish for the poorest and lowest strata of society to look at the wealthier classes and leaders with contempt and distrust. Likewise, he opposed the idea of the richest Romans greedily acting only in their own self-interest. As such, he encouraged them to actively aid the poor as if they were their fathers. It seems that Romulus led by example. The historian Appian of Alexandria even said that Romulus often ruled as a loving father who evidently cared deeply for his subjects. Regardless of whether Romulus was behaving genuinely, he undoubtedly felt that acting in this manner would make it easier to govern his people. In the same vein, Romulus probably believed that his well-to-do subjects should act fatherly and generously to the plebeians. If they did then all parties would clearly enjoy a better relationship because it would in turn cause the impoverished to view the ruling elites more favourably, creating harmony. In this way, they engaged in patronage.[23]

The Roman patronage system, which the ancients later called *clientela*, became a long-standing staple of Roman society for hundreds of years, and it may have originated from the Romulean era. *Clientela* was essentially a social network of individuals who were expected to dole out mutual favours. The rich, who became known as 'patrons' in the system, gave advice, meals, money, legal aid and jobs to their lowlier counterparts, who were called 'clients'. The clients, whom Romulus originally permitted to choose their own patron, performed favours in return for their patrons' munificence. In the later Republican period, they voted for measures supported by their benefactors, joined their armies or simply accompanied them around town. A large following appeared prestigious, and the later Romans equated it with great affluence.[24]

Patrons and clients were bound to each other and expected to reciprocate the system's benefits. The mutual agreements were even passed from generation to generation as the *clientela* system became hereditary. The Romans took *clientela* very seriously too, and they utlimately passed laws related to the patronage network, including forbidding patrons and clients from testifying against one another or suing each other in court.[25]

At this early point in Rome's history, Romulus evidently also formed a mostly unwritten, modest code of laws. They were likely inspired by the Greeks and Albans, but he may have instituted some unique rights and punishments as well. Given the ancient sources' confused accounts, however, it is regrettably difficult to know what laws Romulus enacted at this stage as opposed to later in his tenure.[26]

Romulus busied himself with more than simply laying down laws, though. He created public offices, including the lictors. There were twelve lictors in all. Romulus may have chosen this number because he had observed twelve vultures or because he based the lictors and their numbers on an ancient Etruscan tradition. Whatever the case, the lictors were essentially officers of sorts who served and always accompanied the king, and they carried symbols denoting their employer's office. During Romulus' era, they followed him around, which increased his prestige and advertised his regal authority, but they may have simultaneously served as bodyguards who protected him from harm. The office of the lictors lasted for hundreds of years, well into later Roman periods.[27]

While Romulus created honours for himself, he also empowered the people. He organized them into a voting body in order to allow them to assume the democratic component in his government, but their power was limited. It seems that they only voted on measures when he allowed them to do so. Nevertheless, Romulus could assemble them to elect judges, cast their votes on proposed laws and consider declarations of war. Most of the time, their actual influence over government operations was largely negligible. While the people may not have wielded much real power, they were unquestionably grateful that Romulus had given them this honour.[28]

Romulus rewarded his people with more than just voting privileges. In what must have been one of his more popular decisions, he decreed that each male Roman citizen would be freely granted two *jugera* of land. This was probably the equivalent of only about 1.3 acres. Still, many of the colonists became landowners for the first time in their lives, and it provided some of his poorest adherents a means to help provide for their families.[29]

As Romulus meticulously designed his system of governance and ruled over his people, he continually expanded Rome's walls to shield an even greater plot of land to ensure that Rome could always receive more people. This was also necessary because he kept admitting individuals who sought asylum. During this era, Rome was a beacon for the dispossessed, oppressed and even criminals who sought a second chance. By attracting people from these walks of life, Romulus rapidly increased Rome's size, but it was an unbalanced populace. When Romulus and Remus left Alba Longa to found a colony, their followers were mostly men. Similarly, when Romulus offered sanctuary to all who sought it, a host of males flooded Rome. They hailed from across the region, but an inordinate number of them had questionable backgrounds. Men from the surrounding hills emigrated to Rome, as well as herdsmen from nearby Etruria, but males whose families were Greek in origin likewise relocated to Rome. While Romulus gladly embraced these immigrants, they were mostly men. This left Romulus ruling over an ever-growing male population with very few females, which was problematic. Without women producing children, Romulus would be left leading a people that could only be sustained for one generation.[30]

Romulus' current crop of subjects was relatively secure for the time being. Their king had overseen the construction of a well-fortified settlement that could repel many attackers. He had accepted many immigrants and thus allowed Rome's population to boom. This provided a bevy of military-aged males, which Romulus organized into his army. Beyond this, Romulus was a natural commander. In fact, he was correctly lauded for his military leadership during the coup d'état that ultimately returned Alba Longa's crown to Numitor. All of this meant that his settlement increasingly stood a better chance of being able to withstand invasions from minor kingdoms.

Other communities apparently noticed Rome's rise, but most of the neighbouring towns appeared to have no desire, or at least a justified reason, to challenge Rome. Meanwhile, the more powerful cities within the region simply wrote off the Romans as inconsequential, which turned out to be unwise. Rome was slowly growing in might, but without replenishing its legionary ranks with a new generation of military-aged males, the Roman sense of security would not last long. One of the most obvious ways to address this issue and encourage large-scale procreation was to somehow coax nearby women into marrying the Romans, but this was much easier said than done. In the end, Romulus' struggle to rectify this problem triggered a major conflict, which greatly imperilled the nascent city and left an indelible stain on Rome's reputation.[31]

VI

Consualia

'Armed with swords, then, many of [Romulus'] followers kept
their eyes intently upon him, and when the signal was given,
drew their swords, rushed in with shouts, and ravished away
the daughters of the Sabines.'

– Plutarch

As the months and perhaps years passed, the newly founded Rome
was increasingly secure and continued to flourish under King
Romulus, but he became greatly concerned about his settlement's
future. It boasted many able-bodied men but few women, which made
the procreation needed to populate Rome's future ranks exceedingly
problematic. This posed a real danger too. Without a new crop of offspring, the city would wither away in a matter of decades, if not sooner.[1]

Romulus additionally worried about Rome's lack of binding alliances
with neighbouring kingdoms, whose inhabitants mostly seemed to scorn
the Romans. He discussed his significant concerns at length with the newly
installed senators, who felt that his apprehensions were well-founded. In
response, they suggested that Romulus ought to send diplomatic envoys
to nearby communities to form treaties of alliance that also established
rights of intermarriage between their peoples. If any of these cities
accepted Romulus' invitations, then the Romans believed that they
would greatly benefit. It would permit intermarriage and subsequent
procreation within Rome, and the marriages would solidify meaningful
military partnerships. This would, in turn, increase Rome's standing in
the region as well as provide further protection.[2]

To this end, Romulus dispatched his emissaries, and one by one, they
visited nearby Latin and Sabine towns' governing bodies. The Sabines

were members of an old, bellicose tribe. They had spread across portions of central Italy, where numerous cities claimed Sabine heritage. The Roman ambassadors visited many of these and other cities. They likely included Caenina, Antemnae, Crustumerium and maybe even Fidenae and the Sabines' chief community of Cures. The envoys likely touted the Romans' close relationship to the gods as well as their bravery and self-sufficiency as they proposed friendly treaties.

However, what had started with a glimmer of hope ended in abysmal failure. The ambassadors' foreign counterparts entertained the entreaties without the expected decorum. Some of the towns' leaders purportedly even responded to the Roman proposals by mockingly asking if 'they had opened an asylum for women, for nothing short of that would secure for them intermarriage on equal terms'.[3] Their derisive answers referenced Romulus' asylum on the Capitoline Hill, which provided sanctuary for immigrants before they were awarded Roman citizenship. The surrounding cities' leaders clearly thought that the Romans were a lowly rabble without great wealth or notable accomplishments. As such, the only foolproof method to find women willing to marry them would be to build an asylum for women of ill-repute. These repeated, overt insults left the Romans feeling spurned. Making matters worse, it seems that even Alba Longa's citizens continued to refuse to intermarry with them. This must have particularly stung, given the Romans' relationship and recent history with Alba Longa.

As Romulus' representatives each dispiritedly returned home empty-handed, he was forced to accept that the people within Rome's vicinity intensely disliked and distrusted the Romans. The neighboring communities looked down upon Romulus' undesirable subjects, and understandably so. Rome was comprised of simple country folk and many poverty-stricken Albans, with an inordinate number of fugitives, debtors and maybe even escaped slaves residing there. Furthermore, it appears that an incredibly large number of Rome's citizens may not have even known who their fathers were. Most Latin and Sabine parents from respectable families would have prohibited their daughters from marrying such men. They were considered dishonourable, socially inferior and of illegitimate birth.[4]

There were probably other reasons why the nearby kingdoms rejected Romulus' proposals so quickly. They had anxiously watched Romulus and Remus' exodus from Alba Longa and noticed that one of the brothers' first acts was essentially an armed conflict between their followers. The surrounding monarchs undoubtedly worried that a new, belligerent community of increasing power was developing in their backyard. This was incredibly disconcerting, and their apprehensions continued to grow.

Within no more than a handful of years of Rome's founding, neighbouring kings watched in disbelief as Rome's population apparently swelled. It seemed that their worst fears had come to fruition. A new settlement that was inclined toward war had formed nearby, and it was expanding at an alarming pace. This was a dangerous situation that could threaten their own autonomy. Consequently, when Romulus offered to form alliances with the cities and asked for the right of marriage between their citizens, these communities were more than a little sceptical. They may have worried that this was a ploy to gain dominion over their towns or at least force them into unfavourable alliances. This could draw them into unnecessary wars and/or curb their self-rule. They may have also feared that they might be exploited in order to promote Romulus' ambitions, and they had little desire to help the pugnacious Romans become stronger.[5]

There was no shortage of reasons why numerous communities found various rude ways to say 'no thanks' to the Roman king's proposals. While this understandably generated anger among Romulus' people, the Roman monarch was undaunted and privately refused to take no for an answer. In the meantime, he masked his disgust and acted as though he bore no ill will toward his neighbours. Yet he began to scheme with his lieutenants and other confidants to acquire the females that he wanted for his people. This led to a dark chapter in Rome's history that later Romans struggled to justify.[6]

Upon carefully considering their options, Romulus and his aides devised a clever strategy to entice a host of females to visit Rome. Then the Romans intended on abducting and forcibly marrying them. Romulus felt that his devious plan was warranted on at least two counts.

First, he had initially attempted to act honourably and asked for the right to intermarry with the nearby Sabine and Latin communities' daughters, only to be publicly snubbed. As a result, he felt that the forceful seizure of the maidens was justified. Second, his duty was to defend Rome and provide for its well-being, and he felt that kidnapping the women could help secure his kingdom's future. Without a surge of females within Rome, there could be no procreation, and in due time, the population would decline, endangering the city's future. Moreover, he was under the impression that marriages, even under these unfavourable circumstances, might cause the cities from which the maidens hailed to consider allying with the Romans. He presumably contended that the women would essentially serve as hostages who would dissuade their native cities from attacking Rome, lest the Romans might harm the captives. Over time, as the marriages bore fruit, he hoped that the communities would view the Romans and their descendants as family, and they would become natural allies. As a result, Romulus believed that he must acquire the young women by any means, even dishonesty and kidnapping, to provide the offspring and allies vital for Rome's survival.[7]

When Romulus and his deputies drew up the treacherous stratagem, the Roman king presented it to Numitor, who readily approved it. However, Romulus also wanted the gods' support. So, he swore an oath to a deity named Consus who, among other things, oversaw secret counsels. Romulus pledged that if his ploy was successful, then he would celebrate an annual festival accompanied by sacrifices in the god's honour. Afterwards, Romulus shared his scheme with the Senate, and they likewise authorized it.[8]

Once Romulus' plan took form and all parties were preparing to play their roles, Romulus dispatched messages to communities around Rome, including Caenina, Antemnae, Crustumerium and maybe even Fidenae and Cures. Some of the cities were of Latin origin while others were Sabine, and many were the same towns that had tactlessly rejected Romulus' requests for friendly treaties.[9]

Either around four months or four years and four months (the sources disagree) after Romulus had founded Rome, the notices arrived at their destinations. The letters informed them that Romulus had discovered an ancient, sacred altar, which had been buried and long forgotten. It was either associated with the Equestrian Neptune or the god Consus. This alleged fortuitous discovery was naturally cause for a grand festival to celebrate the altar's finding and end its long-term neglect. Therefore, Romulus announced that he had organized a splendid, multiple-day event. In a feigned exhibition of goodwill, Romulus invited the nearby peoples to partake and enjoy the upcoming celebration, games and sacrifices, which he certainly promised would prove memorable.[10] The festival later became known as the Consualia. It ultimately became a bi-annual Roman holiday that was held on 21 August and 15 December. The Romans celebrated it for centuries, and the holiday included giving horses and mules rest, while adorning their heads with blossoms.[11]

To ensure that the event was magnificent enough to lure the unsuspecting peoples to Rome, Romulus secured ample wealth to bankroll the occasion with his subjects' help. The costly affair required considerable work too. Rome needed to be readied for a sizeable influx of people whom they intended on impressing with their festivities. To meet their goals, the Romans pieced together a programme of celebratory events; they procured a host of animals for the feast; servants likely imported wine and cooked desserts; and they assembled staging areas for sacrifices and spectacles as well as seating for the visitors. Convinced by all of this, the Sabines and many Latins naively viewed the grand celebration as an attractive proposition. It appears that without much consideration, they readily agreed to attend the festivities with their families.[12]

The invitees probably thought that Romulus' official summons was innocent, and that there was no plausible cause for concern. They must have believed that he would never pursue anything inappropriate, for several reasons. They assumed that they were attending a holy celebration. If Romulus acted improperly, then it might be considered a colossal insult to the gods, which could invite their wrath upon Rome. Clearly, Romulus didn't want to risk this, they thought, but they were unaware that Romulus had already enlisted heavenly aid for the plot. What's more, Rome was only one budding city, while the Sabines were an entire tribe that boasted multiple towns. To offend them and many Latins too would unwisely risk war against their combined might. Even the bold Romulus wouldn't take such a gamble, they surely believed. Lastly, Romulus seems to have masterfully played the role of an understanding and respectful king. As each city rejected his proposals for intermarriage and alliances, he successfully disguised his true, spiteful feelings. Thus, the Sabines and Latins apparently never suspected any Roman treachery.[13]

According to the traditional dating, Romulus set the festival's commencement for some time in August 753 BC or 749 BC. The latter date seems more probable, given that it would have taken more than four months to build a city, form a government and prepare a massive festival. Nevertheless, as the anticipated celebration approached and Romulus' plans were firmly in place, eager and inquisitive Sabine and Latin families flowed into Rome. The prospect of free games, presumably drunken revelry and gluttonous feasts excited them. The Sabines and other nearby peoples were also naturally curious about the city of Rome itself. Many had either watched from afar or at least heard of the settlement's swift construction and how its population perpetually increased. While their interest was likely harmless, it seems conceivable that some of those who attended were specifically dispatched to reconnoitre Rome, gather any potentially useful intelligence and report their findings to their superiors. Many members of the surrounding communities were, after all, concerned about Rome's growing might, but the overwhelming majority of their inhabitants evidently ignored such worries, at least for the most part.[14]

There is no precise record of the sequence of celebratory events, but upon entering Rome's gates, hospitable Romans must have warmly greeted the foreign attendees, who eagerly accepted a guided tour of their new city. The first official act of the Consualia, however, was a dramatic public sacrifice to Consus on the newly discovered altar. The rest of the festival consisted of perhaps a series of addresses from Rome's leading men, including Romulus, his deputies and priests. Then there were surely magnificent feasts, an abundance of wine and various physical contests. The Romans spared no expense to make this a grand event.

The celebration's climax was on the final day. It was a competitive horse race, but before the crowds gathered near the racetrack, much of

Romulus' scheme had already come into effect. He had directed many of his subjects to quietly arm themselves with swords, take strategic positions around the track and remain vigilant until he gave the signal to abduct the foreign women. As the anticipated moment approached, the likely drunken attendees congregated around the raceway and jockeyed for the best views. High-ranking Romans, on the other hand, enjoyed reserved seating in the most prominent and desirable locations, which were in sight of the other spectators. Romulus, more specifically, probably sat in a special chair that denoted his importance, which he also advertised by regally dressing in purple.

As Romulus' subordinates eagerly waited for his command, they eyed an audience filled with young, alluring Sabine and Latin women. These were their targets, but many of the armed Romans had no specific woman in mind because Romulus had instructed them to seize whatever virgins that they could. Despite this, more than a few Roman men must have visually combed through the foreign congregation to locate the most beautiful maidens, whom they hoped to make their wives. Yet Romulus had warned his subjects not to violate the women the night of their abduction. They were to remain temporarily chaste.

After Rome's visitors huddled around the raceway, Romulus presumably delivered a few words to announce the race's commencement. Then the horses launched from their starting positions. The spectators watched in great anticipation while the steeds furiously galloped. As they strategically manoeuvred and repeatedly risked crashing, the crowd surely erupted into deafening cheers and gasps, but their delight quickly turned to terror. As the unsuspecting and mostly disarmed foreign crowd reached a point of intoxication and were mesmerized by Romulus' spectacle, the Roman king gave the prearranged signal to launch the assault.[15]

To alert his loyal subjects, Romulus casually rose, removed his purple cloak, adjusted it and draped it over himself once again. He used this sign to metaphorically sound the attack. At that moment, a menacing wave of sword-wielding Romans rushed toward the foreign spectators, who were confused and quickly became panicked.[16]

As the intimidating Roman youths had been ordered, they swept through the crowds and snatched vulnerable young women. Many fathers and mothers struggled in vain to hold onto their daughters and protect them from abduction, but they were no match for the armed men. The parents helplessly watched in horror as the Romans ripped their children from their grasp. While the Romans seized many maidens indiscriminately, others specifically chose virgins for their beauty, in contravention of Romulus' directive. It appears that some of the more affluent Romans requested that their subordinates capture particular women who were selected for their good looks.[17]

In one such purported case, a band of men had seized and were transporting an unwilling young lady to the man for whom she had been captured, but a group of other Romans confronted them along the way. Struck by the young lady's beauty, they demanded that her handlers surrender the virgin to them. Those in possession of the maiden refused because she had been reserved for a well-known and widely admired man named Talassius. Upon learning this, the men trying to steal her away immediately halted their attempts and erupted in a chorus of supportive shouts and applause because of Talassius' high-esteem. Some of them even escorted the young lady and her handlers to Talassius' home as they cheerfully shouted his name along the way. This may have been the origin of the later Roman custom of shouting 'Talassius!' during wedding ceremonies, but the source of this nuptial practice is disputed. The Carthaginian Sextius Sulla, on the other hand, suggested that 'Talassius' was the code word yelled by the Romans who had abducted a woman. Thus, this too could have been the genesis of the eventual Roman matrimonial tradition of exclaiming 'Talassius!'.

Interestingly, other nuptial practices supposedly sprouted from these abductions. Later Roman weddings consisted of the groom ritually pulling his reluctant bride from her mother's arms and carrying his wife over the threshold. This supposedly harkened back to the forceful abduction of the Sabines and Latins. Later Roman women also parted their hair with a spearhead before their weddings, which Plutarch claimed was done in remembrance of the first Roman weddings' eventual connection to war.[18]

Regardless of the customs' origins, the virgins' bewildered family members watched in terror as the Romans abducted their daughters one by one during what appears to have been a lightning-quick operation. It caught the parents off-guard and left them without any immediate recourse, but few, if any of them, endured physical harm. It even appears that while the young armed males were kidnapping the Sabine and Latin women, the Romans encouraged the maidens' families to leave Rome. The Romans probably even provided a convenient, unguarded escape route so that these visitors could flee without any impediment or fear of injury.

In all likelihood, many of the fathers and mothers slunk away from the commotion fairly quickly once they realized that retreat was their best option. They weren't prepared to fight, and didn't have the necessary arms to defend themselves. They probably felt that their only chance of recapturing the maidens was to withdraw, mobilize and devise a coordinated strategy to challenge the Romans. Yet this didn't prevent them from hurling insults at the Romans or denouncing them for their treachery as they quit the city. It's probable that several other families remained behind a little longer than the rest to protest against the events and demand that Romulus redress the Romans' misdeeds. When their petitions were completely ignored, they surely resorted to suppliantly begging, but Romulus' mind was resolutely set. He intended on permitting his subjects to permanently keep the maidens as their wives, and in due time, the remaining Sabine and Latin stragglers despondently left Rome.[19]

Upon exiting the city, Romulus presumably secured Rome from any same-day reprisals. Afterwards, the Romans' attentions closely focused on the frightened young maidens. While the ancient writers didn't clearly disclose the ladies' immediate fates, some of them were unquestionably maltreated. It seems quite possible that following their seizure, an untold number of kidnappers sexually violated many of the innocent virgins against Romulus' orders. Some of the captors may have claimed that they had been overtaken by their passion, which was a wholly inadequate excuse. For others, it may have been little more than a dominant act of aggression meant, in part, to subdue the young women. It may also have served as an indirect way of exacting revenge against the Sabine and Latin parents who had rejected the Romans' earlier invitation to intermarry as well. An undisclosed number of rapes likely transpired as the recently abducted maidens experienced pure horror, which left more than a grievous stain on Rome's early history.[20]

The following day, Romulus chose to speak with the apprehensive women about a few matters. He wanted to explain the situation and reassure them that their futures would be bright and that they would enjoy many rights and privileges. This must have been necessary, given that the young ladies were beyond depressed by their current state and paralyzed by fear. Their new keepers may have already viciously raped many of them, while other virgins expected the same fate or maybe even death. Nearly all of them lamented their future. For all they knew, they were entering a new phase of their life, which might be no different than slavery punctuated by sexual exploitation. The thought of possibly never seeing or even speaking with their beloved family members again additionally distressed the virgins. Considering that many of the abductors were criminal fugitives, any loathsome fate seemed possible. The captured women were rightfully concerned, but Romulus sought to allay their fears.

To achieve this goal, Romulus addressed the kidnapped virgins, and his message to them was clear. The maidens' current predicament was their parents' fault because they had obstinately denied the Romans the privilege of marrying them. Romulus asserted that if the surrounding kingdoms had approved a fair treaty, then this unfortunate turn of events would have been unnecessary. Romulus struggled to defend his actions, but he claimed that there was no reason for the young ladies to be anxious. He declared that they would enter into lawful and respectable marriages with his subjects, and they would live honourable lives. Their children would be free Roman citizens, capable of reaching the heights of Roman society. Moreover, the maidens would essentially enjoy the same individual rights of any free Roman woman, which admittedly was considerably less than that of a Roman male.[21]

Romulus and his lieutenants also tallied the previous day's spoils in order to determine whether they had acquired an adequate number of females. The ancient estimates varied greatly. They ranged from as few as 30 to as many as 683, and most, if not all of the virgins, were apparently of either Sabine or Latin origin. While most of the ancient writers referred to the abducted women as Sabines, it seems obvious that many of them were from cities that housed many Latins.[22] It's not entirely clear which communities were hit the hardest by the kidnappings. Strabo implied that the Sabines suffered the bulk of the abductions, but Livy suggested that Caenina, Antemnae and Crustumerium, which certainly were comprised of many Latins, were impacted to a higher degree.[23]

Aside from the contradictory sources, if Romulus' true goal was to provide a new generation of Romans, then as little as thirty maidens would have been almost useless. As such, the higher estimates might be nearer to the truth. However, if Romulus ordered the abduction simply to spark a war to expand his own domain, as at least one ancient author suggested, then the lower figure may have done the trick. Notwithstanding the numerical discrepancies, after Romulus had taken an inventory of the new female population, he approved as many as 683 Roman bachelors to marry the virgins.[24]

Romulus' pitch to the maidens to try Roman living likely wasn't well received at first. They were surely sceptical of the kidnappers' justifications and intentions. Even if the captives believed Romulus, they couldn't have been excited about marrying lowly fugitives, but Romulus pleaded with the women to consider the merits of marrying into Roman society. He promised that they would be treated fairly, and they had no reason to despair. Many of them must have passionately disagreed, but as time progressed, they learned that Romulus was sincere. He bore no intention to harm them any further. Indeed, he wished to grant them full rights as Roman women. While this realization gradually eased their apprehensions, their fiancés' mostly good behaviour from this point forward assuaged their anxieties even more.[25]

Following Romulus' message to the women, the Roman kidnappers tried to excuse their crimes against the maidens, claiming that they were fuelled by unrestrained desire. Their justification was probably met with immediate resentment, despite Livy alluding to the contrary. The Roman men had acted like barbarians and stolen the virgins, but eventually, the captors began to treat the women with legitimate respect. The young Roman men became affectionate and loving, which the maidens sincerely appreciated and even began to enjoy.[26]

At some undisclosed time, it seems that the women officially wed their abductors. Some of them may have forgiven the Romans and willfully married their grooms, but it's certainly plausible that many were forced into wedlock against their will. Regardless of the compulsory weddings, as many as 683 marriages of some form took place. According to Dionysius of Halicarnassus, Romulus decreed that the ceremonies ought to be performed in accordance with the traditions of the women's homelands. Regrettably, the details of this era's weddings aren't well recorded.[27]

If the ceremonies were anything like the later Roman ones, then the weddings included a sacrifice to the gods to ensure that the appropriate deities approved of the union. There was likely an exchange of vows and a hearty feast with the families involved, *sans* the bride's relatives of course. The less fortunate Romans may have opted for simpler, more casual ceremonies. Others might have refrained altogether from participating in a formal wedding and simply considered themselves married, but a religious man such as Romulus would have likely frowned upon the latter course of action. Nevertheless, while the unions had begun in widespread terror, the marriages largely evolved into heartfelt, romantic partnerships.[28]

In the days and weeks following the mass kidnapping, there were undoubtedly a multitude of matrimonial ceremonies among the patricians and plebeians. Yet Romulus' subjects weren't the only Romans getting married. According to an account that Plutarch recorded, Romulus was also wed at some point. A noblewoman, perhaps of Sabine origin, by the name of Hersilia ended up in his custody, but unfortunately, there's little record of Hersilia or her marriage with Romulus. Differing accounts suggest Hersilia might have actually been a married woman at the time of the abductions. She may have been kidnapped by accident or remained in Rome on her own accord because her daughter had been abducted. Further muddling the matter, Plutarch asserted that she may have married a Roman other than Romulus, but it is possible that Romulus wed her after her first or second marriage.

It's not apparent how Romulus personally gained possession of Hersilia, but it doesn't appear that he physically participated in the kidnappings. He had designed the illicit scheme and gave the order for it to commence, but there is no mention of him madly dashing into the foreign audience and absconding with any of the young women. Instead, Hersilia may have caught his eye prior to the abductions, or following the Sabine and Latin families' withdrawal from Rome, he might have handpicked one of the noblest and most beautiful women from a line-up of those captured. No matter how Hersilia wound up in Romulus' keep, the two purportedly married one another. Their wedding must have been a much more elaborate ceremony than the other Romans enjoyed, given that Romulus was Rome's king.[29]

A multitude of virgins, possibly including Hersilia, meekly accepted their fate, married into the Roman families and slowly began to live the lives of Roman women. Their husbands' sincere affections and relatively good treatment thenceforth mostly allayed the wives' apprehensions. Their parents, however, were still in despair and furious, but they weren't entirely sure how to respond to their daughters' abductions. They probably worried that if they waged war against the Romans, then they would be placing their daughters in an even riskier situation. They were in Roman custody, and the Sabines and other affected peoples unquestionably felt that if they attacked Romulus' subjects, then he might harm the captive women. So, they hoped that they could still retrieve their children through peaceful, diplomatic means.[30]

At some point, envoys from the impacted cities arrived at Rome's gates to confer with Romulus and/or his Senate. The emissaries had cause to sharply scold Romulus and demand harsh punitive sanctions against him. Rather than pursuing this route, it seems that they humbly delivered their requests, which were moderate given the circumstances. They called for the maidens' return and understandably asked Romulus to publicly acknowledge his wrongdoing and apologize. To show their goodwill, they offered to form alliances with Rome once Romulus met these two conditions. Unsurprisingly, the right to intermarry must have been conspicuously absent from the proposed friendly treaty.

Their suggested terms didn't sway Romulus, and since he was in possession of many Sabine and Latin women, he held the upper hand in the negotiations. So, he submitted a counter-offer to the ambassadors, which permitted the Romans to retain the maidens and marry into the foreign families. The emissaries couldn't accept Romulus' proposal following his lawless actions, and they predictably dismissed it. Even so, it seems that their original offer was still on the table if Romulus would reconsider. Despite being guilty of an egregious transgression and the Sabines' and Latins' reasonable terms, Romulus soundly rejected their proposal and the envoys returned home empty-handed.[31]

When they arrived without satisfaction, their countrymen were painfully disappointed. The affected cities' residents had vainly hoped that they could reach a diplomatic solution with Rome, but it was for naught. As a result, the towns' inhabitants, especially the abducted girls' fathers and mothers, were filled with despondency and anger. They even dressed the part of grief-stricken parents and donned garb that represented their dark feelings. They likely wore tattered clothing, while their hair was unkempt, and the fathers remained unshaven so that it invited even further sympathy. Every day that they sulked in public and appeared dishevelled and beggarly reminded their countrymen of their great suffering and Romulus' shocking crime. With these constant spectacles, it was impossible for their fellow citizens to ignore the Romans' misdeeds. In fact, it seems that the parents' decision to wear mourning garb was spurred partly by a desire to incite their countrymen into action against Rome.

Indeed, the maidens' fathers loudly lamented their daughters' pitiable situation and passionately pleaded for the wrongs to be rectified. Many travelled beyond their home towns to recount Romulus' ignominy and demand justice.[32] It appears that the cities of Caenina, Antemnae and Crustumerium had been heavily affected by the abduction. Thus, they needed little prodding in order to escalate the situation, which threatened to evolve into full-blown war with Rome. Yet some of these people had long observed Rome's rise with dread and sought an excuse to prune its growth anway. Romulus' provocation gave them the pretext that they needed to declare war, but the trio of cities preferred to enlist the support of the powerful Sabine nation before attacking Rome. They felt that there were potentially sympathetic Sabine leaders whom they could cajole into aiding them, which would only increase their odds of defeating Romulus.[33]

One such ruler was the aging Titus Tatius, king of the nearby city of Cures.[34] Tatius exerted considerable influence, ruled over the pre-eminent Sabine city and could muster a powerful army. If Tatius could be coaxed into joining forces with the people of Caenina, Antemnae and Crustumerium, then they probably thought they could forever extinguish the Roman menace, and do so with ease. Unfortunately for Romulus, when the envoys reached Tatius and described the Romans' opprobrium to him, the Sabine monarch revealed that he was appalled and felt a sense of duty to defend his fellow Sabines and other allies. This should have been expected, considering that the Romans may have likewise abducted some maidens from his city.

Tatius might have had ulterior motives for involving himself in the situation as well. He may have have viewed the young Roman kingdom as a growing threat that he preferred to eliminate before it was too late, and the maidens' seizure could provide the pretext for war. Regardless of his decision's impetus, many Sabines resolved to join with the other cities and confront Rome. This was both a rescue mission as well as a punitive expedition, and Tatius was charged with leading the Sabine war effort. Thereupon, Caenina, Antemnae and Crustumerium, along with Tatius' Sabines, seemed poised to battle Rome.[35]

Romulus must have foreseen war as a probable outcome long before the maidens' abduction. Consequently, it is conceivable that he had already laid much of the groundwork for a hazardous conflict with his neighbours. He was a forward-thinking individual who undoubtedly weighed the risks and rewards of his actions and believed that chancing an armed conflict in order to gain the virgins was a necessary gamble. However, he might not have believed that Tatius would join the fray, or if Romulus did anticipate this possibility, then he hoped that he possessed the military might and tactical cunning to defeat his united enemies.

Whatever the case, it's not entirely evident when Romulus knew that Tatius was preparing for war, but he ultimately learned of it. As a result, Romulus may have worried about his settlement's future, given that the combined strength of his enemies presented a daunting obstacle. He had gained upwards of 683 maidens through trickery, but he was soon facing a formidable force bent on Rome's destruction. Once Romulus knew that the Sabines had either agreed to war with Rome or were being courted for that purpose, he wisely forwarded deputations to the Sabines in an attempt to dissuade or at least delay them from attacking Rome. It's not clear what their message to the Sabines was, but it worked well enough to help slow their entrance into the war.[36]

While Romulus' adversaries mobilized their forces and prepared to march on Rome, the Romans were dealing with a domestic issue. Rome's newlyweds had either failed to become pregnant or there was a rash of miscarriages among them. This troubled Romulus, who clearly hoped that the marriages would result in a new crop of Romans. Romulus complained, 'What boots [sic] it me to have ravished the Sabine women, if the wrong I did has brought me not strength but only war? Better it were our sons had never wed.' This also distressed the recently married couples, and many of them decided to visit a sacred copse at the foot of the Esquiline Hill and pray to the gods for their aid. While there, according to legend, the goddess Juno nebulously responded to their cries, 'Let the sacred he-goat go in to Italian matrons.'

The goddess' vague instruction confused the Romans, and in order to translate Juno's orders, Romulus consulted an Etruscan augur who had emigrated to Rome. Upon considering the goddess' reply, the seer believed that he understood what was required. He subsequently killed a male goat and cut its skin into strips that were used to flagellate the maidens' backs. This strange ceremony apparently solved the crisis, and Rome soon brimmed with pregnant maidens who later gave birth to healthy children. According to legend, this is one possible reason why later Romans smacked people with goatskin thongs during the Lupercalia festival.[37]

Notwithstanding this strange tale, Romulus had acquired the women and children that he so desperately desired, but it came at a great price. He had robbed many of the surrounding cities of their daughters, and their hometowns appeared willing to unite to defeat Rome. Due to his actions, Rome was quickly entangled in a major conflict that threatened to jeopardize everything that the Romans had laboured to achieve.

VII

Caenina

'Acron, king of the Caeninenses, a man of courageous spirit
and skilled in war, had been suspicious of the daring deeds of
Romulus from the beginning, and now that this violence had
been done the women, thinking [Romulus] a menace to all
peoples, and intolerable unless chastised, at once rose up in
arms, and with a great force advanced against him.'

– Plutarch

As Rome's neighbouring communities united and prepared for
war, they undoubtedly felt confident that they would be able to
defeat the unruly Romans without much trouble. After all, Rome
was a single city, which had only recently been founded. Meanwhile,
the anti-Roman coalition boasted several established settlements and
perhaps even included a broader network of Sabine towns. Given this,
if the allied partners coordinated with one another, then they could
reasonably expect to defeat Romulus and erase Rome from ancient
maps, but Romulus wasn't wholly ignorant of their designs.

Romulus had already learned that King Tatius' Sabines and other
affected communities were seriously beating the drum of war, and as a
result, the Roman monarch probably kept close tabs on them. He likely
received reports from his spies and scouts about his enemies' movements.
He presumably also collected intelligence from the envoys whom he
had dispatched to confer with the Sabines.

Even so, the size of the coalition tasked with slaying Romulus surely
dismayed him, but he was known for his bravery and boldness. As such,
he didn't intend on meekly surrendering, despite his enemies' perceived
advantages. Instead, he probably believed that if he acted carefully

and the gods favoured him, then he stood a good chance of emerging from the looming conflict as the victor. Therefore, he redoubled his efforts to ready his young city for war against many daunting foes.

There must have been widespread exuberance on the side of the impacted cities upon learning that King Tatius and his Sabines would aid them in their efforts to destroy Rome. Yet that excitement gradually waned as the Sabines repeatedly postponed the war. After agreeing to support the other towns, Tatius was painfully slow to act, thanks in part to Romulus' skilled envoys who used diplomatic channels to delay the Sabines' entrance into the conflict. Tatius' inaction rankled his allies and especially irked the people of Caenina. Romulus had wronged them, and Caenina's king, Acron, was particularly wary of Rome's growing power. As a result, the Caeninenses impatiently longed for war with Rome.[1]

Tatius' sluggish response may have stemmed from a confluence of factors beyond simply the Roman ambassadors' tactics. The Sabines needed to discuss the approaching conflict's strategy and preparations at length. Meanwhile, Tatius may have been gradually amassing his forces, which took considerable time. Beyond these matters, his army was sufficiently potent to defeat Romulus' rabble without any help from Caenina, Antemnae or Crustumerium, the overly confident Tatius thought. As a matter of fact, he preferred to wage the war without their aid.[2]

There are a couple of reasons why Tatius might have wished to prosecute the war on his own rather than as a coalition member. He evidently expected Rome to fall with or without assistance from the other cities, given that Rome was a recent and relatively insignificant upstart. Thus, Tatius certainly thought that if Rome's destruction was inevitable and could be accomplished within his sole power, then why should he participate in a grand alliance, share the glory and spoils, and imperil Sabine lives? It appears that he didn't. If he took any risks, then he wanted all of the credit.

These may have been the primary factors that led Tatius to repeatedly delay the conflict, but there was likely more to it than this. He was no fool when it came to waging war, and there may have been other pressing matters and vital considerations that prompted him to postpone the conflict numerous times. He probably wanted to comprehensively gird his subjects, possible allied cities and army for the coming war, which took a significant amount of work. First, he had to continue raising a multitude of troops and train them in tactics and strategy, which, if he was thorough, couldn't have happened quickly.

Second, he may have felt that he should secure Cures and any other cities under his watch before launching a foray into Roman country. He couldn't entirely anticipate Romulus' strategy or how he would potentially respond to an act of aggression. So, Tatius wanted to ensure that his own defences could thwart a Roman assault if Romulus took the offensive. Before they could march on Rome, the Sabines also had to be fortified against possible strikes from third parties, and Tatius needed to acquire a reserve of foodstuffs to keep his soldiers' stomachs full. Without adequate nourishment, his troops would become enfeebled and might succumb to illness, and if they were perpetually hungry, then they could turn on their king, leading to a bloody coup. Therefore, he likely strove to acquire and store excess provisions.[3]

As a prudent king, Tatius needed to address these concerns, and if he did, then they must have taken time. This left the impatient people of Caenina, Antemnae, and Crustumerium increasingly frustrated. However, there's the possibility that Tatius figured if he postponed the war indefinitely, then Caenina, Antemnae, and Crustumerium would battle Rome on their own. This would leave one or both factions weakened, which would ultimately increase his own influence in the region.

Regardless of Tatius' possible reasoning, Caenina, Antemnae and Crustumerium demanded action sooner rather than later, but they couldn't force Tatius and his powerful Sabines to act. The Caeninenses, Antemnates and Crustumerians were seething with anger toward Rome and eventually concluded that Tatius might never give the order to attack the Romans. Thus, they pondered launching a campaign without the Sabines' help. What had begun as a promising coalition of partners was slowly devolving into a fractured force, which greatly improved Romulus' odds of surviving the war.

Tatius' numerous delays especially disgusted King Acron of the Caeninenses. Acron had watched in dread as Rome had grown. He worried that unless he acted swiftly, Rome could soon eclipse all of the other nearby communities and become the region's dominant city. This may have been Acron's principal motivating factor for desiring an armed conflict with Rome. Still, the abduction of many female Caeninenses demanded action and provided him with the justification to declare war on Rome.[4]

Interestingly, Acron shared some of the same traits that made Romulus a great leader. Caenina's king was daring and clearly knew how to inspire his subjects, but he acted impulsively. His planning was less thorough than Romulus', and he was short-sighted compared to the Roman king. Acron had an abundant excess of courage but apparently insufficient sagacity, or at least patience, which was a dangerous combination during times of war.[5]

Regardless of Acron's shortcomings, he was bent on warring with Rome. While the three cities had decided to attack Rome without Tatius, even this ill-conceived plan fell apart very quickly as discord apparently grew among the discontented towns. It seems that the Caeninenses were far more restive than the Antemnates and Crustumerians, whose perceived lack of enthusiasm angered the Caeninenses. Their allies apparently weren't too keen on immediately rushing headlong into battle without first making certain preparations. The Antemnates and Crustumerians were steadfastly determined to attack Rome, but the Caeninenses evidently deemed their delays unacceptable. Consequently, Acron astoundingly opted to march against Rome without the Antemnates' or Crustumerians' help. This was a serious mistake. Even though he had raised a large army, hastening into battle without one's allies was a critical error. The three-to-one combat rule that states that armies ought to be at least three times as large as their enemy in order to likely guarantee victory was just as applicable in Romulus' era as it has been in more modern times. Acron evidently ignored this tenet.[6]

Despite these perplexing gaffes, Acron brazenly advanced into Roman territory and, upon arriving, began building a defensive camp. It was meant to protect his troops during the night and provide them a safe haven in the unlikely event that the Romans obtained the advantage. During or immediately following the fortification's construction, Caenina's monarch unleashed pillaging parties intent on laying waste to the Roman countryside. They subsequently began destroying and seizing crops, livestock and other valuables. They probably also razed more than a few farmhouses.

Acron must have believed that this would serve several purposes. He wanted to prevent Rome's agricultural production from supporting Romulus' war effort, and Acron hoped that the Romans huddling behind the city's walls would feel the sharp pang of hunger if the war became a protracted affair. Acron apparently assumed that this would put the Romans at a disadvantage. By seizing their agricultural output, Acron could potentially achieve these goals. He surely also preferred to use Rome's foodstuffs to support his own soldiers. Beyond this, Acron may have permitted his troops to plunder the countryside because it generally placated soldiers and kept their morale high.

Another reason that Acron may have decided to devastate the Roman countryside was to force Romulus to fight the Caeninenses, preferably under unfavourable circumstances. Acron understood that besieging Rome could be timely, costly and would risk many lives. However, if he could lure Romulus and his troops outside the safety of their walls to defend their farms, then maybe he stood a better chance of quickly defeating them.

King Acron's rationale was sound to some extent, but he badly bungled it in application. First, he either lost the element of surprise or never even obtained it. Romulus became fully aware of Acron's march into his kingdom, perhaps because Romulus' network of spies kept him informed of Acron's movements. Second, upon announcing his orders to advance into Roman territory and plunder the region, many of Acron's men converged on the region like locusts and spread across vast swathes of land. Yet they were dispersed so thinly that they were mostly defenceless against organized counterattacks. Romulus and his scouts observed the vulnerable Caeninenses and immediately recognized their blunders. Seeing that they were exposed, Romulus quietly and swiftly marched his legionaries out and unexpectedly fell upon the pillagers. Romulus' sudden appearance and show of force shocked Caenina's raiders. It's possible that the Caeninenses scrambled to defend themselves against the Romans. Nevertheless, they were no match for Romulus' well-formulated attack, and they fled from the Romans after suffering an unknown number of casualties.[7]

The Caeninenses must have hoped to eventually find sanctuary in their newly constructed camp, but Acron made another grievous error. Either he dispatched too many troops to lay waste to the countryside, while ordering an insufficient number to defend the encampment, or the fortifications were simply deficient. Whatever the case, Romulus learned of the cantonment's location and marched his determined legionaries with speed toward it, and they immediately attacked the camp with ferocity. The Caeninenses struggled in vain to defend the fort, but it was done in vain. Due to Acron's inadequate preparations and the force of Romulus' surprise offensive, the camp fell to the Romans with relative ease.[8]

Following the attack on the Caeninenses and the bivouac's capture, there may have been another, more substantive battle. Romulus had successfully taken the initiative and was threatening to halt Acron's campaign before it started in earnest. To reverse his misfortunes, Caenina's king hastily regrouped his troops in an effort to stave off a humiliating defeat, but the exact manoeuvrings of each army unfortunately aren't clear at this point. Nevertheless, it appears that as Acron was trying to rally his troops and save them from annihilation, the Romans rapidly advanced toward the newly assembled enemy army. The Romans intended on attacking the Caeninenses, but this encounter proved far different from the surprise, lightning assaults that the Caeninenses had previously experienced. This ultimately became Romulus' first known experience in a typical set-piece battle.[9]

It's not evident what formation the Romans used while under Romulus' tutelage. The later Roman legions were generally arranged with the infantry comprising the centre, while the cavalry manned the flanks. The foot soldiers didn't fight in one large grouping. They were divided into smaller tactical units, with gaps in between each group. This permitted the later Roman armies great flexibility, which served them well, but Romulus couldn't have relied on this method of warfare because Livy stated that the Romans didn't adopt it until many years later. Rather, it seems more plausible that Romulus' legionaries lined up in the phalanx, which was a giant mass of infantry tightly packed together, or perhaps some other ancient formation.[10]

Regardless of their arrangement, as the armies lumbered into position, Romulus and Acron diligently made final alterations to their plans and ordered their soldiers into battle array. As the troops anxiously eyed each other, a series of messengers likely exchanged missives between the opposing generals. Romulus and Acron may have even conferred in person, but it quickly became clear that there would be no peace agreement and a battle was inevitable. Interestingly though, the kings challenged one another to engage in single combat before the troops in no man's land, and they accepted and settled on their bout's terms. Before proceeding to the battlefield, Romulus broke away to pledge an oath to the chief god, Jupiter. Romulus vowed that if Jupiter enabled him to slay Acron, he would personally take the fallen king's armour back to Rome where he would ritually donate it to the god. Upon making this pledge, Romulus returned his attention to Acron who was preparing to fight him.[11]

As the two armies watched in great anticipation, their kings proceeded beyond their troops' front lines to meet each other. They were presumably adorned in expensive and ornate armour fit for kings and were armed with gilded swords, shields and perhaps even spears. When they were ready for the contest, they advanced to assail one another in single combat, and the encounter began. There is no record of the actual fight, only its conclusion, but it's safe to assume that it was a ferocious affair. The two probably charged with their swords brandished as they took the offensive. Each would have lunged forward to strike their opponent, while the other parried the blows. The sparring cycle may have occurred an unknown number of times, but Romulus somehow gained the advantage and slew Acron in full view of both armies.

As Romulus mercilessly dealt the deathblow to Acron, a chorus of shouts from the Romans surely interrupted the nervous silence. There was certainly also a deafening clamor as they excitedly beat their spears and swords upon their shields. Meanwhile, Caenina's army watched in quiet horror as their king laid lifeless in a pool of his own blood, but Romulus added insult to injury. The Roman king contemptuously removed his fallen foe's battle garb so that he could ceremonially dedicate it to Jupiter, which offended the already dejected Caeninenses.[12]

Unfortunately for the Caeninenses, this wasn't the end of the day's carnage. Once Romulus had cut down and ingloriously stripped Acron of his armour, the Roman king refocused his energy on vanquishing the remaining Caeninenses. However, at this juncture, they were really in no shape to challenge the Romans. They had been harried while plundering the Roman kingdom, lost their camp – which presumably included their food, supplies and many weapons – and had watched their king die by Romulus' hand. While the loss of their monarch demoralized the Caeninenses, it also left them without a commander. One of Acron's lieutenants or heirs presumably assumed the role of the Caeninenses' senior general, but whoever took control was, like Acron, no match for Rome's king.

After slaying Acron, Romulus readied his troops for battle and sounded the charge against Caenina's dispirited army. No details of the battle are extant, but the result was an overwhelming Roman victory. The fate of Caenina's army isn't exactly clear either. It appears that they were either mostly annihilated or suffered great casualties, while many of the survivors were captured or retreated to safety. One way or another, Romulus had vanquished the Caeninenses' army, and the road to Caenina lay open to the Romans.

Romulus' battlefield success was so complete that no soldiers from Caenina's army were able to adequately block the Romans from advancing on their homeland. Moreover, none of the Caeninenses were able to flee in time to warn their countrymen of the devastating defeat. Seeing the path to Caenina unimpeded and unguarded, Romulus set out to sack the exposed city. When the Romans neared the town, they were pleasantly surprised by what they observed.[13]

Despite the conflict, Caenina astonishingly appeared to be at peace. Caenina's townsfolk were mostly, if not exclusively, ignorant of their monarch's and army's grim fates. There weren't sufficient guards manning the walls, and the city's primary gate wasn't even barred. Romulus must have gleefully observed Caenina's vulnerable state as he gave the order to breach the town. It only took one attempt for the Romans to force their way inside Caenina, where its inhabitants mustered little resistance, and within a relatively short span of time, the Romans easily gained mastery of Caenina.[14]

As the Romans secured the city and set up guard posts, Caenina's citizens probably lamented the gruesome punishments that they expected to face. In the ancient world, it was common for victorious armies to massacre and/or enslave newly conquered peoples. Contrary to such common behaviour, Romulus revealed that he was more merciful than many other ancient leaders. He surprisingly announced that he intended to inflict no further physical harm against the Caeninenses who surrendered. Even though Romulus exhibited his aversion to massacring them, he still punished the Caeninenses and took preventative measures to ensure their future compliance.

Under his proposed peace terms, which may have still needed the Senate's approval, Romulus ordered the Caeninenses to relinquish their weapons and mandated that many of the remaining adult Caeninenses would permanently relocate to Rome. It seems that he suggested that once in his kingdom, they would enjoy the same rights and liberties as any other Roman citizen, but their forced migration would serve several strategic purposes. Romulus surely understood that transferring a host of Caeninenses to Rome would weaken Caenina, given that it would split their population. He might have also done it to encourage intermarriage between the Romans and Caeninenses, which, in time, could foment warm relations and harmony. In the short term, though, it was undoubtedly meant to act as an insurance policy to deter Caenina from rising again. If they did, then they could expect the Romans to kill the Caeninenses in their custody, but Romulus demanded more hostages than just these. He even required that the Caeninenses surrender an untold number of children as captives to the Romans, who would care for them from Rome. This provided the Romans with a secondary layer of protection, which would hopefully dissuade the Caeninenses from ever challenging Rome again.[15]

Beyond this, Romulus proclaimed that large portions of Caenina would be destroyed. Rather than directing his legionaries to raze parts of the city, Romulus forced Caenina's inhabitants to do it themselves, which must have been humiliating. They obediently complied but probably removed all valuables and prized possessions from their homes before toppling them.[16]

It's highly likely that after the Caeninenses hurriedly gathered their treasures together, the Romans decided to pilfer through the priceless troves and confiscate whatever caught their eye. Amassing the spoils of war was always a favourite pastime of soldiers, and Romulus became known for generously sharing plunder with his troops. Yet he commendably didn't commandeer any of the valuables for himself. Nevertheless, by the end of the ordeal, there were conspicuous uninhabited spaces within the town that were denude of wealth, thanks to the legionaries.[17]

With the Caeninenses neutralized as a credible threat to Rome, Romulus and his people had reason to celebrate but little time to do so. Potential enemies still surrounded Rome and wished to do the Romans harm. While Romulus may have preferred to return home, he couldn't do so just yet. Shortly after he slayed Acron and sacked Caenina, another threat emerged, which demanded the king's attention and his army's talents.

VIII

Antemnae and Crustumerium

'Whilst the Romans were thus occupied, the army of the
Antemnates seized the opportunity of their territory being
unoccupied and made a raid into it.'

– Livy

The Roman legionaries were excitedly revelling in their victory
over the Caeninenses, but trouble wasn't far off. The nearby
Antemnates noticed that the Romans were distracted and busy
imposing their will on the Caeninenses. With Romulus and his men
preoccupied, the Antemnates intended to strike Rome and take advantage
of the Romans' supposed unpreparedness. However, this seems to have
been the only well-thought-out element of the Antemnates' strategy,
which mostly appeared no different than the Caeninenses' approach.
With Romulus' legionaries ostensibly distracted, the King of Antemnae
readied his soldiers and advanced into enemy territory. He then divided
his troops into small parties and ordered them to destroy the Romans'
crops, just as the Caeninenses had previously done and regretted.

The Antemnates had seized the element of surprise, but they swiftly
spoiled it by not acting deliberately. Rather than ambushing the Roman
army or rushing directly into the heart of Rome and laying siege to the
city, they occupied themselves with plundering and ravaging the Roman
countryside. This quickly alerted Romulus to their unwelcome presence
within his domain, and he immediately rounded up his legionaries,
cobbled together a strategy and mobilized to meet his latest enemy.
Remarkably, the Antemnates didn't bother to appropriately prevent
Romulus' army from marching toward them unscathed. Making matters
worse for the Antemnates, they committed the same blunder as the

Caeninenses. They thinly spread their army across Roman territory and left themselves defenceless against organized attacks.[1]

Sometime after the Antemnates' initial foray, Romulus and his army stormed out toward them, intent on quashing them in the same manner that they had done with the Caeninenses. When the Romans neared their enemy, Romulus and his deputies reconnoitred the field and finalized their plan of attack, but it didn't need to be overly complex. The Antemnates were in small raiding parties and evidently weren't expecting a large-scale attack at this time. Romulus could essentially catch them unawares and overwhelm them with his superior numbers and organization. Upon recognizing this, his legionaries flooded into the countryside to meet their foes who, despite their best efforts, couldn't counter them. Romulus' troops indiscriminately cut down a multitude of Antemnae's soldiers and captured a host of others, while the rest were put to flight. It was yet another feeble attempt to overcome Romulus, which he easily foiled.

After his latest dominant victory, Romulus resolved to adopt the same strategy that he had employed with the Caeninenses. He marched his troops straightaway for Antemnae, which lay a few miles due north of Rome, with designs to sack the town and teach its citizens that they ought not to cross King Romulus. Following the Antemnates' crushing defeat, their town was an easy target for the Romans, who arrived in short order, stormed Antemnae, burst through its fortifications and captured the city with little notable resistance. Once in control of Antemnae, Romulus and his men likely acted as they had toward the Caeninenses. The Romans must have plundered the city and toppled large portions of the town. The legionaries probably also disarmed its inhabitants and the Antemnates surrendered hostages to the Romans, who transported many of them to Rome.[2]

Following this success, Romulus believed that he could return home, but he felt a great sense of duty to fulfill his promise to offer Acron's armour to Jupiter. Indeed, Romulus conceived grandiose plans for this dedication and arranged a magnificent spectacle for his people to enjoy. For these purposes, he ordered his subordinates to cut down a sacred oak tree that grew in his legion's camp. Upon doing so, craftsmen refashioned the trunk so that Acron's armour could be permanently affixed to it.

Romulus wanted it to serve as a monument assigned to Jupiter, as well as a celebratory memento of the war. As artisans finished the trophy, Romulus gathered together the war's spoils and prepared his troops for a jubilant parade through Rome.

When everything was organized, the triumphant cavalcade marched toward Rome and dramatically entered the city's gates. Rome's celebrated hero and monarch, Romulus, wore a laurel wreath as a crown and donned a royal purple robe, while he held his trophy, the oak tree adorned with Acron's panoply, over his right shoulder for everyone to see. As he dignifiedly strode through Rome, his fawning subjects loudly cheered for him, and they must have simultaneously crowded closer to capture a glimpse of the fallen king's armour. Meanwhile, Romulus absorbed the Romans' admiration as he leisurely passed by the elated attendees.[3]

Also within the triumph were the monarch's victorious troops. They proudly marched in their respective companies and loudly sang songs praising the gods as well as their triumphant general. The spectators watched as the legionaries marched down the city's main thoroughfare, and the onlookers congratulated them. Likely within the parade were livestock that pulled carts laden with the vanquished enemy's booty and weapons. The wagons slowly rolled past the adoring onlookers, who were thoroughly impressed by the grand spectacle. The procession probably culminated with many solemn sacrifices to the gods, especially to Jupiter, to thank them for their favour.[4]

Afterwards, the Romans surely imbibed prodigious quantities of wine and participated in a gluttonous feast. According to Dionysius of Halicarnassus and Plutarch, this was supposedly the origin of Rome's famous triumphs, but Romulus' procession likely differed from the later Roman triumphs, which followed a scripted order. They eventually became celebratory parades filled with gaudy and costly pageantry, meant to express the Romans' gratitude to the gods for a great military success and celebrate the victorious general's accomplishments.[5] However, Livy disagreed and suggested that Rome's first triumph didn't originate with Romulus but with one of Rome's later kings, Tarquinius Priscus.[6]

Regardless of when the first triumph officially occurred, Romulus resolved to fulfill his pledge to dedicate Acron's armour to Jupiter.

To this end, he planned to erect Rome's first temple, where the regal armour would be housed. Romulus intended on dedicating the building specifically to Jupiter Feretrius, because *ferire* meant to smite, which is what Romulus had done to Acron, thanks to Jupiter. Thus, Romulus climbed to the Capitoline Hill's summit and outlined where the temple of Jupiter Feretrius would be built. Then Romulus' engineers began its construction, but it was a humble shrine by later Roman standards. Its longest side was no more than 15ft in length, and it was of simple construction, presumably built of wood and thatch.

When the labourers erected it, Romulus doubtlessly conducted several sacrifices, publicly dedicated the temple to Jupiter Feretrius and ceremonially deposited the trophy of Acron's defeat within the shrine. During the consecration, Romulus declared:

> Jupiter Feretrius! these arms taken from a king, I, Romulus a king and conqueror, bring to thee, and on this domain, whose bounds I have in will and purpose traced, I dedicate a temple to receive the '*spolia opima*' [rich spoils, i.e. Acron's armour taken from his body by Romulus] which posterity following my example shall bear hither, taken from the kings and generals of our foes slain in battle.[7]

As later Roman generations learned, Romulus' slaying of Acron was a notable achievement. In fact, throughout the Roman kingdom and Republic's history, Romulus was one of only three Roman commanders to personally slay their enemy's supreme leader in battle and place *spolia opima* in the temple. The other occasions purportedly occurred in the fifth century BC, when the Roman general Aulus Cornelius Cossus slew Veii's king, known as Lars Tolumnius, and again in 222 BC, when the Roman consul Marcus Claudius Marcellus killed the Gallic king Britomartus.[8] Interestingly, in 44 BC, sycophants authorized Julius Caesar to also enjoy the great honour of depositing the *spolia opima* even though he didn't actually meet the requisite qualifications.[9]

Following Romulus' spectacular celebratory affair, his mind turned toward more practical matters. He had defeated two peoples and sacked their cities, and he wanted to present his peace terms to the Senate to gain the body's approval. Before he was able to convene the Senate, Hersilia, who may have been his wife at this point, greeted him and asked for a moment of his time. She was apparently unaware of Romulus' plans to treat the newly conquered peoples leniently because she was worried about how Romulus might punish them. Other abducted maidens were likewise concerned, and they earnestly begged Hersilia to intervene with Romulus on their relatives' behalf. They hoped that Hersilia could persuade Romulus to grant the conquered people mercy, even though it appears that the Roman king had already decided to treat them with moderation. So, Hersilia boldly approached her husband and presented a well-reasoned argument for exhibiting clemency toward the Caeninenses and the Antemnates.

She stated that Rome would be much more powerful if he excused the defeated peoples' actions and permitted them to become Roman citizens. This would increase Rome's population, expand its economic capacity and boost its military strength. She might have even acknowledged that if he pardoned them, then they might become even more loyal than his current subjects because he would be giving them something that he was justified in taking: their freedom and lives. Moreover, it is plausible that Hersilia hinted that if he pursued this course of action, then he would appear as though he was a magnanimous king. This could aid Rome in its future foreign policy-related dealings, and it would placate many of the abducted females from Caenina and Antemnae.

Romulus paid close attention to his wife's impassioned pleas, and he seemed to agree with her that these proposals could augment Rome's power. Beyond this, he certainly didn't want to reoffend the newly married women by harming their relatives. Therefore, Romulus probably thanked Hersilia for her reasoned thoughts, claimed that he mostly agreed with them and said that he would take them under advisement. He likely cautioned Hersilia to be patient, given that he intended on discussing the matter with his Senate to acquire their approval. Considering that Romulus was king and the Senate was his advisory board, Hersilia must have felt confident the Caeninenses and Antemnates would receive Rome's mercy.[10]

At some point, the Roman king convened the Senate to discuss the Caeninenses' and Antemnates' fates. When the senators assembled,

Romulus presumably delivered a thorough report of the recent conflicts. The remainder of the conversation largely centred around how to treat the newly conquered Caeninenses and Antemnates. The Romans needed to determine what to do with much of their newly vacated land, which was currently under Roman control. In the Senate meeting, Romulus also presented his proposal in which he advocated for sparing all the Caeninenses' and Antemnates' lives. Of these, he wished to permanently relocate many to Rome.

According to Romulus' proposal, those who moved to Rome would be allotted free land, perhaps around two *jugera*, on which to live. Romulus additionally planned to enrol a considerable number, if not all of them, as Roman citizens. Finally, he intended on making Caenina and Antemnae Roman colonies in order to keep a close eye on them and guarantee their obedience. Romulus would confiscate large swathes of their land, maybe around one third, and give it to Romans who wished to become the cities' first colonists. However, no property belonging to the abducted maidens' families was to be seized, which Romulus hoped would completely mollify the wives' lingering anxieties. The Senate respectfully listened to their king. After he finished describing his suggested intentions, the senators fully endorsed and ratified the terms, and they claimed that Romulus' vision was strategic, far-sighted and just.[11]

Upon finalizing and approving the peace agreement, Romulus summoned the maidens who hailed from Caenina and Antemnae to assemble in what later became the Forum, which at this point was just a swampy valley. He requested their presence so that he could present his decision and respond to their appeals. When they nervously entered his presence, they were distressed and fearful, and many immediately fell prostrate before him, pleading for Romulus to treat their family members and countrymen with mercy. In response, he ordered them to remain silent while he spoke. As an awkward silence descended, Romulus stated:

> Your fathers and brothers and your entire cities deserve to suffer every severity for having preferred to our friendship a war that was neither necessary nor honourable. We, however, have resolved for many reasons to treat them with moderation;

for we not only fear the vengeance of the gods, which ever threatens the arrogant, and dread the ill-will of men, but we are also persuaded that mercy contributes not a little to alleviate the common ills of mankind, and we realize that we ourselves may one day stand in need of that of others. And we believe that to you, whose behaviour toward your husbands has thus far been blameless, this will be no small honour and favour. We suffer this offence of theirs, therefore, to go unpunished and take from your fellow citizens neither their liberty nor their possessions nor any other advantages they enjoy; and both to those who desire to remain there and to those who wish to change their abode we grant full liberty to make their choice, not only without danger but without fear of repenting. But, to prevent their ever repeating their fault or the finding of any occasion to induce their cities to break off their alliance with us, the best means, we consider, and that which will at the same time conduce to the reputation and security of both, is for us to make those cities colonies of Rome and to send a sufficient number of our own people from here to inhabit them jointly with your fellow citizens. Depart, therefore, with good courage; and redouble your love and regard for your husbands, to whom your parents and brothers owe their preservation and your countries their liberty.

While Romulus claimed that the Caeninenses and Antemnates wouldn't be impacted by confiscations or forcible relocations, that wasn't entirely true. Romulus had a knack of taking hostages, annexing land and creating colonies. So, when he told the abducted women that the defeated peoples wouldn't be penalized in such a way, he may have been only referring to their family members and their property. Whatever the case, the women were overjoyed by what they heard, and there must have been loud cries of joy and thanks to Romulus for his clemency. After many individually praised him for his compassion, they gradually returned home and resumed their daily lives. Romulus, on the other hand, still had other public matters to attend to. He and/or his subordinates needed to oversee the land allotments for those emigrating to Rome and those moving to Caenina and Antemnae. This was no easy task either. As time progressed, many of the abducted women's family members relocated to Rome in order to live near them. A host of other Caeninenses and Antemnates likewise moved to Rome to start new lives, which increased Rome's population by no less than 3,000 people within a short period. Indeed, after enrolling them, Romulus boasted more than 6,000 males who could bear arms within his city. Rome received many people, but Romans were also departing Rome because Romulus planted colonies in the conquered cities. Each was comprised of only 300 Romans, but that was likely enough to help the distrustful Romulus monitor the towns' activities and ensure their good behaviour.[12]

As Romulus and his lieutenants settled the immigration issues, the Roman king looked to his city's defences and prepared for potential conflicts. There were still other enemies nearby who wanted to harm Rome, including Crustumerium. It was one of the chief cities that, along with Caenina and Antemnae, had clamoured for war with Rome, and its people still harboured hatred toward the Romans. Romulus had already subdued Caenina and Antemnae, but sometime later, the Crustumerians committed an unrecorded provocation against Rome, which demanded a rapid response. Romulus wanted to end the threat against his kingdom once and for all. So, he set out to crush the Crustumerians.[13]

The Crustumerians' role in the affair is somewhat muddled due to conflicting sources, but after the Crustumerians committed an unknown act of war, they dug in and prepared for a confrontation with Romulus. It isn't clear if the Crustumerians were in Roman country or if they waited for the battle in their own territory, which was only around 10 miles north of Rome.[14]

Either way, according to Dionysius, unlike the Caeninenses and the Antemnates, the Crustumerians didn't act imprudently. They laid the groundwork in case the Romans besieged their city and put their army on alert. They also seem to have kept close tabs on Romulus' whereabouts so that they wouldn't be taken unawares as their naïve allies had been. Thus, following the Crustumerians' undisclosed provocation, when and if Romulus chose to advance toward their position, they wouldn't be shocked and overwhelmed simply by the legionaries' arrival.

Just as the Crustumerians had certainly predicted and their scouts informed them, the Romans decided to head toward their position with the intention of eliminating them as a threat. Somewhere along the way, the two armies met. They were both in a state of battle readiness, and their troops bravely manned their stations. Perhaps after Crustumerium's king and Romulus briefly conferred and determined that their terms for peace were unacceptable, the respective generals gave the signal to charge. Each army probably unleashed a lethal salvo of spears and rushed toward their foes as waves of soldiers fiercely smashed into the enemy's shields. The battle raged for some time as both sides boldly and ably fought, but somehow Romulus' legionaries gained the upper hand and ultimately routed the Crustumerians.[15]

A large portion of the Crustumerians likely fled to their home city, where they made final preparations to defend their walls against the Romans who were hot on their heels. Yet when the legionaries arrived outside Crustumerium, they realized that seizing the settlement would be a greater challenge than sacking Caenina and Antemnae. Crustumerium's leaders had prepared their people for the Romans' arrival, but despite the challenges that Crustumerium posed, the Romans directed their energies toward taking the town. There are no details of the siege other than that both sides struggled mightily, but Romulus' men eventually broke through the fortifications and captured the city.[16]

According to Dionysius' account, the Crustumerians fought courageously and mustered a stout defence of their homeland, which impressed Romulus. He had easily defeated the Caeninenses and Antemnates, and he had sacked their cities without much difficulty too. The Crustumerians, however, battled the Romans with commendable vigour and defended their city with surprising determination. Because of their bravery and honour, Romulus informed them that they would not suffer draconian punishments. This was a great relief to the apprehensive Crustumerians, but they still needed to answer for their actions, while simultaneously providing assurances that they would never cross Rome again. Therefore, they probably faced requirements similar to the Caeninenses and Antemnates. Romulus established a colony on their land, and the Crustumerians in all likelihood surrendered hostages and the city's weapons. Given that the

Romans could demand whatever they wished, the Crustumerians escaped rather lightly.[17]

When Romulus felt that he had adequately settled matters in Crustumerium, he and his victorious legionaries proudly marched back to Rome, where they were certainly well received and enjoyed a fitting celebration. For some reason, though, Romulus opted against hosting a triumph for his latest victory. Perhaps he felt that more important matters were pending. Whatever the case, following the series of successful military engagements and public examples of Romulus' clemency, his legend quickly grew. Apparently, entire cities – whose names are mostly lost to us other than the Latin town of Medullia – submitted to him. They doubtless hoped to remain in his good graces, fearing that he was powerful, warlike and bent on conquering all nearby communities, but others seem to have simply craved his protection.

As such, Rome's domain grew and it experienced an influx of immigrants. Indeed, a host of individuals flooded into Rome from across the region. They had heard of Romulus' steady and competent leadership and his forgiving manner of ruling. Considering that Rome was in the ascendant and Romulus seemed to be a man worthy of being king, many decided to emigrate to Rome and start new lives in the burgeoning city. They may have also been lured by an offer of two *jugera* of free land. This increased the size of Rome's army, Romulus' tax base and the city's economic production, which greatly benefited Rome. One such person who relocated to Rome around this time was an Etruscan named Caelius, of whom little is known other than he settled on a hill that was adjacent to the Palatine. It later became known as the Caelian Hill, which became one of Rome's seven hills.[18]

Other individuals learned of Romulus' successes but were less pleased by the news. The Sabines, who were supposed to aid Caenina, Antemnae and Crustumerium, observed Rome's growth with regret. They may have been upset that they had not crushed Romulus' kingdom earlier when it was more vulnerable, and they probably worried that the longer they waited to smite the Romans, the stronger the Romans would become. This, in turn, could imperil the Sabines' well-being and influence in the region. Ultimately, they felt confident that they could still defeat

Romulus but shouldn't postpone their confrontation with the growing Roman threat much longer. So, they more seriously concentrated their efforts on an eventual showdown with Rome, which would be the greatest military threat Romulus had yet faced.[19]

IX

Tarpeia

'Tarpeia, keeping her promise, opened to the enemy the gate agreed upon, and rousing the garrison, urged them to save themselves speedily by other exits unknown to the enemy, as if the Sabines were already masters of the place; that after the flight of the garrison the Sabines, finding the gates open, possessed themselves of the stronghold.'

– Dionysius of Halicarnassus

King Tatius, his Sabine subjects and other allies had watched Caenina's, Antemnae's and Crustumerium's mismanaged conflicts with Rome from a distance. They observed how badly each had been bungled. Rather than banding together and coordinating their war effort, the trio's alliance had splintered. This allowed the shrewd Romulus to pick them off one by one, and every Roman victory left Rome even stronger.

Considering this, Tatius probably wished he hadn't stonewalled Caenina, Antemnae and Crustumerium. Leaving the bellicose cities to their own devices as they prosecuted the war poorly was a costly blunder. It ultimately contributed to their defeats and permitted Rome's influence to quickly grow. Instead of continuing to lament his mistakes or the vanquished cities' fates, Tatius determined that Rome was becoming a grave threat and needed to be pacified. If Tatius didn't confront the Romans soon, then Romulus' kingdom might blossom into a dominant city and surpass the Sabines' influence. Tatius sought to prevent this unfathomable possibility from ever coming to fruition.[1]

Unlike Caenina's and Antemnae's kings, Tatius was an intelligent and skilled leader. While he had committed a serious error by not engaging Rome earlier, he realized his mistake and preferred to never underestimate Romulus again. Consequently, he resumed his war preparations in earnest. According to Dionysius of Halicarnassus, Tatius painstakingly raised an army of least 25,000 foot soldiers and nearly 1,000 horsemen to confront the Romans and bring them to heel. However, it's highly probable that Dionysius or his sources exaggerated the size of Tatius' force. Regardless of this embellishment, Tatius recruited a multitude of troops as secretly as possible because he wished to catch the Romans off guard and gain a strategic advantage. Yet it must have been difficult to covertly raise and train an army of allegedly over 25,000 men. It was even more arduous to do so assuming that Romulus had dispatched spies across the countryside, who assiduously collected helpful intelligence.[2]

As Tatius readied his Sabines for conflict, he must have spent considerable time studying his opponent. The Romans had proven themselves surprisingly wily in their recent engagements. Yet even though Romulus had exhibited his cunning on the battlefield, Tatius felt that the Romans would eventually fall to his Sabines. Rome was still only one relatively minor, albeit ascendant, city. Tatius, on the other hand, was the leader of the power-centre of Cures and a broader Sabine coalition, and he planned on leading an army with a vast numerical superiority. He also hoped to gain the element of surprise, but Romulus had no intention of sitting idly as Tatius marshalled his forces. After Romulus vanquished the trio of cities, he evidently learned of Tatius' intentions and busied himself with strengthening Rome in advance of the Sabine war.

Rome's monarch keenly recognized the significance of the looming Sabine conflict, and he understood that it was one that could determine Rome's future. Thus, he took great pains to adequately fortify his kingdom and raise much-needed troops by any possible means. After auditing his defences, one of Romulus' first orders of business was to augment Rome's Palatine Hill fortifications. The walls were already formidable, but they were clearly not impregnable. Consequently, Romulus commanded his subordinates to heighten and likely reinforce the bulwarks around the Palatine Hill. He probably also tasked his countrymen with erecting additional towers and/or platforms where troops could more easily defend the recently strengthened walls.

Romulus' strategy to enhance Rome's defences wasn't limited to just the Palatine Hill. He aimed to create a network of strongholds to frustrate his enemies and better protect his subjects. While the city of Rome was largely centred on the Palatine Hill, there were other populated hills within the vicinity that Romulus planned on fortifying. On the nearby Capitoline and Aventine Hills, he instructed workers to build stout defences, whereupon they raised two mighty fortresses, one on each hill's summit. These weren't grand citadels by later Roman standards, but they were still imposing. Indeed, the Capitoline stronghold was more defensible than the Palatine Hill fortifications, and Romulus even stored a valuable cache of war supplies within the Capitoline citadel.

These defences must have been wooden structures, largely comprised of a fence made of pikes and surrounded by deep ditches. Once constructed, Roman legionaries garrisoned the fortresses. The point of these citadels wasn't simply to create military outposts to hinder Tatius' offensive, although this was a major factor. Romulus ordered their construction to provide shelter for Rome's vulnerable farmers and shepherds too, and for good reason. During their wars with Rome, the Caeninenses and Antemnates first laid waste to the countryside, seized crops and livestock, and harassed Rome's farmers and herdsmen. Perhaps Romulus feared that the Sabines may adopt the same strategy, and part of the reason Romulus constructed these fortresses was to counter this risk and protect his exposed people. Romulus even raised the ramparts in locations where his subjects could quickly withdraw. Indeed, for their well-being, he decreed that many of his people should spend their nights in the safety of the citadels. Romulus cared for his subjects as though he was their father, and these palisades permitted him to safeguard them as well as hopefully hamper Tatius' designs.[3]

Augmenting Rome's defences and creating military outposts were effective steps in a frantic effort to repel the coming Sabine war machine, but more was needed. Romulus knew that Tatius' troops could vastly outnumber his legionaries unless things quickly changed. Rome had rapidly grown by accepting immigrants into the city and offering citizenship to many Caeninenses, Antemnates and Crustumerians. While this increased the number of men at arms, his legions were still insufficient to resist the Sabine invasion. To address these concerns, Romulus dispatched messengers to plead for assistance from anyone whom he considered a friend of Rome or at least an enemy of Tatius. Unfortunately, Rome didn't have many allies at this time, which isn't surprising given the Romans' abduction of the maidens and the Roman population's largely unsavoury character. Nevertheless, Romulus' grandfather, Numitor, forwarded a host of troops from Alba Longa to assist Rome in its time of need. Numitor also dispatched craftsmen, who were skilled at building weapons and engines of war, to support Romulus.

This wasn't the only foreign aid that Romulus received. Further assistance came from a possibly unexpected source. One of the leaders who received Romulus' desperate plea for support agreed to help. He was an Etruscan named Lucumo, and his relationship with Romulus had only recently warmed. Lucumo hailed from the city of Solonium, which was roughly 12 miles from Rome. He was renowned for his military prowess and boasted a multitude of mercenaries who hailed from regions around the Tyrrhenian Sea, and they too came to Romulus' aid. The nature of Romulus and Lucumo's alliance is shrouded in uncertainty. It seems that Lucumo may have felt some sort of strong ties of friendship with Romulus, and the two presumably established a formal alliance, which bound them. To sweeten the deal, Romulus may have even offered Lucumo and his armies of mercenaries compensation, perhaps in the form of free tracts of land near Rome.[4]

Upon finalizing the agreement, Lucumo set out to assist his new ally. Once Lucumo's mercenaries and Numitor's soldiers joined with Romulus, the Roman king boasted a respectable army. It was smaller than the Sabine king's force, but it wasn't entirely dwarfed by them. Including cavalry, Tatius had cobbled together nearly 26,000 men for his invasion, while Romulus allegedly led a force of 20,000 legionaries and 800 cavalrymen. If these estimates can be believed, then this would be remarkable, given that Romulus had only recently founded Rome, but the troop numbers should be treated with great caution.[5] In fact, modern archaeologist Andrea Carandini calculated that, assuming Rome truly existed around this era, its population was possibly no larger than 17,000–18,000-people strong. This figure includes women, children and the elderly. If this is true, then

Lucumo and Numitor would have had to contribute a massive number of soldiers to Romulus' war effort, which they probably didn't. In reality, it is unlikely that the Romans marshalled an army of over 20,000.[6]

Despite the questionable troop estimates, Romulus and Tatius continued busily readying their kingdoms for war. As spring neared and war seemed imminent, Tatius dispatched envoys, allegedly tasked with finding a diplomatic solution to avoid the impending conflict. This may have been little more than a formality, since Tatius seemed intent on forcefully curtailing Rome's budding influence. Even so, when Tatius' representatives arrived at Rome, Romulus permitted them to enter and address Rome's elders. Thereupon, the emissaries demanded that Romulus surrender the Sabine women whose abduction had sparked the hostilities. The ambassadors also insisted that the Roman monarch commit some sort of conciliatory gestures to give the appearance that justice had been delivered and Romulus had learned his lesson.

Romulus had previously refused similar terms, defeated the Caeninenses, Antemnates and Crustumerians, and had already painstakingly laid the groundwork for the looming war with the Sabines. His previous successes may have fomented a feeling of overconfidence that induced him to believe that Rome might be able to weather the approaching conflict. As such, his uncompromising response to the Sabine ambassadors was predictable. He emphatically stated that the women in question were living relatively happy lives with their new husbands. Therefore, it would be improper to forcibly eject them from Rome. However, Romulus countered that the Sabine representatives should offer other peace terms, and if they were reasonable, then he would gladly accept them to avert an unnecessary war. Considering that the entire conflict centred around the kidnapped women, there were no other possible conditions that could rectify Romulus' transgressions in the Sabines' minds. Following a series of responses and subsequent deliberation, the Sabine envoys departed from Rome empty-handed, and war became unavoidable.

After the failed peace talks, Tatius readied his army to finally invade Roman territory. At the same time, Romulus made his final preparations. He had already augmented Rome's defences on the Palatine Hill, built fortresses on the Aventine and Capitoline Hills and raised an impressive army. Yet he still believed that he could improve Rome's odds of victory. So, when war seemed forthcoming, he decided to station his troops in advanced positions so that they could intercept the Sabines at a safe distance from his citizenry and offer Rome the best possible protection. Thus, Romulus divided his forces into two large groupings. He naturally commanded one and led them to the Esquiline Hill, where they awaited Tatius' arrival. Meanwhile, his trusted Etruscan friend Lucumo oversaw the other division and stationed it on the nearby Quirinal Hill.[7]

Once the Sabine king doubtlessly learned that Romulus was diligently fortifying his kingdom for the invasion, Tatius probably felt that he must act with urgency. He recognized Caenina's, Antemnae's and Crustumerium's failures. He additionally understood that Romulus was an astute general who had already capitalized on the Sabines' original delay in action, and Tatius didn't want to allow the Romans to further strengthen their defences. Knowing that time was of the essence, Tatius finalized his plan, and on one following spring night, he led his army toward Rome, which lay less than 30 miles south-west of Cures. To improve their chances of catching the Romans off guard, they timed their departure so that they would enter Rome under the cover of darkness.[8]

As the Sabine army approached Roman territory in relative silence, they harmlessly passed by the Roman farms. Unlike the Caeninenses and the Antemnates, they didn't waste precious time destroying crops. This would have only slowed their march and given Romulus advanced warning that they weren't far off. Rather, the Sabine troops continued their rapid advance into Roman territory through the night.

When they neared Rome, it was still dark and the Sabines were doubtless exhausted. Nevertheless, they snaked through the valleys between the five hills that comprised Romulus' primary defences. Since it was still nighttime, Tatius probably couldn't entirely perceive the ambit of the Romans' fortifications, nor their strategy. Even so, he surely dispatched scouts to reconnoitre the hills as best they could. They must have reported that Romulus had stationed men on each ridge, but it was too dark to grasp the breadth of Romulus' preparations. As a result, Tatius couldn't justify a dangerous attack on a fortified hill without intimate knowledge of its defences. Furthermore, night battles were always dangerous affairs in ancient times, because armies were just as likely to accidentally fight their own comrades as the enemy. So, Tatius decided to make camp for the time being in the lowland between the Capitoline and Quirinal Hills.

The Sabines initially felt confident that they could vanquish the Romans. They had raised an enormous army and apparently obtained some level of surprise due to their expedition's swiftness. Beyond this, they had entered into the heart of Rome unobstructed and camped their troops amidst Romulus' strongholds.[9] Before dawn, Tatius must have been eagerly making arrangements to build a stout bivouac for his troops and/or subsequently storm one of Rome's hills. Then, if all went as planned, he intended on systematically defeating Romulus in battle and dismantling his fortifications, but as the sun rose, Tatius' optimism slowly gave way to dismay. The extent of Romulus' expansive defences and the size of his army shocked Tatius. In all likelihood, Tatius had assumed that he held a decisive numerical advantage, but he quickly learned from his scouts that Romulus had likewise raised a massive army. There were also other disheartening discoveries: Romulus' fortresses were imposing and couldn't be captured with ease, and Roman legionaries held the most defensible and strategic positions in the area, which left no advantageous posts for Tatius to assume without risking great peril.

Like their former allies, the Caeninenses, Antemnates and Crustu-merians, the Sabines had underestimated Romulus. Unless something changed, their expedition risked ending in complete failure as quickly as it began. Indeed, the Sabines had few possible moves. They were in the midst of a network of formidable defences and facing an army that held the high ground. Meanwhile, they were vulnerable so long as they remained in the valley between the Capitoline citadel and the army stationed on the Quirinal Hill.[10]

Despite the Sabines' shaken confidence, Tatius resolved not to abandon his undertaking just yet. Instead, he surely ordered his scouts to survey Romulus' fortresses and positions more closely in the hope of discovering a weakness. Therefore, Sabine patrols set out to probe the hills. It appears that nothing of great value was immediately detected on four of the hills. Yet one Sabine detachment approached the Capitoline Hill fortress, which was commanded by a Roman prefect named Spurius

Tarpeius. As the reconnaissance team examined the citadel, the Sabines were also being carefully watched. Tarpeius' daughter, Tarpeia, gazed at them from atop the mighty fortress and sensed a great opportunity, but unfortunately, the ancient writers were in disagreement over the following events.[11]

According to the conflicting accounts, Tarpeia began to piece together some sort of scheme. Her goal was either to make Rome's enemies susceptible to Romulus' troops or treacherously betray the Capitoline fortress and her countrymen to the Sabines. Supposedly, she conspired to obtain what the Sabines 'had on their left arms', which was an exceedingly ambiguous objective. As a means of enriching herself, she may have wished for the jewelled rings and golden bracelets that the Sabines wore on their left hands and arms. Thus, she may have intended on betraying the citadel in exchange for Sabine treasures.

Alternatively, to make the Sabines vulnerable to Roman attacks, she might have wanted the shields that the Sabines tightly gripped with their left hands. If she could strip them of their shields, then she'd greatly aid Romulus. Whatever the case, she believed that she knew her father's plans, the routines of the fortress guards and the citadel's architecture well enough to offer Tatius a deal: the surrender of the Capitoline citadel. So, she dispatched one of her assistants through a small passageway to request a surreptitious meeting with the Sabine king.[12]

Tarpeia's maiden easily found the massive Sabine army, at which point, she informed the Sabine soldiers who she was and why she was there. She announced that she had a message of great importance for their king. Tatius was desperate for a piece of encouraging news and was growing increasingly vexed by Romulus' thorough strategic groundwork. When the Roman servant appeared with a missive for him, he grew ever more hopeful.

Thereupon, the messenger either delivered Tarpeia's letter or was given an audience with Tatius or one of his lieutenants. Once they received the communication, the Sabines were intrigued, and they formulated a risky plan for Tatius to meet Tarpeia in secret to allegedly discuss betraying the Roman citadel to the Sabines. They agreed on a time and location for the clandestine encounter. Tatius was thrilled to be presented with a chance to strike a painful blow against the Romans, but he probably also worried that he could potentially be walking into a trap. Nevertheless, he was willing to risk his well-being for the promise of capturing a mighty fortress, and he readily agreed to confer with Tarpeia. Even though he eagerly accepted her invitation, he surely took all necessary precautions against any possible attempts to assassinate or capture him.[13]

Tatius and Tarpeia either settled on that night or one of the following evenings. As the meeting time approached, Tarpeia waited on the Capitoline Hill in anticipation for her father's scheduled departure from the citadel. When he subsequently left, his daughter snuck out of the stronghold for her conference with the Sabine king. However, she may have left under the pretence of gathering water specifically needed for conducting sacred rites. At any rate, Tatius and Tarpeia met at a predetermined location, but both prudently remained a safe distance apart. They were close enough to speak with one another, but distant enough to ensure their own safety if either party acted unfaithfully.[14]

As the two faced each other, Tarpeia informed the Sabine that she could easily betray the citadel to Tatius that night. She revealed that her father wasn't in the fortress, which left the garrison leaderless, and she could unlock the citadel's gates for the Sabines. She also must have known of the guards' timed rotation. So, she could advise Tatius when it was most convenient to attack. She could even urge the garrison's troops to abandon their posts.

Tatius was pleased with what he heard, but he understood that Tarpeia's valuable services wouldn't be free. Perhaps after asking what Tarpeia wanted in exchange for her services, she responded that he needed to be willing to agree to a *quid pro quo* arrangement. She vaguely stated that she desired what the Sabines had on their left arms. Tatius must have assumed that she was referring to their golden armlets and rings, but he seems to have been satisfied with not requesting clarification. After discussing their prospective agreement's details, the two elected to aid one another and decided when and how the Sabines should storm the fortress. To ensure their goodwill, Tatius and Tarpeia even swore oaths to adhere to their pact, and they subsequently left to play their roles in the coming assault.[15]

Tatius rushed to relay the welcome news to his lieutenants and ready his troops for what he hoped would be an easy victory. Meanwhile, Tarpeia quietly re-entered the citadel without raising any suspicions, but what happened next is subject to debate. If she was set on treacherously betraying the fort to the Sabines in exchange for their jewellery, then she prepared to open the gates and help the Sabines seize the stronghold.

However, had Tarpeia's strategy actually been a clever ruse meant to help the Romans, not the Sabines, then things certainly would have happened differently. According to another tradition, she didn't want the Sabines' golden armlets. Rather, she sought their shields so that they would be exposed if they met the Romans in battle. Perhaps even more importantly, per this account, she hoped to inform Romulus of her objective in order to allow him to transfer additional troops to the citadel and possibly ambush the unsuspecting Sabines as they attacked the fortress. So, she sent a servant to deliver her plans to Romulus. Yet after exiting the stronghold, her servant fled to Tatius' camp to inform the Sabine king of Tarpeia's duplicitous scheme.[16]

If Tarpeia was actually trying to aid her fellow Romans, then she must have worried that her message to Romulus had been intercepted because the Roman king never came to her aid. Despite this setback, she could still hope that her bargain with Tatius would result in the acquisition of the Sabines' shields, which could help the Romans, but the Sabine shields weren't worth trading for the citadel. Beyond this, it would have been incredibly dim-witted for Tatius to relinquish his army's shields, and Tatius was no fool. It should be noted that the larger number of ancient historians seem to have believed that this version was a fanciful story with little merit and that Tarpeia was driven by greed and treachery, not patriotism.[17]

Regardless of her true motivations, when Tatius and his troops assaulted the Capitoline Hill fortification in the middle of the night, Tarpeia dutifully fulfilled her end of the disloyal bargain. She unlocked the gates and admitted the Sabines into the citadel. Then she hastily alerted the Roman troops stationed in the fortress. She pleaded with them to save themselves and desert the garrison through passages by which they could safely escape. It seems that the majority of the Roman legionaries fled the citadel without firing a missile or unsheathing their swords. Facing little resistance, the Sabines rushed into the stronghold through the unsecured gates, quickly seized control of the fortress and captured a large portion of Romulus' war supplies.

When Tatius and the bulk of his troops took the Capitoline Hill, it was more or less a ghost town. Its defenders had largely abandoned it, and few, if any, Romans lingered other than Tarpeia. She fearlessly remained in the citadel and patiently waited to be compensated by Tatius, as per their agreement. However, she regrettably learned that treacherous dealings are rarely rewarded honourably. Once the Sabines seized the fort, she either asked for their shields or their golden bracelets. Tatius preferred not to completely renege on his deal with Tarpeia, maybe because he had pledged to adhere to their agreement. Still, he didn't wish to reward a traitor like Tarpeia either. Consequently, he violently flung either his shield or his golden bangles at Tarpeia, stunning and injuring her. Then he ordered his soldiers to do the same as Tarpeia received a violent barrage of blows until she died from the blunt force trauma or the weight of the shields crushed her.[18]

It is certainly possible that Tarpeia had intended on aiding Romulus, and if Tatius had learned of her attempt to undermine their arrangement, then he must have felt that her execution was justified. This could have been accomplished by killing her with what the Sabines had on their left arms. It's noteworthy that years after her death, the Romans celebrated Tarpeia and even offered libations to her on the Capitoline Hill, where she was initially buried until her bones were removed. Such reverence would have been odd if she had betrayed Romulus. What's more, Romans eventually called the hill that she surrendered to the Sabines Tarpeius, after her. While the name ultimately didn't stick, a certain cliff face on the hill still bears her name: the Tarpeian Rock. This is where later Romans hurled condemned individuals to their deaths. While it is unclear whether Tarpeia was guilty of treachery, Romulus assigned considerable blame upon her father, Tarpeius, presumably for creating the circumstances that permitted the citadel's fall.[19]

Aside from the differing accounts of Tarpeia's involvement, Tatius had inflicted a severe blow to the Roman cause without risking much.

When Tatius first arrived in Roman territory, he discovered that Romulus' preparations were thorough and placed the Sabines at a distinct disadvantage. While the two armies were somewhat closely matched numerically, the Sabines were left highly vulnerable because they had no defensible location on which to build a camp. Furthermore, Romulus had either fortified or stationed armies on all of the nearby advantageous locations, which the Sabines couldn't take by force unless Tatius was willing to risk massive casualties. Yet through one act of treachery, he had gained an imposing toehold in the heart of Roman territory and captured a valuable trove of Roman supplies. Very quickly, the balance of the war began to shift in Tatius' favour, and his Sabines' despair evolved into justified hope.

This encouraged the Sabines, but the Romans were forced to cope with the bitter reality that they had passively lost a stronghold to the enemy. While the Romans still maintained highly defensible positions in the area, their enemy now held a major citadel in the midst of the Roman defences. Moreover, the Sabines were no longer as vulnerable to Roman attacks, and they could hold out as long as supplies lasted because their newly acquired garrison was well-fortified.

After exploring the recently captured Capitoline Hill, many Sabine soldiers took up quarters there, guarded their provisions and watched for the enemy. The largest body of Tatius' troops, however, probably didn't camp within the stronghold. They remained outside its walls because the citadel likely wasn't large enough to house the 26,000 people.

Regardless of the fortress's size, Tatius knew that capturing it had brought about a notable shift in the war, but he still needed to defeat Romulus' army and seize the other strongholds to force Rome to accept an unfavourable treaty. Romulus had no intention of surrendering. He had, after all, commendably prepared for Tatius' arrival. While Romulus' initial plan to keep Tatius from gaining a foothold in Roman territory had seemed sound, Tarpeia had undermined it. To achieve victory as the war evolved, Romulus needed to vanquish the Sabine army, recapture the Capitoline Hill fortress and eject the Sabines from his domain. Given these realities and with Romulus' and Tatius' armies encamped near one another, a war of hazardous set-piece battles or extended sieges appeared increasingly likely.[20]

X

Tatius

'If,' [the maidens] cried, 'you are weary of these ties of kindred, these marriage-bonds, then turn your anger upon us; it is we who are the cause of the war, it is we who have wounded and slain our husbands and fathers. Better for us to perish rather than live without one or the other of you, as widows or as orphans.'

– Livy

Tarpeia's betrayal was a painful setback for the Romans, which completely changed the war's dynamic, but there was no time for Romulus to dwell on this. He needed to act decisively and with urgency. So, due to the conflict's changing circumstances, Romulus transferred his legionaries to a more strategic location the following day. He moved them from their entrenched position on the Esquiline Hill to the low ground between the Sabine-held Capitoline Hill and the Roman-controlled Palatine Hill. Rome's primary settlement rested atop the Palatine. Consequently, Romulus' principal objective was to defend it from potential Sabine attacks, while simultaneously applying pressure on Tatius' troops on the Capitoline Hill. Romulus also ordered his Etruscan friend Lucumo to march his mercenaries from the Quirinal Hill toward the low ground between the Palatine and Capitoline hills.

After losing the formidable Capitoline fortress to treachery, Romulus decided not to waste any time. He wanted to deliver the knockout blow to the Sabines, and fast. Thus, upon marching his troops near the Capitoline Hill, Romulus challenged Tatius to battle, but Tatius didn't find it prudent to engage the enemy just yet. Perhaps Tatius was still adjusting his plans or preferred to allow his soldiers to rest, given that they had seized the stronghold the previous night. Regardless of his reasoning, Tatius rejected Romulus' invitation, but the two kings realized that neither could maintain the status quo in perpetuity.[1]

Likely in the succeeding days, there were numerous minor encounters, which left few casualties. Rather than serving to open full-scale hostilities, these tactics may have been used to test their opponent's defences and hopefully reveal their vulnerabilities, but they bore little, if any, fruit. When these probing missions failed to turn the war's tide or expose a weakness, it seems that the monarchs begrudgingly accepted the fact that the armed conflict would be decided by hazardous, pitched engagements.[2]

In due time, Romulus once again offered to give the Sabines battle, and this time Tatius was ready to confront the Romans. After their messengers presumably exchanged a series of communications, the two kings settled on a time and location for the encounter. They agreed to meet in what later became the Roman Forum, which lay between their strongholds. Tatius was happy to consent to battle too. He believed that the circumstances were favourable to his army and that in the worst-case scenario, if the Romans routed his soldiers, then he could simply retreat to the Capitoline fortress and take cover. Furthermore, the prospective battlefield didn't seem as though it would benefit one army over the other. Instead, it seemed to restrict both to a confined area and would ensure a tough contest, but Tatius enjoyed at least one advantage. He held a numerical superiority. As such, he saw little risk in battling Romulus at this juncture.[3]

Precisely what happened next is difficult to determine because the ancient sources contain considerable inconsistencies, but if they are combined, they seem to present a broader picture of what might have transpired. When the battle's date and time arrived, the two massive armies lumbered onto the marshy plain between the Palatine and Capitoline hills, and they anxiously waited for a battle that they hoped would quickly conclude the war. Once in place, the soldiers eyed their enemy from across the field as they nervously secured their weapons. Meanwhile, Romulus and Tatius made last-minute arrangements and gave final orders to their deputies before commanding the troops to advance toward their enemy.

When the armies came within range, they unleashed a salvo of javelins and missiles. The projectiles rained down on their intended targets, wounding and killing an untold number, but the surviving soldiers bravely drew their swords and resumed their advance toward the enemy. When the two armies met, they violently collided into the other as their shields and swords clashed. During the melee, the troops frantically hacked and stabbed at their opponents when the opportunity arose.[4]

The battle was fierce and raged for a considerable time. Each army boldly charged the other, retreated when their advance stalled and then rallied once more. The engagement wasn't marked by constant action. Rather, it must have essentially been a series of mini-battles punctuated by breaks. It was still a ferocious mode of warfare, which exhausted the troops who frequently needed to catch their breath during the lulls in fighting. The halts in action additionally gave the generals the opportunity to recollect their thoughts, reorder their troops and alter their battle plans.

As the engagement continued, the momentum swung back and forth like a pendulum in each army's favour. Each time one side gained what appeared to be a decisive edge, the opposing force responded in kind and negated their foe's advantage. The battle simmered for hours like this until the sun began to set. This heralded the end of the day's combat because neither general was willing to risk a perilous night battle. The Sabines and the Romans were so evenly matched in leadership, numbers, planning and courage that neither could maintain the upper hand. As a result, the battle ended in a costly draw.

As the sun went down, the Romans and Sabines returned to their respective camps for the night. They were exhausted, hungry and desperately needed to tend to their wounded. There was surely a feeling of pride, given that they had withstood their enemy's vigorous attacks, but they were also undoubtedly disheartened by the fact that they had not victoriously concluded the war or even won the battle. In the wake of the day's events, a terrifying feeling that the conflict could drag on indefinitely and become incredibly bloody certainly weighed on the soldiers' minds. There were many grim, visible reminders of the day's carnage too. The battle had left a host of men slain, and their bodies remained strewn about the battlefield because it would have been difficult to collect all of the corpses and dispose of them under the cover of darkness.

Over the successive days, there seems to have been a temporary truce so that the Romans and Sabines could give the dead proper burials. While the recently deceased most likely didn't enjoy the ceremonies that most Romans and Sabines enjoyed during peacetime, funerary attendants presumably performed the minimum necessary rites. After this was completed, the bodies of the commoners were, in all likelihood, cremated or entombed wholesale in a makeshift burial chamber. The fallen noblemen, on the other hand, probably received different treatment. If so, then they were transported back to their homes for more elaborate funerals whereupon they were interred in mausoleums fitting their status.[5]

Following the macabre displays, Romulus and Tatius diligently prepared for another pitched battle. They did all that they could to exhort their troops who must have felt great hesitation over facing their adversaries once again. Despite any lingering concerns, Romulus and Tatius resolved to confront the enemy again and end the war as soon as possible. Once more, they may have exchanged a series of missives discussing the upcoming battle's terms. Just as before, they settled on meeting on the same plain between the Capitoline and Palatine hills, and as the conflict's time neared, the armies' generals drew their soldiers into battle array. According to Dionysius of Halicarnassus, Romulus arranged his troops with a large body of men in the centre and two distinct wings on the flanks. Romulus commanded the right wing, while his friend Lucumo led the left. Unfortunately, there is no direct mention of the Sabines' formation, but it's plausible that it mirrored that of the Romans.[6]

When the soldiers were in position, Romulus ordered his men to charge the Sabines, and the Sabines responded in kind. One of the Sabine generals was a man named Mettius Curtius. According to Livy, Curtius eagerly rushed toward the Romans much more quickly than his men. At the same time, a Roman called Hostus Hostilius, whose grandson later became king, charged faster than any of his countrymen. Consequently,

Curtius and Hostilius met halfway between their armies and engaged in single combat before their soldiers, who watched in great anticipation. It was a fierce contest, but Curtius fought from more favourable ground and ultimately struck the deathblow to Hostilius, who fell before the Roman army, seriously demoralizing them.[7]

Despite Hostilius' death, Romulus urged his troops forward. They obediently followed his orders, and both armies likely exchanged a barrage of spears and drew their swords before they neared one another. Curtius led the Sabine centre. Given his earlier contest with Hostilius, he was clearly a gifted fighter. Yet he was also a competent general, and he exhibited his talents as he led the offensive. Before long, his Sabines reached the Romans. Then the two armies smashed into one another and violently assaulted their foes, but the Roman centre struggled against Curtius' men, who fought relentlessly.[8]

As the battle continued and countless men were struck down, Romulus and Lucumo both experienced great success on the wings. It even appeared they were close to outflanking the Sabines and possibly vanquishing them once and for all. Romulus and Lucumo had nearly tasted victory, but Curtius snatched it from them by overpowering their army's centre. The Sabines ultimately forced the disheartened Roman centre to retreat for safety toward Rome's gates on the Palatine Hill. This left the wings largely detached from the remainder of the Roman army. Very quickly, what initially looked like a potential Roman victory threatened to become a Roman massacre.

Facing possible ruin, Romulus and his wing abandoned their efforts and rushed to the aid of the beleaguered Roman centre. As Romulus arrived to assist them, he launched a potent counter-attack, forcing Curtius and the Sabines to withdraw. Curtius wisely instructed his troops to form an orderly retreat toward their camp, maybe on or near the Capitoline Hill, but Romulus followed them in quick pursuit and was apparently gaining ground on Curtius' soldiers.[9]

In time, Curtius and perhaps a small corps of his shock troops halted their withdrawal and bravely stood their ground to ensure that the rest of his men could reach the safety of their bivouac. Curtius and his rearguard dug in at a place not far from a body of water in what is today's

Forum. As Rome's legionaries approached, Curtius waited patiently and searched for Romulus. When Romulus and Curtius caught sight of one another, each madly dashed forward to fight one another. The generals engaged in single combat, but unfortunately, ancient historians recorded little of this bout other than that Romulus bested Curtius and managed to severely wound him multiple times. In serious pain and suffering from blood loss, Curtius recognized his precarious position and fled, leaping headlong into the lake to swim for safety. Romulus incorrectly assumed that Curtius would drown, considering that he dived into the water while injured and wearing his heavy battle armour. Somehow, Curtius mustered the energy to swim to safety, escape death and eventually reach his camp. According to Dionysius, this was supposedly why the Lacus Curtius, Rome's once-famous lake, gained its name. Even though Curtius survived, Romulus had essentially shifted the battle's momentum back in the Romans' favour.[10]

Following the bout with Curtius, Romulus turned his gaze toward the Capitoline Hill stronghold and Curtius' remaining troops. If Romulus could somehow recapture the fortress and defeat the Sabine army in the field then, combined, the victories would deal the knockout blow to the Sabine war effort. Despite the many wounds that he had incurred during the course of the battle, Romulus organized a body of men and launched an assault on the Sabine-held fortress. The legionaries followed his orders and fought with distinction, but while the assault was underway, a well-aimed stone flung from the Capitoline citadel soared toward Romulus and struck him on the temple. The Roman king nearly stumbled to the ground and appeared severely injured. The sight shocked the Roman ranks and many rushed to his aid. While they saw that he wasn't dead, his chances of surviving the impact seemed slim.

Concerned attendants gathered up the dazed king and transported him to the Palatine Hill for physicians to treat him. When many of the legionaries under his command noticed his conspicuous absence and accounts of his potentially lethal injury spread through the ranks, his troops lost heart and retreated, giving the beset Sabines new life. However, hope was not yet entirely lost for the Romans. The left wing led by Lucumo was still vigorously fighting and experiencing a fair amount of success, but in the heat of battle, a Sabine soldier launched a spear toward Lucumo. It met its mark and lodged in his side. Within a short period of time, Lucumo died, leaving his wing without its commander, and his troops likewise fled.[11]

With nearly the entire Roman army retreating and both of its top generals out of action, the Sabines again seized the initiative and chased the retreating Romans toward the Palatine. Just when Rome's future seemed bleak, an unlikely force staved off defeat. Romulus had previously deployed young, mostly inexperienced men to guard the city walls as a last line of defence. When the battle's momentum turned against the Romans and the Sabines rushed toward the Palatine, these youths stood firm at their stations. They even managed to thwart the Sabine attack at Rome's gates, likely by first pelting the enemy with missiles and then charging out of the gate to bravely meet the Sabines.[12]

Meanwhile, the injured Romulus recovered from his head wound just enough to comprehend Rome's recent reverses. He swiftly returned to the battlefield and urged his men to stand and fight, but they initially ignored his exhortations. Seeing that his army was facing ruin, Romulus cried out to Jupiter and begged for the deity's assistance. The Roman monarch exclaimed:

> Jupiter, it was thy omen that I obeyed when I laid here on the Palatine the earliest foundations of the City. Now the Sabines hold its citadel, having bought it by a bribe, and coming thence have seized the valley and are pressing hitherwards in battle. Do thou, Father of gods and men, drive hence our foes, banish terror from Roman hearts, and stay our shameful flight! Here do I vow a temple to thee, 'Jove the Stayer', as a memorial for the generations to come that it is through thy present help that the City has been saved.

Once Romulus felt that Jupiter had acknowledged his prayer, he yelled, 'Back, Romans! Jupiter Optimus Maximus bids you stand and renew the battle.' Then he joined the sortie with the youths against the Sabines. Upon seeing their king healthy and full of vigour, and possibly being encouraged by Jupiter, the Roman legionaries who had been fleeing were rejuvenated and inspired to turn and fight the Sabines again. During the confused melee, Romulus somehow found time to form his once retreating legionaries into ordered ranks, and the Roman king bravely led a full charge from the front.[13]

The unexpected turn of events shocked the Sabines, and as the tide once again began shifting against them, they struggled to regain the advantage. Their army retreated in the face of Romulus' counter-attack, and they took heavy losses as they fled. Romulus sensed victory and endeavoured to smite the Sabine army and end the conflict. Unfortunately for the Romans, by this time, it was late in the day, and nightfall ultimately saved the Sabines, which meant that the Romans couldn't fully capitalize on their good fortune. Thus, around dusk, both armies parted, leaving a battlefield littered with corpses, and another engagement essentially ended in a stalemate.[14]

According to Dionysius, there was no renewal of battle over the next few days. Instead, the exhausted Romans and Sabines doubtlessly buried their fallen comrades, treated the injured soldiers' wounds and carefully considered their next steps. The previous battles were fought to draws and had left a large number of men dead. As such, neither the Romans nor the Sabines were interested in engaging in another hazardous encounter. Yet at this juncture, the Romans and Sabines had few palatable courses of action available.

The war had become a costly and time-consuming affair, and the Sabines realized that they might not be able to defeat the Romans under the current conditions, at least not easily. It seems that they had three choices. They could carry on with the war, maybe attempt to raise and transport another army to the region to continue battling the Romans, and then try to overwhelm them with vastly superior numbers and fresh troops. Even if they could do this, resuming hostilities had its own risks, and there was no guarantee that they would be victorious. Conversely, they could abandon the war, return home and, on their way, lay waste to the Roman countryside as a punitive measure. This was an unsatisfying option, though. Retreating back to their homeland without vanquishing their enemies would be humiliating because they would essentially be conceding defeat. Their only other option was to request conditions for a tolerable peace treaty. Perhaps, they hoped, they could coax the Romans into accepting very lenient terms so that both factions could honourably end the war while saving face.

The Romans were weighing their options too, but they were even more puzzled than the Sabines. The Romans had been unable to eject the Sabines from their homeland, despite all of their preparations and repeated efforts to defeat them. Worse still, the Sabine conflict had resulted in a host of Roman deaths. If Romulus resolved to continue the war, then the Romans could possibly expect the Sabines to completely destroy their countryside and slay an entire generation of Romans. The Sabines were tenacious foes, and the truth was that the Romans might not be able to defeat them. If the Romans fought and lost, then they could expect painful terms. On the other hand, if they sued for peace at this juncture, then they worried that they might have to surrender the captured maidens. Their seizure had prompted the war in the first place, and Romulus believed that they were necessary for Rome's future. Relinquishing the females would be an admission of guilt and recognition of their defeat. Beyond this, the Romans feared that if they offered peace, the Sabines might demand incredibly harsh terms. Romulus, his Senate and perhaps his lieutenants deliberated over this vexing topic for days, but there were seemingly no acceptable choices.[15]

More than just influential men were considering the Sabines' and Romans' predicaments. Romulus' wife, Hersilia, called an assembly of the kidnapped maidens to discuss the conflict and their desire for peace. Most of the women felt that there was no benefit to the war, at least from their perspective. The conflict pitted their fathers and brothers against their husbands, whom most had sincerely learned to love. Furthermore, many of the women were either pregnant or had already given birth to children fathered by their abductors. Because of this, the women were unwilling to see the war between their loved ones continue. If anything, they wanted peace with moderate terms and goodwill between the peoples.

To achieve this goal, they requested a conference with Romulus and his Senate, and their petition was surprisingly approved. When the time came to converse with Rome's leading men, the women presented their pleas for peace and discussed how harmful the war was on themselves. Then they asked for permission to meet with their Sabine relatives on the Capitoline Hill to demand that they cease warring with their husbands. The Romans had few viable options, and consequently, they agreed to allow the maidens to try to obtain a friendly and mutually acceptable treaty between the peoples. Still, there was evidently a degree of distrust with regards to the women. This seems evident because the Roman men only permitted wives with children to travel to the Sabines' camp. While they were away, their progeny was mostly placed in their husbands' custody, probably to serve as hostages to ensure the women's obedience and return. However, if the wives had multiple children, then they were permitted to take at least one of them along to introduce to their relatives.

After Romulus and his Senate approved the Sabine and Latin women's requests, the females dressed in funeral garb and carried many of their children with them as they exited the city and approached Tatius' camp. Their sudden appearance surprised the Sabines. For the first time since their abduction, the women were reunited with their male relatives. Once they were rejoined, there were likely tears of joy and long, warm embraces, but very quickly, the maidens turned their attention to official business. Thereupon, they begged for an audience with the Sabine elders, which was duly granted.[16]

Subsequent to the women's arrival, Tatius and his senior advisors must have privately convened because they were confused and sceptical of the maidens' abrupt appearance. Of course, the Sabine warriors were thrilled to be reunited with them, but why had the Romans allowed them to travel to the camp and why were the women asking for an audience with the Sabine elders? Tatius wasn't sure of their intentions, but he wanted to find out. Thus, the Sabine monarch permitted the women to meet with him and his lieutenants, and as the conference commenced, he asked them to explain why they had come. Hersilia replied that they were present to plead for peace between their fathers and husbands. She assured the Sabines that a fair and mutually beneficial agreement could be obtained, but Tatius and his deputies weren't moved to immediately agree to their impassioned pleas. The young women sensed this and fell prostrate at the Sabine leaders' feet until they agreed to do everything within their power to make peace. Then they sent the women on their way.[17]

Upon dismissing the women, Tatius and his confidants discussed how they should proceed, and they ultimately fulfilled their promise. With the intention of negotiating peace terms, they opened communications with Romulus. Both parties seem to have been filled with great hope that the war could be nearly at its end. In the spirit of peace, the Romans and Sabines readily agreed to an armistice until they could obtain a final accord.[18]

Plutarch and Livy claimed that this was not exactly the cause of the truce. In their account, during the last Roman-Sabine battle, as the Sabines retreated from the final Roman counter-attack, there was a lull in the fighting. According to this tradition, it was not yet dark, and during the stop in action, the Sabines re-formed ordered ranks to meet the oncoming Romans who were in quick pursuit. Seeing that the Sabines were quickly making tactical adjustments, Romulus presumably did the same with his legions. Then with each army facing one another again following hours of tough fighting, numerous deaths and varied fortunes, they prepared to hazardously re-engage their foes. However, the encounter promised to leave large swathes of the Roman and Sabine soldiery dead. Ignoring the risks, the two obstinate commanders gave the order to recommence the battle, and projectiles began soaring across the field, striking unsuspecting troops as the opposing forces advanced toward their bitter adversaries.[19]

Just as the armies were nearing each other, the Romans and Sabines suddenly halted their advance. They stared in confusion and awe as an amazing spectacle unfolded. A large number of abducted Sabine women, with unkempt hair and tattered clothing, fearlessly poured into the midst of the battlefield seemingly in a fit of hysteria. Some of them even did so while cradling their newborns. As the women ran across the field, they begged the Romans and Sabines to quit their quarrels as they didn't want to see their husbands and kin kill each other. They appealed to their relatives, exclaiming, 'If you are weary of these ties of kindred, these marriage-bonds, then turn your anger upon us; it is we who are the cause of the war, it is we who have wounded and slain our husbands and fathers.

Better for us to perish rather than live without one or the other of you, as widows or as orphans.'[20]

This dramatic display and the wives' reasoned entreaties visibly moved the soldiers, who hoped for lasting peace. As the battle died down, Hersilia and other well-spoken maidens continued demanding that the factions' leaders end the senseless conflict, but the women also led by example. No matter whose flag each soldier fought under, the women provided the troops with food and water, gathered the wounded and transported them to their homes. Meanwhile, many of the abducted females spoke at length about how well their husbands had been treating them, and the women even introduced their offspring to their Sabine families. Following these sensational events, Romulus and Tatius agreed to call a truce until they could concur on a final peace agreement.[21]

Aside from the differing accounts, one way or another, the abducted women brought the conflict to a standstill and Romulus and Tatius to the bargaining table. Still, the kings needed to settle on a lasting peace accord. After agreeing to an armistice, Romulus and Tatius personally met to thrash out the treaty's details. They conferred in the *Comitium*, which was on the Via Sacra between their armies. The Sabines likely stated that they couldn't return home if the maidens were still possessed by a foreign, hostile kingdom. Furthermore, they couldn't end the war in a weakened state, especially if they had nothing to show for it. Conversely, Romulus preferred to retain the abducted women, while at the same time stipulating that any peace accord must strengthen his city. So, Romulus and Tatius eventually agreed to a clever compromise. The Romans and many Sabines would merge into one enlarged, more powerful state, which would retain Rome's name. The young Romulus and aging Tatius would both remain kings, who would serve concurrently and as equals in their unified city-state.[22]

The proposal was creative and benefited both parties. Romulus and Tatius could each boast of multiplying the number of men at arms, which greatly secured the newly unified state. This compromise additionally permitted the Romans to keep the maidens because the Romans were no longer members of a belligerent, alien kingdom. They were now the Sabines' fellow countrymen. Therefore, this agreement sidestepped the problem of leaving the women in the hands of thieving foreigners. Moreover, the maidens' parents legitimized the marriages by paying the Roman husbands handsome dowries. This treaty even encouraged mingling of the populations. Any Sabine who wished to relocate to Rome was permitted to do so and enjoy full rights as a Roman. Many eventually moved to Rome, which substantially increased the city's size. In fact, Rome doubled its population in short order. Still, the Sabines and Romans made some concessions. Rome would be their capital, and each citizen would be called a Roman. Yet the citizenry as a whole would henceforth be referred to as Quirites, allegedly after Tatius' hometown of Cures, although this etymology is disputed.[23]

To finalize the agreement, Romulus and Tatius swore oaths to be faithful to the treaty and uphold its provisions. They subsequently erected altars near the Via Sacra, where the dual monarchs presumably conducted sacrifices to solidify the agreement and seek the gods' blessing for their compromise. They saw no abnormalities in the sacrificial beasts' entrails, which suggested that their agreement didn't offend the gods. Then the Romans and part of the Sabine nation officially became one kingdom and peace was reached. Finally, the conflict was over, which permitted the soldiers to return to their homes or remain in Rome to resume their private lives.[24]

While the accounts of the Sabine war suggest it happened over the course of a single campaign, Dionysius contended that it lasted three years. This seems suspiciously long, given the narratives, but not impossible. It is, however, plausible that Dionysius included conflicts with the Caeninenses, Antemnates and Crustumerians in his calculation.[25]

Regardless of the war's length, once at peace, Romulus and Tatius turned their attention toward civil matters in order to organize the newly unified kingdom per their treaty's terms. They needed to enact additional laws and institute mandatory religious observances within their recently merged domain, and they were required to do so in concert with each other. Even though Livy reported that they governed in seamless unity, they certainly must have found ruling alongside an equal a major adjustment that was more than a little difficult.[26]

Duarchy

'Thenceforward the two kings exercised their joint sovereignty with perfect harmony.'

– Livy

The majority of the Romans and Sabines must have been overjoyed upon learning that Romulus and Tatius had reached a lasting peace agreement. The two kings were likewise relieved that they were able to avert a protracted and even bloodier war. In exchange, they were required to cede some of their regal power and sovereignty to their former adversary. Under their terms, the newly unified state would essentially be ruled by a duarchy, which consisted of two kings who theoretically wielded equal power.

While Romulus and Tatius publicly embraced the new treaty and heralded it as a clever compromise, they doubtlessly experienced some growing pains. After all, they weren't accustomed to ruling alongside a partner, but the kings tolerated their newly diminished, albeit still powerful, roles for everyone's best interest. They began working in unison, and even though the co-monarchs resolved to rule together, it seems that they found it prudent to live in separate parts of the expanding city. As such, Romulus considered the Caelian and Palatine Hills his home. He had already been residing on the Palatine Hill since before Rome's founding and naturally preferred to remain there. So, he continued living on the Palatine at a location likely near the Steps of Cacus, which today overlooks the Circus Maximus.[1]

Romulus' home wasn't far from a place where, according to legend, a flowering cornel tree grew, but this was no common hardwood. It was a testament to Romulus' brute strength. Earlier in his life, he hurled a javelin made of cornel wood while he was standing on the Aventine Hill. When the athletic Romulus gripped the spear and thrust it with all of his might, it allegedly soared from the Aventine Hill to the Palatine, where it landed with great force. It penetrated the ground so deeply that nobody could retrieve it from the soil, despite many attempts. Eventually, the shaft sprouted and grew tall and hearty, and Romulus looked after it with religious-like care. During later Roman times, the Romans cherished the sacred tree. Whenever it appeared sickly, Romans would exclaim, 'Water! Water!', and rush to empty water vessels onto the tree to ensure its survival. In spite of this devotion, the great Julius Caesar accidentally killed it, or at least one of its descendants, during a construction project. Aside from the tree's untimely demise, considering that it was a monument of sorts to Romulus' own physical prowess, it makes sense why Romulus chose to reside near it.[2]

Tatius, on the other hand, had previously seized the Capitoline Hill during his war with Rome, and he took up permanent residence there and eventually considered the Quirinal part of his domain as well. Remaining on the Capitoline Hill may also have been part of the peace accord in order to placate Tatius. If he retained possession of the captured hill, then he might appear as though he was a victorious conqueror, which could augment his prestige. Whatever his reasoning, Tatius' dwelling was atop the hill not far from where later Romans erected a temple in honour of Juno Moneta, the supernatural guardian of the city's funds.

The kings' decision to live separately was wise. If the erstwhile foes literally lived and ruled beside each other, then there was a higher likelihood that problems might arise. Constant contact could lead to public spats, fierce disagreements and even open contempt. They had already prosecuted wars against one another, and they probably still privately viewed each other as rivals. Consequently, there must have been a palpable tenuousness to their peace. The last thing they needed was to create a risky environment that might breed antipathy. So, they prudently lived apart.[3]

Even though they quartered on different hills, once united as co-kings, Romulus and Tatius worked in concert with each other and laid down new laws, regulations and religious institutions, but the ancient writers were often confused over when certain of these were enacted. Many believed that some of these early laws were ratified solely under Romulus during Rome's initial founding, while others thought they came into effect during the duarchy. Romulus had previously established many rules on his own, but it's more likely that a multitude of Rome's primary laws date to this era.[4]

Given that Rome was rapidly expanding, there was plenty of business demanding the kings' attentions. Rome's citizenry had doubled following the war. Perhaps because Rome's growing population began to increasingly take residence on nearby hills, one of Romulus and Tatius' first acts was to annex two of the ridges. As such, they officially added to their domain the Quirinal and Caelian hills. The former was due north of the Palatine Hill, and the latter directly east of the Palatine.[5]

Upon appending new hills to their kingdom and combining their people, Romulus and Tatius needed to fully integrate the Sabines into Roman society. Under their agreement, the Sabines were treated as Roman citizens, and they seem to have received most, if not all, of the same rights. However, Maurus Servius Honoratus claimed that the Sabines weren't necessarily the Romans' equals. He stated that they were barred from voting for magistrates, but in all other ways, they enjoyed the same privileges as any Roman.[6]

While there might have been a degree of inequality, both kings relied on a group of elders who wielded considerable influence. Romulus had already created the Senate, and it appears that likewise, Tatius also had an advisory body of elder aristocrats. As had previously been the case, Romulus continued relying on his Senate. Similarly, when Tatius assumed the role of co-king, he brought along his councillors, who numbered around 100 or maybe less (the ancient sources differ).

During the early days of the dual kingship, each monarch separately consulted their councils from their respective hills before acting in unison, but eventually, Romulus and Tatius decided to create one single Roman Senate. The reasons for this are pretty clear: each king wanted his own senior advisors to impact the other king's thinking; the monarchs probably wished for greater transparency and collaboration between the Romans and Sabines during the decision-making process; and Romulus and Tatius strove to create a legitimate unified government. All of this was accomplished by proceeding henceforth with only one Senate, consisting of both Romans and Sabines. Consequently, either fifty or 100 illustrious Sabines (the ancient authors provided conflicting reports) were inducted into the Roman Senate.[7]

Romulus and Tatius additionally reorganized the recently consolidated people in order to more easily rule over them and help the kings cater to their needs. In fact, the monarchs divided their citizenry into three large bodies, often called tribes. Sadly, it's not clear whether the populace was arranged into tribes based upon territory, ethnic background or occupation. Nevertheless, members of the first tribe were named for Romulus and were called the Ramnenses; the second grouping became known as Tatienses after Tatius; and the third were the Lucerenses. Unfortunately, the ancient authors disagreed over the latter's origin. The Romans purportedly either named the tribe for the well-known grove where non-citizens often took refuge and asked for asylum, or for Romulus' deceased friend Lucumo.[8]

Probably in order to reduce the kings' administrative burdens, each tribe was assigned a senior official called a tribune, who presumably helped assemble and organize the tribes. In all likelihood, he additionally presented the tribes' concerns to the kings and guaranteed that the tribes fulfilled their primary functions, including conducting sacrifices, but the tribunes didn't work alone. A seer was required to oversee the tribes' communal sacrifices and ensure that the Romans understood the gods' wills.[9]

Each tribe was further divided into ten *phratries*, also known as *curiae*, which were led by officers called *curiones*. Some ancient historians believed that the *curiae* were named for the abducted maidens who helped secure a peace agreement. Others rejected this premise because some of the *curia* shared their appellation with physical places. Regardless of their names' origins, each *curia* was subdivided by ten, and a *decurion* commanded each subdivision. The reason Romulus and Tatius created these divisions and subdivisions seems quite simple. Romulus had empowered his subjects with the right to vote, and it was less complicated for the ancient Romans to vote on certain measures and political candidates when assigned to specific wards. Moreover, it would make it easier for them to fulfill their religious and even civic duties, and the *curiones* and *decuriones* could help with all of this.[10]

Romulus required each *curia* to specifically appease certain deities, and he erected banquet halls where the *curias'* members could feast together and praise the gods. He even created a college of sixty priests, two for each *curia*, to help the wards conduct the proper rites and sacrifices. However, every *curia* had the right to elect their own priests, who served for life, but they were required to be over 50 years old, of unquestioned morality and have no physical deformities. In many cases, the priests' wives and children helped them perform the rites. Yet if the holy men had no offspring, then, in accordance with Greek religious customs, they were permitted to choose the most handsome boy and girl within the *curia* to assist them.[11]

There were other considerations that prompted the kings to reorder their citizenry. To govern over the growing population and conduct the necessary censuses, the people needed to be organized, and apportioning them to different tribes and *curia* helped the kings accomplish this. Relying on the tribal divisions additionally permitted the kings to more easily order specific blocs to assemble so that the monarchs could address them on various issues, including calling them to war.

For some reason, the use of these specific tribal names died out following Romulus' reign, but the notion of dividing Rome's population into tribes remained in the eternal city for centuries. Even the office of the tribunate became a mainstay, but it was different than the one Romulus created. Later in Rome's history, there were a variety of different types of tribunes, including the consular tribune, military tribune and plebeian tribune. They fulfilled different military and civic leadership functions.[12]

While Romulus reportedly established the office of the tribunate, he, perhaps with Tatius' help, also created at least three centuries of knights. As the word suggests, they numbered 100 people per century. This was possibly the early origin of the Roman equestrian order, whose members became incredibly influential and powerful in the later Roman Republic. They essentially became a wealthy, non-patrician business class that enjoyed many privileges that the impoverished plebeians didn't. Whereas many ancients traced the names Ramnenses, Tatienses and Lucerenses to Rome's first tribes, Livy differed. He asserted that these, or similar names, were the monikers of the first three centuries of knights. Whatever the case, they may have had special duties. At some point, Romulus established a company of full-time, intimidating personal bodyguards called the Celeres. There were 300 members of the order whom Romulus either appointed or the Romans elected. Some believed that the ancient equestrians were the same as the 300 Celeres.[13]

As Rome expanded, the kings established a new form of government and organized their people, but Romulus and Tatius were eventually confronted by Rome's insufficient laws. Romulus had previously established statutes and delineated certain rights for his subjects. Yet Rome was still an incredibly young city, and Romulus had only been a ruler for a limited amount of time. As a result, Rome's legal code was evidently somewhat sparse, and this demanded the monarchs' action. The laws that they may have eventually enacted together, or at least those recorded by historians, seemed principally related to divorces and families in general, which is unsurprising.

There were few women living in Rome during its first few years. Thus, Romulus apparently deemed statutes regarding marriage unnecessary at the time, but that soon changed. After Rome's population boomed and intermarried, there was probably a subsequent spike of unhappy marriages and various kinds of marital disputes. This exposed the legal code's insufficiency regarding divorces, spurring the kings' response. Consequently, likely around this time, Romulus and Tatius codified laws related to marriage and families.[14]

The dual kings proclaimed that when a man and woman married, they owned and shared their property together and should view their union as holy and inviolable. If their marriage was troubled, then they were encouraged to cope with each other's shortcomings. However, women were expected to adapt to their husbands' preferences and meekly behave as if they were the men's possessions. Despite officially venturing to preserve marriages, according to Plutarch, a husband was permitted to divorce his wife. He could only do so without facing a penalty if she had committed certain offences, including adultery or attempted murder. Yet a divorce might not be necessary because a woman's act of adultery was technically punishable by death. Women, alternatively, were not awarded the same liberties as men. They were forbidden from obtaining a divorce on their own accord under any circumstance, but considering that females enjoyed very few rights in antiquity, this is not surprising.[15]

Notions of fidelity and the aversion to divorces essentially became laughable to later, more promiscuous Roman generations. The early Romans, on the other hand, allegedly didn't take marriage laws lightly. Dionysius and Aulus Gellius even claimed that no divorces occurred within Rome for hundreds of years. Supposedly, the first Roman to dissolve his marriage was Spurius Carvilius, who left his beloved wife because she was unable to bear children. While he was given permission to divorce his wife, the Romans loathed him for leaving her.[16]

Roman women were often unfairly treated, but Romulus and Tatius made a few concessions to them. For example, when a man decided to divorce his wife for a reason in which his bride was not legally at fault, he was required to surrender half of his property to the woman. He was further obliged to conduct a sacrifice to assuage the gods' displeasure and dedicate the rest of his property to Ceres, the goddess of motherly love. Females were awarded other privileges too. If a husband died but his family survived him, then his property was bequeathed to his wife and their children. Men were also compelled to keep vulgarity to a minimum around women and politely permit them the first right of passage when they crossed paths on a public street. The law additionally forbade women from observing males in the nude, unless of course they were married. Romulus and Tatius must have sincerely believed that if a woman saw a naked man, then the spectacle could corrupt the female, leading to infidelity. Indeed, the Romans considered exposing one's self to a woman so reprehensible that the male in question could be executed for the offence.[17]

There were other statutes aimed at fortifying good character, including prohibiting women from drinking alcohol lest they act immorally and commit adultery. Romans apparently took this law very seriously. For instance, one Roman woman decided to help herself to some wine during Romulus' reign, and in response, her husband, Egnatius Mecenius, bludgeoned her to death with a piece of wood. Since his wife had broken the law, Romulus absolved Mecenius of any wrongdoing and refused to penalize him, but there was a clear double-standard. Men could consume as much wine as they pleased without the same concerns.[18]

While ancient historians chronicled Romulus' many laws, others noticed what they believed were glaring omissions in the legal code. Plutarch, for example, found it strange that the dual monarchs didn't assign a stiffer penalty for committing parricide, the act of murdering one's own parents. Later Romans considered it one of the vilest crimes, but Romulus likely didn't feel that it was appropriate to impose a harsher punishment for the offence. He loved his countrymen as if he was their father, and as such, any murder seemed like a crime against a family member and was perhaps just as abhorrent as parricide in his eyes. Regardless of Plutarch's disbelief, parricide allegedly didn't occur in Rome for several hundred years, which may demonstrate why a special parricide law wasn't needed. The first recorded instance of the crime either involved Lucius Hostius sometime subsequent to the Second Punic War (218–201 BC) or during Gaius Marius' fifth consulship (101 BC) when Publicius Malleolus murdered his mother.[19]

Not every one of Romulus' new laws specifically related to marriage or morality. Some set long-lasting traditions for Roman youths. Following a decree from the kings, Roman children were required to wear a *bulla*, a protective amulet meant to ward off malevolent spirits. The law also obliged youths to be clothed in what became known as the *toga praetexta*, an unwieldy, purple-bordered woollen garment, which must have been stifling in the summer. It denoted the children's youth and may have even signified their special protection under the law. They dressed as such until they came of age and could don the attire of a young adult, which was accompanied by a major celebration in later Roman times.[20]

The traditions and laws that Romulus created affected more than children's attire. He also focused on ensuring that children would be compliant so that there would be order in Roman families. To this end, he laid down laws outlining the requirements for youths and gave fathers ownership of their offspring. Romulus decreed that youths must obey their parents, even in the face of harsh treatment. Indeed, they could be abused and exploited. Fathers could even disown their children and evict them from their homes for whatever reason they saw fit. The paternal ownership of children additionally meant that fathers could sell their sons into slavery, but when a man's son won his freedom, his father was allowed to put him up for sale again. Yet Romulus limited the number of times the same child could be sold to three. Apparently, he thought that more than three was simply too much.

Paternal control over children went beyond this. Patriarchs essentially had ownership of their descendants for their entire lives and could even kill their progeny in some instances. While this was allowed, Romulus strongly encouraged his subjects to raise all male children and at least the first-born female. Yet he decreed that children younger than 3 years old could only be deprived of their lives under certain circumstances. If they were born with physical deformities, then they could be killed by exposure, but only after the parents displayed proof of the handicap to their five closest neighbours. If a father or mother violated these requirements, then they could forfeit half of their property as punishment.[21]

The surge of new laws certainly caused a rise in criminal and civil cases, which necessitated judges to preside over such hearings. As kings, Romulus and Tatius also served as the state's supreme magistrates. Upon announcing their laws and the corresponding penalties for violating them, they could regularly hold court. They probably needed to, considering that Rome had grown and so had the number of disputes. Romulus eventually chose what became the Forum as the location where he presided over civil and criminal trials. While there, Romulus demonstrated that he believed justice delayed was not justice at all because he required that all trials be quick and punishments swift.[22]

Once the legal proceedings concluded in public view, he either acquitted the innocent or sentenced the guilty. In cases where there may not have been specific laws defining the appropriate punishments, Romulus decided to assign penalties that he believed were proportionate to the crimes. He had ample help executing sentences too. Romulus' lictors and his corps of baleful bodyguards, the Celeres, accompanied the king during the judicial proceedings and were more than willing to assist him. Sometimes, Romulus even tasked his lictors or the Celeres with beating or beheading the guilty, which must have produced a shocking and gory spectacle that instilled fear in the Romans. While this understandably seems overly draconian, most other times he preferred to penalize the guilty with fines whereby he would confiscate a portion of their livestock. He probably felt that this was a preferable method of ruling. It taught his subjects valuable lessons without denuding his kingdom of important human resources due to superfluous executions. Furthermore, it didn't inspire the same magnitude of antipathy that capital and corporal punishments did.[23]

It's improbable that Romulus realized that many of the traditions that he supposedly created would last well into Rome's Imperial period, but some of them allegedly did. These laws mostly served real purposes too. The early Roman family laws may appear strange and sometimes unforgiving, but Romulus and Tatius' intent is apparent. They preferred marriages to last and result in as many children as possible. Romulus and Tatius hoped that their laws would help accomplish these objectives and permit Rome to thrive for generations to come.

Many of the co-rulers' laws and penalties for breaking them were designed to fortify Roman families and protect the Roman state. Yet Romulus might have had other reasons for pursuing such goals, given that he was starting a family as well. This meant that he witnessed marriage's struggles firsthand and felt that he knew what laws would protect the unions and keep them intact. According to ancient traditions, Romulus and Hersilia wed at some point. While Hersilia must have been initially furious about being kidnapped and forced to marry a man she felt was little more than a wild savage, she sincerely fell in love with Romulus. She even advised him and may have played a major role in concluding the Sabine War. This demonstrates the respect that Romulus felt for her and the influence that she wielded.

After their wedding, the two began to build a family of their own, and Hersilia apparently gave birth to at least two children over a period of time. It's impossible to pinpoint exactly when Romulus and Hersilia started to procreate. It could have begun like it did for so many of his subjects in the days leading up to the great Sabine War or during the extended peace following the formation of the duarchy. It seems more than likely that one, if not both, of Romulus' children were born during the period of peace when Romulus would have been at home and not overwhelmed with pressing existential issues like war.

Whatever the case, Romulus reportedly sired two children, first a girl named Prima and then a boy called Aollius. Almost nothing is known about them, which begs the questions of whether they really existed and if so, did they survive childhood? This cannot be known for certain. However, if they lived past their young, more vulnerable years, then given that they were Romulus' offspring, the pair were undoubtedly pampered and lived in the royal estate on the Palatine. As they grew older, Romulus surely groomed them for leadership roles in the kingdom that he diligently shepherded, and the young prince and princess received the best elementary education possible. They may have even studied at Gabii like Romulus had allegedly once done.[24]

Romulus was building a family and his kingdom was blossoming. Indeed, Rome's outlook was much brighter since merging with Tatius and many of his Sabines, but uniting with them created other positive by-products. The surge of citizens increased the number of men who could bear arms, and as a result, Romulus doubled the size of his legions from 3,000 foot soldiers and 300 cavalry per legion to 6,000 infantrymen and 600 horsemen.[25]

Romulus did more than just enrol Sabines into his army's ranks. He adopted at least one piece of their military equipment as well. Prior to joining with the Sabines, the Roman legionaries carried a circular shield, called a *clipeus*. It was apparently styled after those used by the hoplites of the Peloponnesian city of Argos. Meanwhile, the Sabines carried oblong shields, which later ancients may have envisioned as the Roman *scutum* of subsequent eras. This offered better protection and may have been of sturdier construction. The Roman *clipeus* had served Romulus' troops well enough, but the Sabines' shields were of higher quality. During the recent war, Romulus observed that the longer, more durable Sabine shield functioned noticeably better in battle and gave Tatius' troops a distinct advantage. Thus, Romulus and his legionaries adopted the Sabines' shield, but it is important to note that Livy disagreed and claimed that Rome didn't abandon the *clipeus* for the *scutum* until hundreds of years later.[26]

Aside from this, the blending of Roman and Sabine society wasn't limited to the legions. While both peoples boasted their own proud, timeworn traditions, they also strove to respect each other's customs, which was necessary to help the two cultures coalesce. The Romans and Sabines already had their own unique religious observances, but upon merging, none were cancelled. The newly consolidated peoples embraced every single annual celebration that each group had previously observed as their calendar of celebrations greatly expanded. A few new holidays were even created following the unification.[27]

Romulus and Tatius established 1 March, which was the first day of the Roman year at the time, as the Matronalia. This holiday, among other things, celebrated the abducted maidens' role in ending the recent war, according to Plutarch. The monarchs additionally formed a feast called the Carmentalia, which women especially held in high esteem. It was eventually held on 11 and 15 January. During the Carmentalia, some Romans celebrated Fate's role in overseeing healthy human births. Successful pregnancies and deliveries were clearly important to Romulus.

Perhaps around this time, Romulus and maybe Tatius officially established the Lupercalia as a Roman holiday, which was essentially a purification ritual. It later fell on 15 February, which the Romans considered an unlucky day, but the Romans and Sabines couldn't adopt each other's holidays if they didn't agree on the calendar. So, the Sabines conceded to the Romans and accepted Romulus' system of months.[28]

The Sabines surely appropriated some of Romulus' personal habits as well. Romulus continued conducting augury before any major public business to ensure that he enjoyed the gods' approval. The Sabines evidently embraced this tradition, but the Romans and Sabines needed to give the gods the proper care and attention in other ways too. In order to continue appeasing the deities, Romulus created the Arval Priesthood, which consisted of priests who conducted specific sacrifices. This brotherhood survived well into the Imperial period. In Romulus' day, it was comprised of twelve priests, including Romulus and Acca Larentia's eleven other surviving sons. While they oversaw sacrifices, such offerings weren't required for all events and gods. Sometimes libations were acceptable. Most of Romulus' subjects used wine in their ceremonial libations, but Romulus personally preferred using milk.[29]

As the new Roman society was taking shape, the kings redeveloped the physical city of Rome in many ways too. Homes and temples sprung up across their domain as thousands of Sabines relocated to Rome. The dual kings probably also spent considerable time creating formidable defences on the newly annexed hills, the Quirinal and Caelian. Beyond this, Tatius may have even built an administrative building and a palace fit for a king on the Capitoline Hill.

The most ambitious construction project was evidently a joint effort. Romulus and Tatius wanted to create a communal area that was convenient to those living on the Capitoline, Palatine, Caelian, and Quirinal hills. Yet there was one major problem. The area between these hills was swampy, but Romulus and Tatius were undaunted by this obstacle. Instead of choosing a different location, the kings ordered their men to clear the foot of the Capitoline Hill of trees and drain the swamp as best as possible, causing the Lacus Curtius to dwindle in size.[30]

This must have been an arduous and time-consuming undertaking, but it paid dividends because it purportedly resulted in the creation of the famous Roman Forum, which still exists to this day. However, there was some ancient disagreement over whether a later Roman king founded the Forum. Nevertheless, in time, the Forum served as a religious and municipal centre and busy marketplace.[31] After draining the Forum and preparing it for use, Romulus only allowed it and other similar spaces to be opened as marketplaces every eight or nine days. He believed that it was better for his subjects to remain toiling in the fields or engaging in warfare than trading and mingling aimlessly in communal areas. He thought that if they stayed busy in their occupations, then his people would have less time to be corrupted and engage in illegal acts like adultery.

While Romulus wished for his people to remain actively employed, he specifically delineated which professions were appropriate. Interestingly, free men were only allowed to work in agriculture or serve in the legions. Romulus banned citizens from participating in other occupations.

Still, additional work needed to be done, and Romulus allowed slaves and foreigners to complete the tasks not prescribed for Roman citizens.[32]

Aside from issuing employment edicts and preparing the Forum, Romulus and Tatius took on other major undertakings. The co-monarchs erected religious temples and altars that eventually dotted the Roman landscape. While warring with Tatius, Romulus pledged to Jupiter that he would dedicate a temple to the god in exchange for the deity's assistance. Romulus ultimately believed that he had benefitted from the god's favour. Thus, he aimed to keep his promise, and one of his first building projects of this period was creating a temple worthy of Jupiter Stator (stayer of the flight). When it was completed, it stood on the Via Sacra near the northern end of the Palatine Hill. This was close to the spot where the Romans made their stand against the Sabine onslaught following Romulus' prayer.[33]

Perhaps after its construction, Romulus and/or Tatius installed temples and altars devoted to Saturn, Saturn's wife Rhea, and Vulcan, the god of fire. Romulus built the latter using one tenth of the spoils that the Romans had seized during one of their previous wars. Romulus additionally continued the tradition of serving Vesta and employing Vestal Virgins. Indeed, many writers imputed him with bringing the cult to Rome whereupon he tasked the Vestal Virgins with overseeing a sacred fire. While Romulus introduced this venerated cult in Rome, it was Tatius who built a temple for the goddess, where the Vestals could perform their duties. However, some ancient historians attributed the first construction of Vesta's temple to one of Romulus' successors.[34]

Whatever the case, Romulus and Tatius honoured other gods too. There were areas within Rome that were dedicated to the goddess Diana, who is associated with nature, and Enyalius. Beyond this, the kings placed altars in every *curia* across Rome, which were devoted to Juno who watched over the state. Tatius even dedicated building projects to the sun and moon, guaranteeing that no possible deity felt neglected.[35]

Romulus also concentrated on terrestrial matters, including instituting a plan for governing the kingdom when he was away on business. To address this matter, Romulus created the role of the *praefectus urbi*, who served as his temporary replacement and acted in the monarch's stead when he was away at war or on diplomatic missions. During such absences, the *praefectus urbi* ensured that the justice system continued to function and that emergencies were addressed. Romulus apparently had a preferred lieutenant for this post named Denter Romulius, who was a senator, but little is known about the man. Despite this, it seems that before long, Romulus called Denter Romulius and/or the Senate to temporarily govern on his behalf. After all, someone needed to supervise Rome on a short-term interim basis because its kings were forced to defend the kingdom.[36]

XII

Cameria

'[Romulus and Tatius] engaged in one joint undertaking, the expedition against the Camerini; for these people, who kept sending out bands of robbers and doing great injury to the country of the Romans.'

– Dionysius of Halicarnassus

For the first five years of Romulus and Tatius' dual reign, Rome was mostly at peace. This was likely also an era of prosperity. Without war, its inhabitants could concentrate on private enterprises and enriching themselves. Meanwhile, Rome's borders grew as the kings annexed nearby hills, and its population boomed. New building projects carpeted Rome's domain, and its kings established new laws and administrative procedures that served Rome well. Considering what the ancient historians recorded, it seems that the Romans were in the midst of a period of economic expansion, while simultaneously enjoying the security provided by their army's size and leaders' reputations.

Despite this harmony, numerous nearby cities were distrustful of the Romans. They had anxiously watched Rome clash with other cities as its regional power ballooned. At this point, several of these communities probably had little desire to risk a confrontation with the Romans. Since joining with the Sabines, Rome could raise massive armies, which were led by shrewd, military-minded men, Romulus and Tatius. It would take a considerable force and a canny strategy for Rome's neighbours to seriously challenge Rome. Therefore, many within the region felt that they couldn't countenance the hazards of challenging Rome for some time, but it ultimately occurred.

One episode, which only Dionysius of Halicarnassus recorded, supposedly interrupted this welcome period of peace. There was a neighbouring town named Cameria, which was originally a colony of Alba Longa, and its people were called the Camerini. Many of them were little more than unscrupulous robbers who were apparently supported by Cameria's corrupt government, and numerous gangs of Camerini frequently roamed the countryside in search of plunder. They often journeyed to the edges of Rome's domain, where they evidently harassed its citizens and sometimes seized their belongings when the opportunity arose. The Camerini were guilty of many things, including stealing livestock, raiding farms and even ambushing and robbing unsuspecting Romans as they travelled the countryside. The Camerini's endeavours were fruitful too. They despoiled an unknown number of victims, and after the Camerini had stolen what was available, they retreated to safety before the Romans could react. These wanton incursions presumably started as a few isolated incidents, but the Camerini must have greatly increased their raids once they found them highly profitable.

It mustn't have taken long for the Romans to discover that the pillaging parties hailed from nearby Cameria. Victims of their attacks may have overheard their attackers' dialects, noticed clothing that might have been traditional for the Camerini or simply observed them returning home. Regardless of how they learned of their origin, the forays surged, and Rome's subjects demanded that the wrongs be addressed forthwith. At first, it's probable that this seemed like only a relatively minor diplomatic issue that could be resolved in the courts or by alerting Cameria's leadership, but Romulus and Tatius discovered otherwise.

It's not entirely clear whether the Romans first tried to capture the lawless Camerini. If they did, then their attempts ended in failure because the matter escalated into a major diplomatic dispute. To Romulus and Tatius' credit, they didn't immediately use the raids as an excuse to invade and conquer Cameria. Rather, when the situation could no longer be ignored, the Romans dispatched emissaries to speak with Cameria's leaders. The envoys urged them to help end the devastating attacks, which was hardly an inappropriate request. The Romans wanted justice, and they evidently petitioned the Camerini to capture the malefactors and perhaps try them in one of Cameria's courts or convey them to Rome, where they would be judged and punished. The Camerini either steadfastly rejected the Romans' petitions or gave the pretence of acceding to them to temporarily appease the Romans. Whatever the case, soon enough Romulus and Tatius concluded that Cameria's government was officially harbouring and abetting the fugitives, and the Camerini had no desire for justice.

At some point, Rome's ambassadors returned home and may have informed Romulus, Tatius and the Senate that the Camerini bore no intention of halting the incursions into Rome. Still, the Romans didn't immediately abandon hope that the Camerini would eventually acquiesce, see the error of their ways, and convict and punish the bandits. Indeed, the Romans continued to plead with the Camerini to act justly, but following every respectful Roman request, the Camerini failed to cooperate.

In the meantime, it's possible that Cameria's government may have emboldened the plundering parties, who probably continued harassing the Romans. In time, Rome's elders discussed how to address the situation, and Romulus and Tatius determined that they couldn't permit the Camerini to unjustifiably attack their increasingly impatient subjects any longer. The Roman monarchs felt that they must defend Rome's inhabitants and decided to confront the Camerini with overwhelming force. Consequently, the kings assembled their people, explained the situation and prepared to teach the Camerini a lesson. Perhaps after temporarily putting the *Praefectus Urbi*, Denter Romulius, in charge of Rome, they subsequently marched their legions toward Cameria.

The Romans advanced an unknown distance and met Cameria's troops, who were apparently expecting them. Then the two factions dug in for a set-piece battle, but the Romans enjoyed critical advantages. Considering that the campaign against the Camerini was a joint expedition prosecuted by both Romulus and Tatius, the Romans were definitely led by more capable commanders than their foes. This wasn't the Romans' only benefit, though. With Romulus and Tatius' combined might, it's safe to assume that the Romans outnumbered the Camerini.

Regrettably, there are few details of the conflict, other than there was a pitched battle of some kind, but the Camerini simply couldn't withstand the Roman war machine. Romulus and Tatius enjoyed an overwhelming victory. Still, the co-monarchs weren't satisfied with slaughtering the Camerini army. They intended on creating an environment within Cameria that would hopefully guarantee the Camerini's good behaviour for years to come.

To this end, Romulus and Tatius marched their legionaries on Cameria. When they arrived they surrounded and laid siege to it. Unfortunately again, Dionysius provided no specifics of the operation other than the Romans successfully stormed the city and assumed mastery of it. Certainly, when they captured Cameria, feelings of regret and fear swept over the town's inhabitants, and they would have had good reason to be concerned. The Romans had laboured to find a diplomatic solution to Cameria's numerous transgressions, even though the Camerini had repeatedly wronged the Romans. Each time, the Camerini had either indefensibly dismissed Rome's reasoned petitions or simply failed to address them after promising to do otherwise. Now Rome was in total control of Cameria, and the Romans forced the Camerini to obediently accept their non-negotiable terms.[1]

Upon sacking Cameria, the Romans doubtlessly plundered the city to some extent and shared the spoils amongst themselves. Romulus, on the other hand, declined to personally accept any of the booty, as was his policy. Romulus was apparently restrained, but his legionaries weren't. The scene within Cameria was chaotic due to the frenetic looting. Perhaps when it concluded, Romulus and Tatius informed the conquered Camerini that as punishment – and to ensure Rome's safety – the Camerini would forfeit one third of their land to the Romans, which was a painful requirement. Romulus and Tatius subsequently announced that the Romans would send colonists to inhabit the newly acquired land. They were intended, in all likelihood, to closely observe the Camerini in case they decided to confront the Romans again. Furthermore, Romulus and Tatius declared that the Camerini were to be stripped of all their weapons. This seemed to be a wise decision, given how treacherous the Camerini were. Considering their many misdeeds against the Romans, Romulus and Tatius preferred Cameria to exist only in a weakened, vulnerable state. It also seems plausible that the Roman kings demanded that the individual pillagers, who had been harrying the Romans, be tried. If they were, then the Romans surely found them guilty and punished them.[2]

After Cameria's resounding defeat and the resulting peace accord's enactment, numerous Romans excitedly set out from Rome to form a new colony at Cameria. After making the short journey, they established homes on land formerly controlled by Cameria, but the Camerini grew incredibly embittered and craved revenge against the Romans. As long as they were deprived of weapons and may have had Roman troops watching over them, there was little that they could do. Yet in relatively short order, most of the legionaries returned to their homes. This left the Roman settlers alone amongst the supposedly disarmed Camerini.

Even with the colonists remaining vigilant, the Camerini began plotting to regain control of their land and eject the unwelcome settlers. Contrary to Romulus and Tatius' stipulations, the Camerini presumably smuggled weapons into Cameria, organized themselves and started harassing the Romans who had relocated there. This was an inadvisable move, but they accosted and robbed the Romans anyway. They were willing to do whatever they could to encourage the Romans to leave, while simultaneously stealing their valuable property.

This naturally didn't sit well with Romulus and Tatius, who lost all patience with the belligerent city and decided that the time for diplomacy was at an end. As a result, they raised their legions a second time to settle matters once and for all. However, the Camerini evidently had surreptitiously reacquired weapons on a large scale in case the Romans decided to ever march on them again, which they did.[3]

Following the Camerini's recent provocations, Romulus and Tatius led their legions out of Rome, and they were determined to soundly repress the Camerini menace. Once more they battled the Romans, and even though virtually no details of this encounter are extant, what is clear is that the Camerini couldn't contend with the legionaries. Romulus and Tatius easily defeated them, but the highly irritated co-rulers weren't in a forgiving mood, given the Camerini's repeated offences. Therefore, they required the Camerini to surrender even more property, which was subsequently distributed among the Romans. Then Cameria as a whole officially became a Roman colony, but it seems that a large number of

Camerini were either allowed to remain in Cameria or at least live within the vicinity.[4]

Romulus and Tatius could have completely neutralized the Camerini by massacring the town's inhabitants, but they opted to show mercy. While the Romans deprived the Camerini of a fair amount of their land and property, they didn't execute them wholesale, as was often the case in the ancient world. In fact, Romulus even allowed the Camerini to relocate to Rome and live as Roman citizens if they wished. While some couldn't bear the thought of living under their vanquishers' rule, many must have felt that this was their only option. As such, some 4,000 Camerini accepted Romulus and Tatius' offer and emigrated to Rome, while many Romans relocated to Cameria to colonize the newly vacant land.[5]

This temporarily settled matters, and peace reigned again in Romulus and Tatius' growing kingdom. As before, the kings turned their attention toward civil and religious matters. Regrettably for them, lasting peace and the duarchy weren't permanent or even long-lasting fixtures of the Roman kingdom. New challenges and risks emerged that threatened the kings and their burgeoning city-state.

XIII

Laurentum

'But in the sixth year, the government of the city devolved once more upon Romulus alone, Tatius having lost his life as the result of a plot.'

– Dionysius of Halicarnassus

While Romans previously had plenty of cause to complain about Cameria's thieving subjects, Rome also housed more than a few lawless bandits of its own, which is unsurprising. Romulus had originally enlarged Rome, in part, by admitting a multitude of undesirable fugitives into the city, and many of them likely never reversed their illicit ways. In fact, an untold number of thieves of various ethnic backgrounds, including Sabine, resided within Rome. One such band of criminal Sabines caused great turmoil and happened to be close associates of King Tatius. One of its members was even Tatius' relative. Very similar to the lawless Camerini, these unruly Sabines committed despicable acts. They formed a gang of ruffians who stalked the countryside and ruthlessly robbed unsuspecting people of their belongings.[1]

On one such criminal expedition, the Sabines departed from Rome intent on robbing vulnerable travellers, and they fully expected to return laden with booty. As they discreetly traversed the countryside, they entered the realm of Laurentum, which was about 20 miles south-west of Rome. The bandits patiently waited for easy prey to appear, and they were not disappointed. After some period of time, they stealthily observed a group of Laurentian herdsmen dutifully tending to their livestock.[2]

The Sabines quietly lingered as they watched from afar for a moment when the shepherds were most susceptible to attacks. Eventually, a favourable circumstance arose, and as it did, the bandits launched a pre-planned ambush upon the unsuspecting Laurentians. The robbers then rushed forth with their weapons drawn and scattered the herdsmen's flock, causing chaos and confusion among the Laurentian shepherds. During the pandemonium, the Sabines clashed with the unprepared Laurentians, but they were no match for the organized gang members. The Sabines probably overpowered the Laurentians without much difficulty, wounding some and killing others.

Once the shepherds were mostly subdued or had escaped, the Sabines began seizing their property and absconding with their livestock. Then before a well-organized assault could be launched from Laurentum, the gang members fled the scene. This left the surviving victims free to collect their dead comrades who were shamefully strewn on the ground, and return to their homes.

When the herdsmen arrived in Laurentum, they described the terror that they had endured to their friends and relatives. Before long, the Laurentian authorities also learned of the unprovoked attack and some of their countrymen's deaths. The incident enraged the townsfolk, and they rightfully demanded swift and sure justice. Fortunately for the surviving victims, they somehow learned that the attackers were of Sabine origin and hailed from Rome, and they even discovered their identities. Perhaps following a speedy but thorough investigation of the attack, Laurentum's leaders empowered envoys to travel to Rome. They were tasked with exposing the infractions that had been perpetrated against Laurentum's people and respectfully petitioning the Romans to promptly and justly redress the wrongs.

As the emissaries dignifiedly entered Rome and gained an audience with Romulus, Tatius and the Senate, they explained that a gang of Sabines, who called Rome home, had committed an egregious crime against their people. The ambassadors subsequently suggested that the accused should be surrendered to the Laurentian government to stand trial for their misdeeds and accept their punishments. It's pretty clear that the crimes infuriated Romulus, who was ready to see the offenders disciplined forthwith. Tatius, on the other hand, was probably somewhat agitated by the news but was noticeably more reserved than Romulus, at least initially.

Despite Tatius' curious reaction, Romulus readily agreed with the ambassadors that the guilty individuals should be conveyed to the Laurentians to be judged. Tatius, however, interjected and strenuously disapproved of this plan. The accused Sabines were associates of Tatius, and he privately wished to shield them from the Laurentians' wrath. So, he proposed what initially sounded like a rational response to the envoys' demands. He stated that the men in question were Roman citizens, and it was not fitting to surrender his own subjects to a foreign city without first being found guilty of the crimes for which they were accused. He explained that as Roman citizens, they enjoyed the protection of the state and its system of due process. Therefore, if the emissaries sought justice, then they needed to direct the victims to officially file charges against the accused in a Roman court, whereupon the implicated Sabines would be judged. Only after this and their conviction would he even consider surrendering the men to the Laurentians.

Romulus and Tatius had ruled jointly with relative harmony for around five years, but this episode seems to have been the first instance in which the co-monarchs were publicly at odds with one another. As co-kings, they needed to concur on all important matters before proceeding, but they differed over how to respond to the Laurentum debacle. As a result, Tatius' dissenting opinion essentially vetoed Romulus' plan to transfer the alleged robbers to Laurentum. This greatly frustrated Romulus as well as the ambassadors, who hadn't anticipated this possibility.

It appears that the emissaries weren't prepared to accept or reject Tatius' offer, which would have allowed the victims to introduce charges against the Sabine bandits in Rome. The Laurentians may have seen through Tatius' clever retorts and believed that he was simply preventing the criminals from being punished for personal reasons. The Lauretians probably thought that even if charges were brought against the criminals in Rome, then the trial would be a travesty, given Tatius' involvement. After what must have been a testy exchange, the envoys angrily left Rome to report back to Laurentum's leaders.[3]

Tatius' intervention disappointed and exasperated Romulus. Tatius seemed like a fair leader during most of his tenure as a Roman king, but to

Romulus, Tatius now appeared as though he was purposefully impeding justice. Romulus was perhaps also more than a little suspicious of Tatius' close connection to the accused bandits. While there is no evidence suggesting that Tatius was involved in the actual crimes, he took great pains to prevent the criminals from being punished, which Romulus noted. Yet there was little that Romulus could do since, as co-rulers, he and Tatius were equal partners.

As Tatius had prescribed, the accused Sabine men remained free, at least until someone formally brought charges against them. There is no doubt that the gang members were thankful to King Tatius for blocking a motion that would have allowed their extradition to Laurentum, but they were still at risk of severe punishment. If the envoys reached Laurentum with Tatius' message, returned to file charges and the Sabine bandits were convicted of theft and murder, then that would pose a major problem for the criminals. Contrary to what the Laurentians thought, the criminals may have worried that Tatius wouldn't be able to conjure up a compelling, reasoned argument to spare their lives if this occurred. After all, they certainly thought, Tatius would be hard-pressed to justifiably protect them from punishment, especially if they were convicted of homicide. To prevent this from transpiring and to punish the emissaries for demanding justice, the murdering thieves decided to take matters into their own hands.

Around this time, the Laurentian ambassadors had begun making their way back home, but as the sun started to set, they made camp for the night. They pitched their tents at a suitable location on the side of the road that led back to their homes. After some discussions and maybe dinner, they retired for the night, but unbeknownst to them, they had been followed and were being watched.[4]

The Sabine men whom they had attempted to extradite had followed them ever since their departure from Rome, and they quietly waited for a favourable moment to attack the ambassadors, which soon materialized. While the emissaries slept, the gang maliciously inched toward the camp. Seeing that the envoys were wholly defenseless, the Sabines silently entered the Laurentian tents, slit many of the sleeping men's throats and stole their valuables.[5]

Committing thievery in addition to murder might have just been a crime of opportunity. Alternatively, they may have stolen the Laurentians' belongings in an effort to stage the murder so that it would appear as a robbery gone awry. In this way, perhaps they hoped that they wouldn't be suspected of being involved in the crime. Rather, it could be blamed on random highwaymen. Despite their possible motivations for seizing the property, at least one member of the Laurentian mission awoke, realized what was afoot and managed to escape into the night. The band of ruffians evidently didn't expect that there would be any survivors. To their disappointment, there were, and one or more of them fearfully fled back to Laurentum, where they reported the attack on the sacrosanct ambassadors.[6]

Laurentum's leaders were furious, and rightly so. Not only had the Romans denied them justice on their own terms, but the very same men whom they had tried to extradite had murdered their emissaries in cold blood. Laurentum's citizens were incensed too, but Rome wasn't just facing Laurentum's ire. The atrocious crimes and Rome's feeble response to them shocked and angered other cities that were likely allied with Laurentum. These communities believed that Rome was protecting thieves and murderers in the same way that Cameria had aided their unruly citizens.

As reports of Rome's inexcusable treachery spread rapidly throughout the region, Romulus and Tatius hosted numerous envoys from cities across central Italy who loudly complained about Rome's dishonourable behaviour. However, Rome wasn't just the recipient of a flurry of criticism. It was also the target of conspicuous threats. Most of the ambassadors essentially shared the same clear message: swiftly right the wrongs suffered by the Laurentians or else face war from a united front from all corners of the region. As Romulus anxiously entertained the foreign messengers, the situation quickly threatened to spiral out of control, which could jeopardize Rome's very existence.[7]

During this episode, it's obvious that Romulus and Tatius grew apart as Romulus largely blamed his co-ruler for the avoidable scandal and its potentially hazardous effects. Meanwhile, Tatius exacerbated matters because it seemed that he wasn't taking the controversy seriously, which further agitated Romulus. He preferred to deal with the perpetrators properly and immediately, but Tatius delayed action at every turn, causing a growing schism between the kings.[8]

While Tatius had attempted to shield his associates from punishment, Romulus had heard enough from the envoys about the Sabine gang's despicable behaviour. Romulus knew that the bandits were guilty, and he perceived that Tatius was no longer acting as a just king. He additionally understood that the diplomatic controversy threatened to evolve into a full-scale armed conflict. Romulus wasn't willing to risk war and Rome's survival over a criminal justice issue, especially when some of his subjects and his joint ruler were to blame. Ultimately, Romulus resolved to circumvent Tatius and take matters into his own hands. He concluded that he must ensure his people's safety and guarantee that the criminals would be judged and punished, even if that meant disregarding Tatius' authority.

After deciding to rectify the misconduct and consulting the Senate, whose members agreed that Romulus should deal with the issue himself, he convened some of his loyal deputies. He instructed them to do what he believed should have been done all along: apprehend and transfer the gang members to Laurentum. Upon receiving Romulus' orders, his lieutenants assembled their subordinates and set out to locate the offenders.[9]

It appears that Tatius initially felt powerless to thwart Romulus and the Senate, and in the end, one by one, Romulus' men found and captured the criminals. Romulus' deputies then handed them over to the Laurentian emissaries who had returned to Rome seeking justice. When they obtained custody of the criminals, the ambassadors were relieved knowing that the vicious offenders would finally receive their comeuppance and an unnecessary war would be averted. They were also grateful that Romulus had advocated for justice from the beginning and had given the order to capture the Sabine thugs. The envoys appreciated this and never forgot it.

While Romulus' actions pleased the Laurentians, they enraged Tatius. At some point, perhaps when the offenders were being conveyed to the Laurentian ambassadors, Tatius decided to insert himself into the developing events. He pitied his comrades' probable fates and denounced the extradition to his allies. Tatius knew that he couldn't persuade Romulus or the Senate to free the perpetrators, but he felt great sadness for the Sabines. Many of those in custody were his friends, and one was a relative. He knew that if they were transferred to Laurentum, then the Laurentians would almost certainly execute them. Despite Tatius' vociferous complaints, Romulus had already instructed the Laurentians to go in peace and take the murderers with them, and they subsequently exited Rome with the offenders in chains. At this moment, there was little that Tatius could do other than loudly object to Romulus, which would have been altogether pointless. Still, Tatius had not yet resigned the idea of saving his countrymen.

Somehow, without arousing suspicion, Tatius plotted with his trusted companions to free the Sabine prisoners. He ordered some of his closest aides to raise a small armed force and leave the city on his command. When they were mobilized, he gave the word, and they departed, likely in unassuming bands so as not to alert Romulus of their designs. Once they were beyond Rome's gates, Tatius assembled his soldiers into a larger body and rushed to reach the Laurentian convoy before it arrived in Laurentum.

Tatius and his troops had no difficulty outstripping the ambassadors' slow-moving column, which was presumably comprised of both old and young men with plenty of baggage. Unlike the Laurentian ambassadors, Tatius' men were heavily armed, battle-hardened and prepared for a skirmish. Moreover, they must have greatly outnumbered the Laurentians. Thus, when Tatius and his Sabines reached the emissaries and demanded that they release the prisoners, the Laurentians had no choice but to obey. Thereupon, Tatius' troops apparently unbound and freed the Sabine gang members. It doesn't seem that Tatius inflicted any physical injury upon the Laurentians, but in all likelihood, he threatened them with violence until they complied with his demands. Regardless of Tatius' intimidation tactics, after the Laurentians transferred the perpetrators to him, he evidently allowed the ambassadors to return unscathed, albeit furious, to Laurentum.

The Laurentian envoys safely reached their home and again reported on Rome's outrageous misdeeds, but it seems that the Laurentians were at a loss over how they should respond to the latest offence. Interestingly, war with Rome wasn't their primary choice. They understood that Romulus was their ally and further recognized that the Roman people weren't necessarily their enemy either. Only Tatius and a few bandits were. Because of these realizations, and the fact that they thought so highly of Romulus and Rome presented a daunting military force, they still weren't willing to risk an armed conflict with Rome. The Laurentians felt that they should explore other options first, given that there was dissension between the two kings, and Tatius and his associates were their only real foes.[10]

Meanwhile, Tatius returned to Rome and resumed his position of power. However, a few matters aren't apparent. It's uncertain whether he brought the criminals back to Rome, as Dionysius of Halicarnassus implied, or if he wisely instructed them to disappear into the forests until things calmed down. If he were acting prudently, then he wouldn't have marched back to the Capitoline Hill along with these offenders. This would have tipped Romulus off to the bandits' location whereby Romulus could have rounded them back up and delivered them to Laurentum. Beyond this, it would have been a highly provocative move to publicly parade these individuals through Rome, considering their crimes and Romulus' original plan to return them to Laurentum. It's also not evident just when Romulus learned that Tatius had saved his fellow Sabines, but Romulus' lieutenants somehow became aware and certainly informed Romulus of it fairly quickly. This guaranteed that the remaining days of their joint reign must have been incredibly awkward, given they had been actively working against one another.[11]

Even though there was an obvious and very serious rift between the monarchs, they endeavoured to give the appearance of a harmonious working relationship for the good of their kingdom. Besides, there was other business that they needed to address, including conducting critical religious rites. Put simply, for the time being, they had to move on from their feud, despite the fact that they both doubtlessly viewed this quarrel as far from settled.[12]

As Rome's supreme leaders, Romulus and Tatius served pre-eminent civic, military and even religious roles, and not long after Tatius freed his associates, the monarchs were required to participate in an annual ritual. Once a year, they travelled to Lavinium to offer Rome's ancestral deities oxen sacrifices, which ostensibly ensured Rome's success and prosperity. Matters were still contentious in Rome, but Romulus and Tatius temporarily suspended their simmering dispute for this solemn event, but attending the ceremony should have concerned Tatius. First, he was travelling outside the safety of Rome, where his enemies could possibly ambush him. Second, Lavinium wasn't far from Laurentum, and the Laurentians could easily gain admittance into Lavinium. Unlike Rome, Romulus and Tatius couldn't control who entered Lavinium. Consequently, Tatius probably expected the presence of a few malcontents who might censure him. Yet, as a king, he felt that they would do nothing worse than hurl verbal insults in his direction, which he could tolerate for the sake of making proper sacrifices to the gods.

On the given date, Romulus, Tatius and their attendants arrived in Lavinium to respectfully conduct the rites. They probably didn't receive an overly warm welcome from the Lavinians because of the ongoing controversy with the Laurentians, but the Romans had surely expected this. When the time came, Romulus and Tatius approached the sacrificial altar. As Tatius was participating in the ritual and busily killing and dissecting an ox, trouble arose. A torrent of angry Laurentians, who were related to those who had been slain by Tatius' friends, rushed toward him in what was a preconceived attack. Some wielded ceremonial knives, while others grasped spits used to hold carcasses over fires as they cooked. With these instruments, they stabbed and slashed at the Sabine king as all of Lavinium and Romulus watched the dreadful spectacle. After bleeding out over a short period of time, the elderly Tatius' last breath escaped his battered body. Finally, the Laurentians had gained revenge for the Romans' offences and dishonour, and they had removed the only obstacle to justice: Tatius.[13]

Tatius' murder was a major escalation that could easily have resulted in war. Assassinating another city's king, especially as he led religious ceremonies in a foreign city, was simply an inconceivable act that normally warranted an armed conflict. At the very least, it generally merited immediate executions, but at the time, Romulus was mainly focused on retrieving Tatius' bruised and bloodied corpse and giving it a proper funeral. The Lavinian government apparently had no plans to abuse Tatius' body, nor did they wish to keep it. So, the Lavinians didn't challenge Romulus when he took custody of the corpse and transported it back to Rome.[14]

To prove the Laurentians' goodwill toward Romulus and maybe return to his good graces, many of them followed him back to Rome, loudly praising him for his fair dealings along the way. When Tatius' body arrived there, it was likely received with shock and mixed emotions. Tatius had largely been a good king, and many of the Sabines certainly favoured him. More recently, though, he had committed some questionable acts, which offended a number of his subjects.

Notwithstanding the conflicting feelings, the Romans gave Tatius an elaborate funeral fit for a king. They subsequently entombed his remains on the Armilustrium, a north-western portion of the Aventine Hill. This was possibly the same hill where Remus, Pleistinus and Faustulus were laid to rest. Even though Tatius had acted shamefully during the last days of his life, many of those in Rome celebrated the deceased Sabine. In fact, years after his death, the Romans honoured him with ritual liquid libations, generally of wine. If Romulus similarly honoured Tatius, then it would have consisted of milk, since that was his preference.[15]

Even though Tatius had perished, the ongoing dispute between Rome and Laurentum was still smouldering. Tatius and his companions had wronged Laurentum several times, but its leaders realized that their enemy wasn't Romulus or the Romans. It was Tatius and a group of criminal bandits. Yet the Laurentians had murdered one of Rome's kings, which was an unbelievable offence that normally demanded swift action. However, Romulus understood that Laurentum had endured numerous offences and that if anyone deserved to be penalized, it was only the handful of vigilantes, not the Laurentians as a whole. Therefore, he didn't view Laurentum as warranting punishment, but its citizens were still concerned for their well-being. Some of their countrymen had, after all, murdered Romulus' joint ruler in cold blood.[16]

Plutarch asserted that Romulus delayed any punitive actions against Tatius' killers and the ambassadors' murderers. It's not clear why he would have waited, unless other events interrupted him or Romulus simply preferred to move on from the Laurentian scandal. Regardless of his reasoning, it eventually became clear that he could no longer postpone justice. The Sabine bandits and the Laurentians who had assassinated Tatius needed to be judged in order to assuage the gods' displeasure, given the calamities that followed. There was apparently an outbreak of plague, and it even allegedly rained blood in Rome. This naturally terrified the superstitious Romans. When the exact same events were observed in Laurentum, there was a general consensus that these prodigies were proof of the gods' umbrage over the murderers going unpunished.[17]

To avert Romulus' retribution against their homeland and the gods' anger, the Laurentians dispatched search parties to hunt down and capture those responsible for Tatius' murder. Once they had all been rounded up, the Laurentians delivered them in chains to Romulus to punish as he saw fit. Upon assuming custody of the prisoners, they humbly spoke to the king and attempted to excuse their actions by stating that they had killed Tatius only because he had permitted the murder of their relatives and friends. They claimed that Tatius had wronged them, and they only sought to balance the scales of justice. Romulus already knew this. Even so, they pleaded for mercy and justified their actions, and their testimonies moved Romulus. As such, he forgave them for murdering Tatius. Then he released them as free men. To further show his goodwill toward the Laurentians, Romulus even re-formed a treaty of friendship between Rome and Laurentum.[18]

It appears, at least according to Dionysius, that the Sabine bandits were never brought to justice. They evidently fled beyond Rome's reach, where they remained free, but Romulus wasn't pleased with them simply living in anonymity as fugitives. So, he officially exiled them from Rome and forbade them from receiving fire or water from any of his subjects. While this was more or less a symbolic penalty, it seemed to appease all of those involved.[19]

Plutarch, on the other hand, disagreed with Dionysius. He claimed that the Romans captured and surrendered those who had murdered the

Laurentians to Laurentum's government. The Laurentians subsequently tried and punished the accused Sabines, but unfortunately, Plutarch was silent on the topic of their sentences. If Plutarch's account is accurate, then the Laurentians probably killed the offenders. Either way, after passing judgement on all parties, Romulus went a step further and performed some kind of purification rituals to ensure that he allayed the gods' fury. The execution of justice and rites that Romulus conducted apparently worked because, in time, the plague supposedly subsided, which seemed to prove that the final outcome pleased the gods.[20]

Following Tatius' burial, there were murmurs that Romulus wasn't as upset over Tatius' assassination as one might expect, especially since he had freed those responsible for Tatius' murder. Romulus and Tatius had been co-rulers for more than five years by the time of Tatius' death, and they had formed a partnership that worked well throughout most of their reign. Yet many felt that Romulus should have been more distraught over Tatius' untimely passing. Some thought that Romulus appeared relieved and that Tatius' death pleasantly contented him. This caused many to theorize that Romulus was pleased to have Tatius gone for one or two reasons. Romulus may have believed that Tatius deserved his gruesome fate, given his inexcusable involvement in the Laurentian scandal, but more likely, Romulus desired to rule as a single, supreme leader again. Thus, Tatius' assassination might have accomplished two ends that Romulus supported.[21] Perhaps to placate the Sabine partisans who believed that Tatius' murder gratified Romulus, the monarch chose to honour Tatius by dedicating a priesthood to the deceased co-monarch.[22]

After Tatius' death, the Romans opted against replacing him with another Sabine and perpetuating the duarchy. Indeed, Strabo claimed that the Roman people approved a plan to reinstitute the monarchy rather than continuing the dual kingship. Once more, Romulus was Rome's only monarch, but he may have had doubts over whether his kingdom's Sabine faction would accept him as such. Fortunately for Romulus, his apprehensions were mostly unfounded. The Sabines largely bore great respect for Romulus. Despite rumours asserting that Tatius' assassination relieved Romulus, the Sabines mainly held him in such high regard that some viewed him as an altruistic, caring deity. This was an immense social promotion for Romulus, and while he received a great amount of admiration, many of his subjects simply cowered in fear before him, which may have appeared as reverence. Regardless of their reasoning, the Roman populace readily embraced him as their only monarch.

Within a short period of time, the city effortlessly transitioned from a duarchy back to a monarchy, but the government retained many of the laws and norms that Romulus had previously enacted with Tatius. Yet some changes were necessary. Without a co-king, Romulus' workload doubled. So, he more frequently relied on the Senate to assist him as its members assumed some of the increased duties. This seemed to help, and somehow, Romulus and his kingdom emerged from this scandal largely unscathed. However, there was trouble brewing on the horizon, which demanded Romulus' attention.[23]

XIV

Fidenae

'The people of Fidenae considered that a power was growing up too close to them, so to prevent the anticipations of its future greatness from being realised, they took the initiative in making war. Armed bands invaded and devastated the country lying between [Rome] and Fidenae.'

– Livy

While Rome and Laurentum were in the midst of their diplomatic dispute, other nearby cities were watching closely to see how Romulus would react to the controversy. During the course of the Laurentian scandal, several kingdoms forwarded deputations to implore Romulus to oppose Tatius' will and allow the Sabine criminals to be punished or else face a war against a coalition of towns. This turned out to be unnecessary, but Romulus, on the other hand, could have marched his legionaries on the Laurentians for their participation in Tatius' assassination. Despite having cause, by the end of the Laurentian episode, Romulus chose not to invade Laurentum.

This earned Romulus plaudits from around the region. When leaders from several cities learned of Romulus' propensity toward justice, they likely renewed treaties of friendship with the Romans or formed new alliances with them. Certainly, Romulus had diligently amassed an impressive list of allies prior to the Laurentian debacle, but after agreeing to newly formed treaties, Rome seemed increasingly secure from potential outside attacks.[1]

Rome boasted many alliances, and Romulus' steady leadership and foresight safeguarded the Romans. Even so, it wasn't entirely immune from threats posed by other cities. As Rome's regional influence increased, there were certain communities whose leaders weren't thrilled by Rome's newfound position of territorial authority. In fact, some were wholly distrustful of Romulus and his growing settlement, just as King Acron had once felt.

One such city whose people had closely watched Rome's rapid growth was Fidenae. It was originally established as a colony of Alba Longa and had since become a large and powerful city, which was less than 8 miles north of the much younger city of Rome. The Fidenates viewed Romulus' kingdom as a dangerous upstart whose burgeoning power needed to be reined in before it gained control over Fidenae. The Fidenates may have also harboured a long-standing grudge against the Romans because, according to Plutarch, they had quarrelled with Rome over the stolen maidens' fates. Thus, they might have wanted blood for more than one reason, but they weren't entirely foolish in their attempts to thwart Rome's ascendancy.[2]

While the Fidenates wished to see Rome's downfall, Romulus' legionaries were skilled and seasoned opponents. The Fidenates knew that Romulus had routed numerous armies with relative ease, augmented his own army and enlarged his kingdom by merging with many Sabines. Moreover, Rome enjoyed treaties with many nearby towns. All of this made Rome a formidable foe, and the Fidenates knew that if they were to counter Rome, then they must patiently wait for a moment when Rome was vulnerable.[3]

Before long, what appeared to be a promising opportunity presented itself. The Fidenates doubtlessly learned that Rome was in the midst of a diplomatic squabble with the Laurentians and their allies. Since Romulus was preoccupied with the Laurentian issue, this probably seemed like a tempting time to attack the Romans. However, for the time being and for whatever reason, the Fidenates opted against invading Rome, but when the Laurentians assassinated Romulus' co-ruler, Tatius, this provided another enticing opportunity. Much of Rome's newfound strength was due to uniting with his Sabines, but with Tatius dead, there was reason for the Fidenates to believe that internal disputes might weaken Rome's standing. Tatius' death and Romulus' unsympathetic response to it could theoretically create dissension within Rome, the Fidenates may have thought. As a consequence, it might cause the powerful Roman/ Sabine state to splinter, reducing Rome's overall strength.

The circumstances grew even sweeter for the Fidenates. Around this time, Rome was in the midst of a crippling famine. The Roman situation was so dire that Romulus called on his allies to provide supplies to sustain Rome's considerable population, which was quickly becoming hungry and frail. It seems that Romulus even resorted to requesting aid from his former foe, Crustumerium. Following Romulus' official requisition, the Crustumerians dutifully complied and forwarded provisions, including grain, to Rome.[4]

During this period, the Fidenates felt confident enough to launch an assault against the Romans, who appeared increasingly impaired with each passing day, and the Fidenates' strategy seemed to have been based on Rome's current predicament. First, since Tatius had been recently murdered, the Fidenates likely hoped that internal strife would keep the Romans from satisfactorily uniting against them. Second, the city was on the verge of starving, which the Fidenates planned to exploit.

They intended on applying more pressure on Rome by laying waste to the countryside and seizing life-sustaining provisions. They assumed that this would weaken the Romans enough to allow the Fidenates to defeat them in battle, which the Fidenates envisioned as the next step in their strategy. While the ancient historians claimed that the Fidenates' plan stemmed from their desire to reduce Rome's strength, there may have been another contributing factor. Their decision to attack Rome may have, in part, been spurred by the ongoing famine in another way as it may also have affected the Fidenates. Perhaps they saw war with Rome as a means to provide the nourishment that their people needed, while simultaneously curtailing Rome's growing influence.

Either way, once the Fidenates finalized their ambitious plans to vanquish Rome, they stealthily waited for an opportunity to impair the Romans even further. Soon enough, they located rafts on which the Crustumerians were shipping grain and other provisions to Rome. Seeing that these vessels were insufficiently guarded, the Fidenates attacked them, probably as the ferries were being loaded or unloaded. Without facing much danger or resistance from the rafts' defenders, the Fidenates forced their way aboard the boats and commandeered the critical supplies, killing several Romans and/or Crustumerians in the process.[5]

Their assaults weren't limited to capturing a handful of transport ferries, though. The raids continued as bands of Fidenae's soldiers ventured deeper into Rome's territory. The armed Fiednates confiscated precious livestock, stripped the land of its produce and must have torched many Roman farms in the process. Romulus quickly learned of the Fidenates' organized incursions into his kingdom, which were clear justifications for war. All of this greatly disturbed the king, especially considering the Fidenates' close proximity to Rome.[6]

Romulus was already grappling with many troubles, including Tatius' death and food shortages, and the Fidenates' tactics intensified the already dire situation within Rome. He needed to swiftly respond to the Fidenates' affronts because they were stealing what little food remained in the countryside, destroying rural homesteads and were not far from Rome's gates.[7]

Despite the ancient writers' narrative of the supposed effortless transition from duarchy to monarchy, it's probable that Romulus had doubts about whether Rome's entire populace accepted him. If so, then he surely worried that war with Fidenae could potentially imperil his position in Rome. Leading a force to confront the Fidenates would take him away from his kingdom, where he couldn't personally supervise affairs. If he left, then there was a chance that a few discontented Sabines might venture to orchestrate a coup and place a usurper on the throne, even though a clear majority embraced Romulus as their rightful, sole king. However, if Romulus didn't immediately address Fidenae's attacks, then that might lead to starvation within Rome and generate widespread dissatisfaction among his subjects. This could also result in a revolt. Given the risks, Romulus chose a cautious but prompt initial response.

After enduring Fidenae's wanton attacks, Romulus elected to exhibit strength with prudence by dispatching emissaries to Fidenae to obtain answers and demand satisfaction for the Fidenates' transgressions. This was the proper diplomatic protocol of his day, and if Romulus wanted to avoid an armed conflict, then it was a wise first step, but in the interim, he formed a battle plan in the event that a war broke out.

Following his orders, the ambassadors travelled the relatively short distance to Fidenae, where they were admitted and given an audience with the city's chief men. At the behest of Romulus, they asked Fidenae's leaders to explain why pillaging parties had been violating Rome's borders and seizing supply vessels. After all, Rome had not committed any infraction against Fidenae to deserve such disrespect. Thus, Romulus' representatives insisted that the perpetrators be held responsible forthwith. Beyond this, the ambassadors declared that they expected the Fidenates to do everything within their power to correct their countrymen's misbehaviour and repay what had been stolen from the Romans. The deputation unequivocally stated that if these requests weren't fulfilled and the raids continued, then war would be forthcoming. It's conceivable that they closed their orations by reminding the Fidenates of Romulus' intimidating reputation as a shrewd military commander and the fates of all of those who had crossed him.[8]

There is no detailed record of the conversation between the Roman envoys and the Fidenates, but one thing is certain: the Fidenates failed to comply with Romulus' demands. As such, the ambassadors began their trek home without satisfactorily settling the dispute, and the Fidenates, likely hoping to spark a winnable war, probably continued their sporadic raids to enfeeble the Romans prior to the inevitable conflict. As a result of the incursions, Romulus certainly strengthened his position in Rome just in case any disgruntled Sabines wished to challenge him for his crown. He subsequently assembled the three tribes, inspected them, and he and his deputies enrolled into his legions citizens not overly affected by the famine. Once he had raised an army that he felt was capable of vanquishing the Fidenates, he must have hurriedly trained the legionaries and informed them of the roles that they would play in his grand strategy. Then, possibly after leaving the *Praefectus Urbi*, Denter Romulius, in charge of Rome, Romulus marched his soldiers toward Fidenae.[9]

The belligerent Fidenates had inexcusably rebuffed Romulus' emissaries, and in response, the Romans had threatened them with a devastating military response for their provocative actions. However, precisely what happened next is difficult to discern, considering the conflicting accounts.[10] According to Dionysius of Halicarnassus, Romulus resolved to invade Fidenae's territory and conduct a punitive, plundering expedition, although this could have been done to lure the Fidenates into an ill-advised battle. Whatever the case, Romulus planned to teach them a lesson. As such, his legionaries poured into Fidenae's realm with overwhelming force and pillaged the city's outskirts of its wealth and produce. The expedition appears to have been relatively short, which essentially consisted of raiding, but during the process, Romulus accomplished several goals. He recouped some, if not all, of the Romans' losses and demonstrated that attacking his people would not go unpunished.[11]

Plundering Fidenae's countryside was only one step in Romulus' stratagem. He likely also intended on defeating Fidenae's army, sacking their city and eliminating the Fidenates as a future threat. Consequently, he instructed his troops to march closer to the city. When they were around a mile from the town, Romulus ordered them to make camp and erect ramparts to protect themselves from surprise attacks.[12]

When the Romans had constructed their fortifications, the king commanded a small group of soldiers to stay behind and guard the bivouac. Thereupon, Romulus exited the newly built camp with the majority of the foot soldiers and cavalry, and they neared Fidenae. As they approached, he divided his force again. He instructed a detachment of legionaries to surreptitiously take shelter in a nearby thicket of brush to conceal their location and make it easier to ambush the enemy. Afterwards, Romulus led his remaining foot soldiers and all of his cavalry towards Fidenae's walls.[13]

To coax the Fidenates out of their city's safety, Romulus and his cavalry purposefully advanced in a disorganized manner in order to appear vulnerable to a counter-attack. Then he launched a nominal assault on the town's walls. Seeing Romulus' apparent brazen strategy, which looked disorderly, the Fidenates believed that they could score an easy victory. Therefore, they opened their gates and their troops flooded out to attack Romulus' soldiers. The Romans mustered only minimal opposition to the assault, which was all part of Romulus' plan. His cavalry and legionaries subsequently retreated, hoping that the Fidenates would impulsively follow them, but they didn't, at least at first.

In the wake of the Romans' initial withdrawal, the Fidenates retired to their hometown and barred the gates, but Romulus again returned to harass them and their fortifications. This cycle continued an untold number of times, whereby Romulus charged towards Fidenae's walls in a bold but vulnerable manner. Then the Fidenates chased them away as the Romans marshalled little resistance, and the Fidenates returned to their city. Apparently, during the chaos, Romulus' subordinates somehow managed to damage the rivets securing Fidenae's gates without arousing much suspicion. Romulus realized that this could make sacking Fidenae much easier when the time was right.[14]

The familiar sequence of attacking and retreating continued, but Romulus' strategy ultimately bore fruit. As the Romans once again withdrew from the Fidenates' counter-attack to purposefully draw them further out, the Fidenates finally walked directly into Romulus' well-formulated trap. Despite their previous tactics, this time they chased the Romans and advanced an unknown distance, and Romulus' division eventually gave the impression of inviting the Fidenates to battle. Frustrated with the Romans' strategy, the Fidenates eagerly accepted. As combat began and Romulus' smaller contingent clashed with the larger force of Fidenates, the legionaries broke rank and retreated, just as Romulus had instructed them to do. The Fidenates, believing that a major victory was within their grasp, rashly chased the fleeing Romans beyond Fidenae's safety. However, they had no inkling that the Romans were in the midst of a planned tactical retreat.[15]

As Romulus led his cavalry and foot soldiers away from Fidenae's troops who were giving chase, he reached an area adjacent to the grove concealing the bulk of his army. When the Fidenates were passing the dense copse, the troops who were quietly hiding within it sallied forth and attacked the Fidenates' exposed and very surprised flank. Naturally, this distressed Fidenae's army, but matters soon turned even worse for them. While struggling to deal with the initial Roman ambush, the soldiers Romulus had left to guard his camp exited their fortifications and assaulted the Fidenates' other flank.

When his enemy was being harassed on both wings, Romulus evidently commanded his retreating troops to form organized ranks, turn about face and advance toward the Fidenates' centre. Very quickly, what had appeared to the Fidenates as a promising battle began to look like a looming disaster. They were being attacked from at least three different sides, and if they couldn't form a quick and orderly retreat, then they would be annihilated and perhaps so would their countrymen who were huddled inside of Fidenae. Consequently, shortly after Romulus' contingent turned to attack the Fidenates, they frantically fled for their lives back to Fidenae.[16]

The Fidenates apparently discovered newfound strength because they vigorously fled for their city's safety much more rapidly than they had poured out of it to confront Romulus. Unfortunately for the Fidenates, the Romans were in quick pursuit and determined to achieve a total victory over their unruly foes. As Fidenae's retreating troops were frenziedly entering their city's gate, the Romans arrived and began to force their way into the city too. Following the Fidenates' defeat at the hands of the Romans and the chaotic retreat, the remnants of Fidenae's army weren't able to repel the charging Romans. The legionaries either reached the city before the Fidenates were able to bar the main entrance or else the Fidenates managed to secure the gates, but it didn't matter. Somehow, Romulus' troops had previously damaged its rivets to such a degree that they were able to easily force the gate open, leaving Fidenae largely defenseless. Subsequently, on the first attempt, the armed Romans entered Fidenae and seized complete control of the city.[17]

According to Pliny the Elder, a Roman named Hostus Hostilius was the first to enter Fidenae, but other ancient historians claimed that Mettius Curtius had killed Hostus Hostilius during the earlier war with Tatius. There are several possible explanations for this. Either the battle with Fidenae occurred at an earlier juncture, Hostilius actually survived the Sabine War or Pliny was mistaken. Regardless of this confusion, Romulus identified Hostilius as the first Roman to breach Fidenae's gates, and as a result, Romulus awarded him a ceremonial crown of leaves for his valour.[18]

Aside from acknowledging Hostilius' exploits, Romulus needed to address the Fidenates' wrongdoings. Romulus had laboured to reason with the intransigent Fidenates after their repeated raids into Roman territory. Romulus had even dispatched ambassadors to resolve the dispute diplomatically. Yet the Fidenates had persistently refused to change their ways, which led to the Roman invasion.

Given what Romulus had endured, the Fidenates should have expected severe punishments. While the Roman king's terms were harsh, he exhibited a noticeable degree of mercy, at least after dealing with the war's ringleaders. Romulus ordered those responsible for the raids on his territory to be immediately rounded up. Then they were convicted and perhaps executed or exiled. Romulus subsequently declared that Fidenae's inhabitants had consistently proven untrustworthy and dangerous, and therefore, he was leaving behind a permanent garrison consisting of 300 Roman legionaries to monitor the quarrelsome Fidenates. In addition to this stipulation, Fidenae became a Roman colony, and Romulus proceeded to confiscate a large portion of their land, which he redistributed among his subjects. Supposedly around 13 April (although the year is unknown), 2,500 Romans took possession of it and permanently relocated there. When this invariably irked the Fidenates, he probably urged them to be thankful that he had decided against summarily massacring the town's entire population.[19]

King Romulus must have been thrilled to have defeated the Fidenates, but he didn't have long to bask in his own glory. There were many other critical matters that required his attention. Tatius had died not long before, which meant that Romulus wanted to continue solidifying his position in Rome and he assumed a much larger workload than before to compensate for Tatius' absence. Thankfully, the Senate was able to relieve some, but not all, of the burden of governing.[20]

Following the conflict with Fidenae, Romulus certainly longed for peace and wished to address these domestic issues, but trouble broke out in a familiar quarter. The Camerini, whom Romulus had reprimanded twice before, still harboured deep-seated grudges against the Romans. They felt spurned, given that the Romans had defeated them in battle, commandeered much of their land and property, and planted a colony in what was once their domain. As such, the embittered Camerini waited for an opportunity to reclaim their honour and their land. Like the Fidenates, they believed that Rome was currently at a distinct disadvantage and, consequently, could be defeated. If they vanquished the Romans, then the Camerini wagered that they could restore their own standing in the region, recover their land and eject the Roman settlers from their city.

They had previously watched as food shortages and an epidemic that was associated with the Laurentian scandal's fallout impaired Rome. While the calamities' intensities might have diminished, the Camerini may not have been privy to this information. Still, they were aware that Tatius' death could mean problems within Rome, and they had also witnessed a serious conflict with Fidenae. Therefore, the Camerini concluded that Rome was vulnerable and concentrating on other issues, which might make it easier to defeat them.

Because of all of this, the dissatisfied Camerini apparently assembled in secret and drew up a strategy to reclaim their land. When they were ready to proceed, they orchestrated a devastating foray into the district that Romulus had appropriated from them. While many Roman colonizers probably bore arms and were ready to defend their families and homes, their struggle against an organized force was futile. The Camerini swarmed their homesteads, killed many Romans and forcibly evicted the rest. When the Camerini had recaptured their land, the emboldened raiders may have even attacked territory long held by the Romans in order to denude it of plunder and confiscate the property. Within a short period, the Camerini had enlarged their domain to its previous size and maybe even larger.[21]

Without a doubt, the Camerini expected Romulus to respond to their provocations, but they believed that Rome was under incredible duress because of the many aforementioned crises it faced. Therefore, the Camerini thought that any reaction would either be considerably delayed or insufficient to regain Rome's losses. Once again, to their detriment, the Camerini underestimated Romulus' and Rome's resolve.[22]

The settlers whom the Camerini had expelled fled to Rome and informed an enraged Romulus of the Camerini's actions. He had encountered the Camerini on the battlefield at least twice before, and he had defeated them each time in convincing fashion. Yet Romulus had previously opted for mercy. He didn't order mass executions, nor did he evidently deprive the entire population of their city. After punishing and largely forgiving the Camerini for their earlier offences, they had acted dishonourably again and committed an act of war against Rome. This demanded a decisive response. Following the conflict with the Fidenates, Romulus obviously preferred to enjoy a lengthy respite to address civil matters related to the recent plague, famine and Tatius' death. Instead, he was called to his subjects' defence.

Romulus likely didn't bother forwarding envoys to discuss possible peace terms with the Camerini. If he did, then it was merely a formality because war at this point was a foregone conclusion. In the previous conflict with the Camerini, he had dispatched emissaries to Cameria, but his diplomatic attempts had all ended in complete failure. As a consequence, the veteran monarch, who had ruled Rome for a little less than 16 years at this point, must have wasted little time. He swiftly reassembled his legionaries and marched to confront the belligerent Camerini for a final time. He advanced toward them and easily found the enemy army, and the Romans and Camerini subsequently prepared for combat. Unfortunately, the ancient writers recorded little about the battle, other than the two armies engaged in a deadly contest. However, the Camerini demonstrated again that they were no match for Romulus' battlefield skill nor his experienced troops. Rome defeated the Camerini, and 6,000 of their soldiers died in this battle alone. Considering the Camerini's repeated offences, Romulus wasn't satisfied with simply routing one of their armies on this occasion. He aimed to finally extinguish the Camerini threat.[23]

After slaughtering a large part of the enemy army, Romulus continued his advance and marched on Cameria itself. It's not apparent if he conducted a siege of any length or if his troops simply forced their way into the city immediately. One way or another, Romulus managed to breach its walls, and his troops assumed unchallenged control over Cameria. While Romulus had been widely known for his many acts of clemency, the Camerini had exhausted his patience. So, he unleashed his troops to freely plunder Cameria, where they looted whatever they wanted and surely violated many of Cameria's women. Romulus also gave orders to arrest those who had been behind the latest revolt, and when they were in custody, the Romans remorselessly killed them.

Sometime later, Romulus re-established the Roman colony that the Camerini had taken, and he placed a garrison in Cameria that was capable of keeping the surviving Camerini in check. He additionally gave orders to permanently seize half of their remaining land, which displaced a host of Camerini who were forcibly relocated to Rome, where they lived under Romulus' distrustful eye. On 1 August of an unknown year, Romulus awarded Romans, who were twice in number of the transplanted Camerini, the confiscated property in Cameria where they took up residence.

When Romulus believed that matters were sufficiently settled in Cameria, he gathered his soldiers, who were weighed down by the spoils of war. They subsequently marched back home to participate in Rome's second triumph. Just as before, Romulus entered Rome and participated in the celebratory procession. In all likelihood, he wore a laurel wreath and purple toga as he dignifiedly strolled through the city and by his adoring subjects. Within the parade was one of the most treasured pieces of plunder that the Romans had seized during the invasion of Cameria: a gleaming bronze four-horsed chariot. The Romans who lined the city's roofs to espy the pageantry were certainly awestruck by the chariot's gaudy appearance.

During the triumph, Romulus' victorious legionaries boisterously marched into the city and passed by their countrymen, who shouted their support and warmly waved to the troops. Beasts of burden probably pulled wagons loaded to the brim with valuables captured during the latest conflict, which must have created a breathtaking spectacle. By the end of the triumph, there were presumably sacrifices to honour and thank the gods for Rome's good fortune. Then the whole city, with the exception of the recently displaced Camerini, celebrated a grand feast and drank prodigious amounts of wine.

Either during the festivities or perhaps shortly thereafter, Romulus again proved his scrupulous commitment and reverence to the gods. Romulus determined that the ornate bronze chariot should be dedicated to a deity, and he chose Vulcan, the god of fire, as the recipient. During Romulus and Tatius' dual kingship, they had built a temple to Vulcan, which was likely where Romulus permanently placed the magnificent gilded carriage.

Deities weren't the only ones receiving great honours. Apparently, Romulus also desired recognition beyond what his second triumph provided. Indeed, he commissioned the carving of a statue of himself. It depicted the goddess of victory triumphantly crowning the Roman king. When artisans completed his stone likeness, it was accompanied by text that boastfully summarized his many achievements. Then labourers placed the stone sculpture prominently near the bronze chariot.[24]

Romulus' stature had been steadily increasing ever since founding Rome. Very early into his reign, he probably bragged about being the son of Mars. Some Sabines, and many Romans too, eventually viewed him as a sort of benevolent deity, which blurred the lines between god and man. Yet when he funded the creation of his statue, he was assuming honours that seemed more fit for a god than a human at the time. In fact, by placing the carving near the bronze chariot that he dedicated to Vulcan, Romulus was allowing his societal standing to elevate to almost a godlike level. He seemed to have enjoyed his newfound prestige as a demi-god and vainly wished to advertise it with his statue. What's more, he sought to publicly and permanently display his successes in text for everyone to see. A humble shepherd may have raised Romulus, but his character was evolving as he increasingly seemed to exhibit arrogance and egotism rather than humility.

Despite his changing personality, after vanquishing the Camerini and Fidenates, enlarging Rome's domain and providing free land for many of his subjects, Romulus' popularity likely boomed. His subjects mostly loved or at least feared him, and they either embraced or tolerated his character changes. They did so because many of them surely believed that he had given them prosperity and security, which they appreciated. Even so, lasting peace had been elusive for the Romans, and the lull following Fidenae's and Cameria's defeats was also short-lived.

XV

Veii

'The contagion of the war-spirit in Fidenae infected the Veientes. This people were connected by ties of blood with the Fidenates, who were also Etruscans, and an additional incentive was supplied by the mere proximity of the place, should the arms of Rome be turned against all her neighbours.'

– Livy

Romulus' impressive victory over the Fidenates didn't go unnoticed by others in central Italy, including the Veientes, who were the era's most powerful Etruscan people. Veii's leaders had watched with regret as Rome's strength increased. Indeed, within a relatively short period of time after Rome's founding, Romulus had tasted great success. He had planted several colonies, gained dominion over numerous nearby cities and grown Rome's population. He had even destroyed all armies sent to confront him, apart from the Sabines who joined with the Romans. While Rome was a young city that showed great promise, Veii was much more established. It had supposedly been founded many years before, and it was one of, if not the, pre-eminent city in the region. Certainly, Veii aspired to retain its position of prominence, but Rome seemed to be experiencing a meteoric rise that could eventually rival Veii's own influence. What was probably most unsettling about Rome's ascendancy was that the city was situated less than 12 miles south-east of Veii, and for the apprehensive Veientes, that was simply too close for comfort.

Veii's people undoubtedly viewed Rome as a pugnacious city-state intent on conquering every town in the region. Given that nearly constant war had marked Rome's short history, this was an understandable sentiment. Even though Veii's king had monitored Rome's conflicts and subsequent growth, he must have originally written them off as an insignificant upstart. Rome had since expanded to such a degree that its borders were not far from Veii's. This naturally distressed the Veientes, and Veii's leaders evidently advocated for military action against Rome before it was too late. Yet until the Romans committed a major infraction against the Veientes, they didn't feel that they could justifiably declare war on the burgeoning kingdom. Therefore, they waited for an excuse to attack Rome. Soon enough, one appeared, and the pretext centred around Fidenae's supposed Etruscan connections.

Romulus had previously battled the Fidenates and turned the once independent city into a Roman possession. Fidenae was originally a colony of Alba Longa, which meant that many of its citizens were likely of Latin and Trojan origin, but Livy asserted otherwise and claimed that its inhabitants were actually Etruscan. Either way, Fidenae was situated in an area where there was considerable mingling between the Latins and Etruscans and, inevitably, there were many Etruscans residing in Fidenae. While the Veientes were ethnic Etruscans, they couldn't simply justify igniting a conflict with Rome because there were some non-Veiente Etruscans living in the now-conquered city of Fidenae.

Considering the close proximity between Veii and Fidenae, it's highly probable that some of their inhabitants were linked by marriage. They may have even formed treaties that closely allied the two towns, even though the ancient historians make no mention of it. So, there were possibly bonds between the two peoples. As a result, it seems the Veientes believed that they could devise a reason, albeit an apparently specious one, related to the Fidenates to declare war on Rome. They hoped that this would permit them to prune Rome's rapid growth, keep its powerful legions at bay and perhaps profit by despoiling Rome's countryside. Before proceeding with their plans and attacking, however, the Veientes needed to exercise a degree of diplomacy.

Armed with superficial justifications, Veii's king dispatched emissaries to Rome, where they were given an audience with Romulus and/or his Senate. The envoys probably spoke eloquently and described how the Romans had offended the Veientes by vanquishing the Fidenates. They demanded that Romulus surrender the city, order the Romans within Fidenae to leave the town and restore all of the property and sovereignty to the Fidenates. The ambassadors unequivocally stated that this was the only remedy for their quarrel, because they claimed that either Fidenae belonged to Veii or enjoyed an especially close relationship. The emissaries also undoubtedly spoke of the Fidenates' supposed Etruscan origins and maybe about the host of marriages between Veientes and Fidenates as evidence of their intimate ties or even treaties of alliance. After the Veientes described all of their grievances at length, they strenuously encouraged Romulus to accept their terms. Only then could war with Veii be averted, according to the envoys. In closing, the Veientes must have subtly alluded to their fearsome prowess in battle.[1]

The Senate and/or Romulus impatiently listened to the Veientes' list of questionable complaints. Yet the Romans of this era, and even later Roman writers, disregarded the Veientes' objections as wholly baseless, which legitimately seems to be the case. Romulus presumably explained that neither he nor anyone else knew that Fidenae supposedly fell under Veii's dominion. Indeed, all evidence pointed to the contrary. He certainly also reminded the emissaries that the Fidenates had committed gratuitous acts of aggression against Rome that demanded an immediate response. They needed to be punished in a way that protected Rome from further assaults. Moreover, the Roman monarch surely asked why the Veientes had not intervened during Rome's war with Fidenae. If they claimed possession of Fidenae or at least very close ties with the Fidenates, then why didn't they come to their aid during the conflict? The Veientes had only become involved once Rome conquered the city. Thus, Romulus firmly rejected the Veientes claims and refused to abandon Fidenae.[2]

The exchange between Veii's ambassadors and the Romans was certainly heated, and upon failing to achieve their goal of securing Fidenae, the envoys stormed out of Rome and returned to Veii. The Veientes might have hoped that they could eject the Romans from Fidenae, acquire the city and limit Rome's authority without any bloodshed. Still, they were more than amenable to the idea of open war with Rome. The Veientes were a mighty people who felt confident that they could smite the young Roman kingdom, and they appear to have concluded that war was the surest method of achieving their goals. While removing the Romans from

Fidenae would curb Rome's growth to an extent, a successful war with Romulus' kingdom could result in Rome's complete demise, which the Veientes evidently sought. Consequently, as the emissaries departed from Rome, both the Romans and Veientes realized that they would soon be at war.

In all likelihood, the Veientes knew that it was unlikely that Romulus would passively accede to their groundless demands. As such, Veii's king had probably already put his troops on high alert. However, when it became clear that war was forthcoming, he preferred to invade Rome without giving Romulus any advance notice. Romulus, on the other hand, grasped the seriousness of the situation and thought a conflict with Veii was inevitable. As a result, when Veii's emissaries withdrew from Rome, he must have requested his battle-hardened legionaries to be ready to confront the Veientes at a moment's notice, although Romulus mustn't have desired a conflict with mighty Veii, given that the Veientes were a powerful people. Therefore, until they officially committed an act of war, Romulus and his subjects remained at peace but prudently vigilant. As with Romulus' other wars, what happened next is subject to debate, due to the differing ancient accounts.[3]

According to Dionysius of Halicarnassus, when the Veientes felt confident in their preparations, they advanced toward Fidenae. They probably did so as quietly and quickly as possible, hoping to obtain the element of surprise so that capturing the city would be much easier. Contrary to their plans, Romulus' scouts learned of the Veientes' advance and quickly informed the Roman king of the turn of events. He swiftly mobilized his legionaries and marched posthaste to Fidenae, arriving before the Veientes.

In due time, the Veientes reached Fidenae and were likely disappointed to discover that Romulus had anticipated their strategy, but they still felt assured that they could defeat Rome. So, Romulus and Veii's commander permitted their troops to engage their enemies, resulting in a massive battle. Each army fought with valour for hours, exchanging a barrage of missiles and participating in forays and counter-attacks as they struggled to gain a decisive edge. Yet neither the Romans nor the Veientes could permanently maintain a significant advantage. So, neither side could celebrate victory. The armed engagement ended in a draw, and as night approached, the two exhausted armies parted.[4]

Despite a disappointing start to the war, the Veientes refused to abandon their efforts, but while they were tending to their wounded and resting, Romulus was diligently planning for their next battle. During the night, he gladly received additional troops from Rome, and he instructed them to covertly remain on an elevated and somewhat distant area behind the Veientes' army. He directed them to quietly linger there and stay out of sight until he ordered them to attack. Thereupon, they obediently took their position and waited.

On a subsequent day, armed combat erupted again between the Romans and Veientes, but at first, the battle's strategy and tactics appeared no different than the previous engagement. The two armies locked in a deadly struggle without either side gaining a discernible advantage. Each side took turns smashing into the other as their shields and swords clashed, causing a deafening commotion. All the while, the troops desperately fought for survival. As this transpired, Romulus signalled the legionaries hidden behind the Veientes to launch their ambush. When they received their orders, they sounded their advance, flew down from their elevated location and loudly charged into the exposed rear of the Veii's exhausted lines. This threw the Veientes into confusion, and facing Romulus' ambuscade, they abandoned their battle stations and fled before the Romans could slaughter them.[5]

Their only line of retreat was to try to ford the Tiber River and, as a means of attempting to escape annihilation, without thinking, many of them imprudently dived headlong into the waters. They were wounded, weighed down by their bulky and heavy armour, exhausted from armed combat and many simply didn't know how to swim. Thus, a host of Veientes drowned during their frantic withdrawal. While the Romans didn't personally slay a large number of Veientes in this battle, the frenzied retreat led to the deaths of an inordinate number of Veientes. This left Veii vulnerable to attack, but Romulus opted against marching on Veii itself because it was so well fortified.[6]

This should have been the end of the conflict, but the Veientes obstinately refused to surrender. Instead of suing for peace, they raised an even larger army than before from their own thinning ranks and their Etruscan allies, and they returned to Fidenae to challenge Romulus again. As before, a terrible battle broke out, about which little is known other than that the Romans managed to gain the upper hand, leaving a multitude of Etruscans dead. The Romans routed their opponents, captured their camp and its supplies and seized a host of prisoners, perhaps even including Veii's elderly commander. It was an absolute Roman victory, which left Veii with few viable options. After all, Plutarch claimed a total of 22,000 Etruscans died in this war, and even unbelievably asserted that Romulus slew more than 7,000 himself. Regardless of this obvious exaggeration, even following Romulus' massive success, he ultimately didn't besiege Veii, probably because of its formidable defences. Nevertheless, the Romans had comprehensively defeated the Veientes, primarily thanks to Romulus' leadership. As a result, the Veientes eventually began to consider seeking peace with Rome.[7]

As the Veientes licked their wounds and the legionaries returned home, Romulus and his men enjoyed his third triumph on the Ides of October (15 October). Just as before, he proudly marched through Rome as his adoring subjects cheered for their triumphant king. Among the procession were great displays of his latest victory. Veii's despondent leader may have moped along in chains, as he was humiliated by the crowd's jeers. The Roman guards prodded the other captured Veientes along as they doubtlessly also endured a barrage of insults. Some soldiers carted whatever booty they seized past the Roman onlookers, who probably gasped at the size of the captured fortune and beheld the bulk of the victorious legionaries. The celebration likely culminated in solemn sacrifices and exuberant feasting and drinking.[8]

Rome had achieved a spectacular victory over the Veientes, captured many prisoners and acquired a great amount of booty. In the wake of Rome's overwhelming victories over Veii, the Veientes were forced to open peace negotiations with Romulus. At some point, repentant ambassadors from Veii journeyed to Rome to confer with Romulus and his Senate. The Veientes had been soundly defeated and had little leverage. Thus, they prepared for the worst, but surely begged for Romulus' restraint. Romulus possessed nearly all of the bargaining power during the negotiations, while the Veientes enjoyed little. So, the envoys anxiously waited as he delivered his suggested peace agreement to them.

Romulus demanded that the Veientes cede a large amount of territory to Rome, including the region named the Septempagium. This consisted of land near the Tiber River, and Romulus also stipulated that the Veientes relinquish their claim to the salt mines at the mouth of the Tiber, which the Romans would annex. Furthermore, the Romans insisted that the Veientes convey fifty well-respected countrymen to Rome to serve as hostages and ensure that the Veientes adhered to the agreement. Finally, Romulus suggested that Rome and Veii should form a 100-year treaty of friendship, guaranteeing that the cities would be at peace for generations to come. After receiving Romulus' moderate terms, the humbled Veientes accepted and officially surrendered.[9]

So that no one ever forgot these conditions, Romulus required that the agreement be engraved on pillars for everyone to see. After both parties agreed to the conditions and began adhering to them, Romulus freed the Veii's prisoners of war. Just as he had done in prior conflicts, the Roman monarch stated that any of the Veientes who preferred to remain in Rome could do so. If they chose to stay, then they would live as Roman citizens whom he would reward with free land. While many of the Etruscans quickly returned home, most of them surprisingly accepted Romulus' generous offer. They became Roman citizens and received property on which to settle, perhaps around two *jugera*.[10]

At last, peace reigned within Rome, thanks to Romulus' guidance, successful wars and skilled negotiations. Following mighty Veii's defeat, Rome established itself as one of the premier city-states in central Italy. Under Romulus' leadership, the city's *pomerium* had expanded to the point of including three different gates, and nearly 50,000 men of military age lived under Romulus' rule. Romulus had defeated all of the nearby communities who had dared to confront him. Among those whom Romulus hadn't vanquished, none could deny the Romans' prowess on the battlefield. It seems that no neighbouring city felt confident enough to challenge Rome's position as the region's premier power. This ensured Rome's safety for at a least generation, but despite finally achieving peace, all was not well in Rome.[11]

XVI

Apotheosis

'It was the pleasure of the gods, O Proculus, from whom
I came, that I should be with mankind only a short time,
and that after founding a city destined to be the greatest on
earth for empire and glory, I should dwell again in heaven.
So farewell, and tell the Romans that if they practise self-
restraint, and add to it valour, they will reach the utmost
heights of human power. And I will be your propitious deity,
Quirinus.'

– Romulus

At some point, perhaps while Romulus was engaged in one of
his many wars, his grandfather Numitor died, likely due to his
advanced age. Numitor had served two stints as Alba Longa's king,
and he owed his second reign largely to Romulus and his deceased brother
Remus. Likewise, Romulus was Rome's monarch because Numitor had
graciously permitted it, and he had even provided Romulus with critical
aid during his war with Tatius. Numitor and Romulus clearly enjoyed a
warm relationship. They gladly helped one another when necessary and
must have genuinely felt indebted to the other, and for good reason.
Without their mutual intervention, neither of them would have become
heads of state, at least for a second time in Numitor's case. Given their
rapport and that Romulus was Numitor's only known surviving male
relative, Romulus was the obvious choice to succeed Numitor as king of
Alba Longa.

As Romulus learned of his elderly grandfather's death, messengers
also informed him that Numitor had bequeathed Alba Longa's throne
to him. If Romulus desired it, then he could simultaneously be king of

the Albans and the Romans. The Albans were probably certain that the ambitious Romulus would eagerly leap at the chance to append Alba Longa to his expanding domain. After all, Romulus had been busily growing his young kingdom since its founding. Plus, ruling over Alba Longa would greatly increase Romulus' authority and prestige, but he interestingly passed on the opportunity to unify the Albans and Romans into a single, cohesive city-state. Instead, he tactfully declined the offer and announced that the Albans should manage themselves with a new form of government.

The primary reason Romulus chose to allow Alba Longa to remain independent, instead of merging the Roman and Alban kingdoms, is a bit of a mystery. Romulus had spent his career tirelessly expanding his borders, but when given the chance to peacefully annex Alba Longa, he strangely declined. Plutarch claimed that Romulus chose this route in order to curry favour with the Albans, but this assertion is suspect. Romulus didn't necessarily need to solicit their support since the Alban crown had legally devolved upon him, although it is much easier to rule over the willing than the unwilling. The truth was that he apparently didn't require any additional consent from the Albans. He could simply assume control over them so long as there wasn't a highly organized attempt to reject his claim to the throne. However, once he refused the Alban crown and decided to empower the Albans to govern themselves, it is possible that he strove to improve Roman/Alban relations. Maybe he wished to gain their favour in order to ensure that the cities would remain closely allied to one another and permit their peoples to intermarry.

There may have been some ongoing issues that prompted Romulus to allow the Albans to remain free of his direct control. It's clear that the Albans largely disliked the Romans, and understandably. The Romans predominantly hailed from less than desirable social classes and behaved poorly. Before Romulus founded Rome, the Albans seemed determined to quickly eject Romulus' rowdy associates from their city. After Romulus and his people built Rome, the Albans declined an offer to intermarry with the lowly Romans. While it seems that Numitor had willed his kingdom to Romulus, the Albans had absolutely no desire to be associated any closer to the Romans than was necessary. This meant that while Romulus had a clear legal claim to Alba Longa, its inhabitants must have loudly denounced the notion of becoming Romulus' subjects.

This left Romulus in a bit of a quandary. He had been granted the right to annex Alba Longa. If its subjects refused to accept him as king and he wasn't mired in another conflict, then he could attempt to seize Alba Longa by force. Had this scenario transpired, the Albans may have still rejected his rule in time. After considering his options, Romulus evidently concluded that controlling Alba Longa wasn't strategically necessary or worth the headache. So, he politely turned down the offer to become Alba Longa's king.

Romulus still needed to institute an Alban government, though, and he may have selected a form that he felt would be the least likely to challenge Rome. Upon concluding that a new regime ought to manage Alba Longa, Romulus certainly met with many of the city's leading men and its council of elders to design a mutually approved system of self-governance. Kings had long ruled Alba Longa, and even Romulus seemed to wholeheartedly support a monarchical form of government in Rome's case. Even so, he decreed, presumably along with the approval of Alba Longa's senior officials, that monarchs would no longer govern Alba Longa. Instead, Romulus planned to create an Alban government which enjoyed increased democratic involvement.

According to the system that Romulus authorized, the Albans were awarded the right to appoint their own chief executive on an annual basis. The Albans were surely wary of those who wielded nearly absolute power and embraced this great privilege. While the exact authority and role of the new executive post isn't entirely known, it's plausible that it was very similar to a kingship with the caveat that the Albans would elect their rulers annually. In all probability, the new position retained the king's role as the supreme military commander, the government's executive officer and chief justice. Yet the post's power and authority must have been greatly reduced from what the original Alban kings once enjoyed. Interestingly, Plutarch believed that Romulus' decision to institute such a government in Alba Longa may have planted the seeds of desire for a republican form of government within Rome, although this didn't come to fruition for centuries.

It's probable that Romulus chose an alternative to a monarchy for a couple reasons. First, there may not have been any clear candidates other than himself who could realistically aspire to be king. Second, given the close relationship between Rome and Alba Longa and that Rome was technically an Alban colony, he didn't want to institute a new Alban monarchy that might challenge Rome's subsequent line of kings. He may have worried that future Alban monarchs might try to assert a degree of suzerainty over Rome.

Romulus undoubtedly wanted Alba Longa to be weak enough to never extend lordship over Rome, but strong enough to remain a key Roman ally. Therefore, in Romulus' opinion, requiring Alba Longa to elect a new leader every year might leave Alba Longa's influence somewhat diminished. In Romulus' mind, this system may have prevented any individual from spending a lifetime amassing great power. Thus, he hoped that Alba Longa would never become the dominant player in the Alban-Roman alliance. Romulus obviously preferred Alba Longa to become the subservient partner in their relationship. At the same time, Romulus could capitalize on the act of giving the Albans the right of self-governance to ingratiate himself to them, perhaps leading to the right to intermarry with their population.[1]

While Romulus may have laboured to gain the Albans' favour, he had been gradually losing key support at home. Rome's initial government was essentially a limited monarchy in which the people enjoyed some voting privileges and the Senate wielded considerable influence. Despite this, as time progressed, Romulus increasingly assumed the role of an absolute monarch. He became ever more tyrannical later in his life, and he regularly even circumvented the Senate, which greatly irked its influential members. Indeed, he acted haughtily and cruelly toward them and the patrician class in general.

The Senate became frustrated to the point of loathing Romulus. Toward the end of his long reign, he openly ignored the Senate's advice and formal role, and he periodically bullied them into becoming his rubber stamp. Romulus still convened Senate meetings, but instead of hosting respectful and conversational sessions, the senators sat in fearful silence while he barked demands at them. As Romulus abandoned much of the governmental forms that he had originally instituted, he generated a great amount of enmity within the powerful patrician class. Its members were immensely wealthy landowners who employed much of Rome's populace and boasted large client lists, which meant that offending the influential patricians was inadvisable.

Romulus' actions may have annoyed the broader citizenry as well, but he didn't violate their trust, rights or power enough to cause widespread dissension among the plebeian class. Rather, they largely viewed Romulus positively. However, there was a sizeable corps of newer citizens who felt disenfranchised because they believed that Romulus preferred the old Romans to them. This apparent bias grew out of Romulus' habit of appointing the old citizens into positions of power or showing them favouritism in the court system. This must have left the newly enfranchised Romans feeling neglected and unhappy.[2]

Romulus' actions as a supreme judge caused great concern and disdain among some of his people too. One such episode exemplifies this. A band of Romans had attacked and robbed the inhabitants of several nearby cities. The Roman king unyieldingly refused to permit these criminal actions to continue, and he ordered his lieutenants to apprehend the bandits. Once they were in custody, Romulus quickly passed judgement and sentenced them to a grisly death. Then the criminals were likely bound and transported to the Capitoline Hill's Tarpeian Rock, which was roughly 80ft high. After Romulus' agents had taken the perpetrators there, one by one, they flung them from the precipice in front of a captive and shocked audience. This harshness was doubtlessly sobering.

Supposedly, this wasn't the first instance of Romulus' penchant for penal cruelty, which produced some unease amongst the plebeian class. In reality, Romulus probably excused his actions as necessary to maintain harmony within his kingdom and peace with neighbouring cities. A band of robbers had caused the strife between himself and Tatius years before. As such, he knew how important it was to act quickly and decisively in response to criminal activity, but these punishments didn't sit well with some of his subjects, perhaps even those from Rome's original class of citizens. Many Romans viewed such sentences as blatant examples of vicious inconsistency. They wondered why Romulus exhibited such brutality to his own people, while frequently granting clemency to foreign soldiers. The Romans had apparently seen this behaviour on numerous occasions too. They witnessed Romulus forgiving the people from cities that had warred with Rome and killed legionaries. Yet, when several Roman brigands committed acts of thievery, they were gruesomely executed. This left a bad taste in a host of Romans' mouths.[3]

Romulus created powerful enemies within his kingdom, but he didn't seem to care. He yearned for complete control over Rome and felt that he could insulate himself from any serious challenges, including assassination attempts or even large-scale rebellions. He had diligently worked to earn his legionaries' support, and it worked. His soldiers loved him almost unconditionally and were steadfastly loyal to him. He knew that if a revolt or full-blown civil war broke out, then he could count on his loyal legionaries to obey his bidding. Given that they were seasoned veterans, he presumed that they could successfully quell any possible uprisings.[4]

While his troops protected him during times of war or from prospective civil disturbances, he knew that they didn't immunize him from assassination attempts, but he laboured to address this. Earlier in his career, he formed an armed personal guard of equestrians to secure himself from any plots against his life. The 300 members of the Celeres were constantly in the king's presence to offer him around-the-clock protection and punish those whom he saw fit.[5]

As time passed, Rome's king grew increasingly arrogant and assumed more power, honours and privileges. He had already accepted a statue celebrating his own achievements and apparently permitted some of his subjects to view him as a godlike leader, but he grew vainer and even despotic. Indeed, he seized greater authority and wished to flaunt it as well. He had previously created the role of the lictors, who were tasked with following him around and bearing the signs of the monarch's office, known as *fasces*. They also apparently beat with staves whoever Romulus pointed out, and they even carried thongs with which to bind men whom the king wanted subdued. Romulus' whims gradually seemed increasingly capricious and violent as he enjoyed ultimate power. He even commissioned the construction of a special throne from which he could leisurely issue decrees and address his subjects and emissaries. This was an unnecessary advertisement of his puissance.[6]

At some point during his reign, he began regularly donning regal garb to publicize his role still further. He wore a bright red tunic and purple-bordered toga called a *trabea*, which denoted his position of influence. This made Romulus the first Roman to wear purple garments, at least regularly, and he apparently did so to exhibit his power. All of this greatly concerned some of his people, especially the patricians, who probably viewed these actions as simply vulgar displays of wealth and authority.[7]

As Romulus' reign proceeded, these gaudy spectacles of royal influence and public slights against the patricians grew more frequent and egregious. His behaviour slowly became unbearable, and thus, the patricians must have very quietly searched for acceptable remedies to the worsening situation. However, one single event might have been the final straw for the senators.

After vanquishing the Veientes and agreeing to a peace agreement not approved by the Senate, Romulus once again found new ways to insult the senators. He decided to settle his troops on the land recently seized from the Veientes without the Senate's authorization, or the people's for that matter, which rankled many. Furthermore, under the peace accord's stipulations, Rome housed hostages from Veii to ensure that the Veientes adhered to the treaty's terms. From the Romans' point of view, these captives were the primary factors guaranteeing the Veientes' compliance. Yet one day without warning, Romulus convened the Senate and informed its members that he was releasing the hostages so that they could return home.[8]

The extant sources do not elaborate on Romulus' rationale for freeing the hostages. Regardless of his reasoning, the Senate clearly disagreed with Romulus and felt spurned by his actions. After all, Romulus hadn't sought their advice on the matter, but he likely informed the upset senators that his mind was set. He was king, and they were merely an advisory board. Therefore, he felt that he had the authority to ignore them. Romulus obviously offended the senators, who held some well-founded apprehensions over his actions, which they thought might permit Veii more easily to challenge Rome again. This may have been the moment that the senators and the other patricians reached the point of exasperation with Romulus and began considering ways of reasserting their power and voiding Romulus'.[9]

Sometime after Romulus' unilateral decision to release the hostages, a remarkable moment in Rome's history purportedly occurred. The exact circumstances are somewhat confused due to differing accounts, but the general story is largely the same. One day in early July, Romulus either called an assembly of the tribes who met near the Goat's Marsh on the Campus Martius, a large field north-west of the Palatine Hill; convened the Senate in the temple of Vulcan; or mobilized his legionaries on the Campus Martius. Whichever version is true, a large number of disgruntled senators were present at his speech. While Romulus was delivering his address, a massive storm erupted. There was a torrential downpour, terrifying peals of thunder and even reportedly a solar eclipse, much like the one supposedly during Romulus' conception. The Romans who were present fled to take shelter from the tempest. Even Romulus' Celeres abandoned him to seek safety. However, a band of senators refused to leave Romulus' side, despite the violent storm.[10]

The tempest didn't last long, nor did the solar eclipse. When the skies cleared and the sun reappeared, the Romans returned to where Romulus had been standing, only to find that he had inexplicably vanished. There was no trace of him or even a thread of his royal garb remaining. He was simply gone. The worried crowd affixed their gaze upon the patricians who had huddled near Romulus during the storm. The people demanded answers from the aristocrats because they feared that the nobles might have assassinated their beloved king. When pressed further, the senators alleged that they had witnessed a supernatural spectacle. At the age of 54 or 55 and a 37 or 38-year reign (the sources differ), they asserted that King Romulus was no longer on earth. They claimed to have been present as he miraculously ascended into the heavens to be with his godly father, Mars, at which point Romulus also became a deity. The bulk of the Romans blindly accepted the senators' questionable tale and quickly departed from the scene to praise their new god and beg for his blessings.[11]

While the patricians' dubious yarn satisfied much of Rome's populace, a vocal minority of less naïve Romans were incredibly suspicious of the senators. These sceptics believed that the aristocrats had somehow treacherously assassinated Romulus. There are a few different extant narratives of the king's disappearance that discounted the supernatural ascension into the heavens, and while the versions vary to some degree, many suggest that the aristocrats perpetrated a sinister plot. One or all of these accounts may have circulated immediately following Romulus' death too.[12]

According to a few accounts, while Romulus was addressing the tribes, the army or the Senate, the senators rushed their king and viciously slew him. To keep their deed a secret, they either hid the corpse, perhaps by sinking it into the Goat's Marsh, or cleaved the king's body into smaller pieces, which the senators subsequently concealed within their togas. Then they proceeded to secretly bury his dismembered remains. Not only would this have been done to help them hide their abhorrent crime, but it may have additionally made each senator culpable. This guaranteed all of the senators' cooperation and discretion, but it could have served another purpose too. The senators may have believed that if each of them possessed a piece of Romulus' body, then they would inherit some of his authority.

It seems that the Senate might have been planning on assassinating Romulus for some time. They were simply biding their time and waiting for the right moment to launch their plot. Fortunately for them, the storm and eclipse conveniently provided the privacy that they needed to slay Romulus. Given the flurry of rumours, a sizeable cadre of Romans rejected the tale of Romulus' apotheosis and began calling for more believable answers, which endangered the patricians' safety.[13]

The senators had good reason to fret. If the plebeians concluded that the nobles had been responsible for Romulus' death, then the alleged perpetrators could face serious punishments. They certainly worried about being executed, possibly by being thrown from the Tarpeian Rock. As the controversy simmered and conspiracy theories spread, the senators either received some very fortunate news or concocted a clever story, which ultimately allayed the people's concerns.

Sometime after Romulus' suspicious disappearance, a man named Julius Proculus came forward and described an amazing experience. Proculus was one of the initial Roman colonists who originally hailed from Alba Longa and may have been one of Julius Caesar's ancestors. Regardless of his descendants, he claimed to have come face-to-face with Romulus following his disappearance. Proculus alleged that when he was walking down a road on the Quirinal Hill, he looked up and caught a glimpse of the deceased king, adorned in resplendent armour and appearing regal and godlike.[14]

The stunned Proculus asked Romulus, 'O King, what possessed thee, or what purpose hadst thou, that thou hast left us patricians a prey to unjust and wicked accusations, and the whole city sorrowing without end at the loss of its father?' Proculus reported Romulus' reply:

> It was the pleasure of the gods, O Proculus, from whom I came, that I should be with mankind only a short time, and that after founding a city destined to be the greatest on earth for empire and glory, I should dwell again in heaven. So farewell, and tell the Romans that if they practise self-restraint, and add to it valour, they will reach the utmost heights of human power. And I will be your propitious deity, Quirinus.[15]

Romulus purportedly continued, 'Go tell the Romans that it is the will of heaven that my Rome should be the head of all the world. Let them henceforth cultivate the arts of war, and let them know assuredly, and hand down the knowledge to posterity, that no human might can withstand the arms of Rome.' After announcing that he had become the god Quirinus, the deity of the Roman state, he instructed Proculus to ensure that a temple was built in his godly honour on the Quirinal Hill. Sometime later, the two parted, and Proculus excitedly rushed to relay his supernatural experience to other Romans, who were impressed by his account.[16]

Ordinarily, Rome's suspicious naysayers would have disregarded a tale such as this at face value, but there are several reasons why it wasn't. First, both the aristocrats and the plebeians respected Proculus.

They held him in high regard for his honesty and virtuous mode of living. Thus, when he spoke, people automatically expected the truth, but he was trusted in this case for another reason too. He was once very close friends with Romulus. This placed more stock in his tale because most felt that one of Romulus' loyal confidants wouldn't lie about such a thing. Nevertheless, there were a few Romans who were still understandably sceptical. So, Proculus proceeded to swear upon Rome's most sacred objects that the experience he recounted was factual.

After this final display, most, if not all, of Rome accepted his account as true, and Proculus' story calmed the distrust and anger brewing within Rome. Even so, it seems highly probable that Proculus and the senators fabricated the convenient tale in order to save their lives and ease the tension that threatened to erupt into widespread violence against their class.[17] Regardless of whether they did or not, the Romans officially deified Romulus and recognized him as the god Quirinus. Even in ancient times, there was some disagreement over why the name Quirinus was chosen. Some believed that it was derived from the word for citizen, given that Roman subjects as a whole were called Quirites. Others claimed that it had some connection to Romulus' purported father, Mars. A number of Romans said it was related to *quiris*, the Roman word for spear. This may have denoted Romulus' prowess in war, a prized spear that was on display in an area of the Forum called the Regia, or because a statue of Juno leaned on a spear.[18]

Aside from Quirinus' etymology, the deity may have been a previously existing entity within Rome's pantheon of gods. If this was the case, then Romulus simply merged or re-merged with the deity, but there was ancient disagreement over this too. Some historians debated whether Quirinus came into existence upon Romulus' apotheosis or predated him. Either way, the Romans thenceforth considered Romulus a god named Quirinus. To show the proper respect for Romulus, as Rome's first king and as a god, the Romans built a temple in his honour on the Quirinal Hill.[19]

According to Plutarch, certain long-held Roman celebrations were linked to Romulus' disappearance. A day in early July was called the People's Flight and the *Capratine Nones* because, Plutarch claimed,

Romulus' ascension ostensibly occurred on the Nones of July and may have transpired near the Goat's Marsh, and the Latin word for a female goat was *capra*. Thus, every year on this date, the Romans celebrated the People's Flight/*Capratine Nones* by offering sacrifices near the marsh. Yet other origin stories for the People's Flight existed in antiquity that weren't related to Romulus. Whatever the case, during the holiday, as the time of the sacrifice neared, the attendees yelled out random Roman names as if they were in a state of confusion and were seeking help. Many Romans were thought to have originally done this after they fled the tempest and returned to find that Romulus had vanished.[20]

Even though Romulus had allegedly disappeared, a few ancient authors apparently believed that a tomb had been constructed for him. It was allegedly built in the vicinity of the speaker's rostra in the *Comitium*. However, this begs the question, if Romulus disappeared, then why did he need a tomb? There are a handful of possible answers. Romulus may have constructed a mausoleum for himself before his death, and afterwards, it might have remained empty. The ancients may have exaggerated the circumstances of his mysterious disappearance and mythical apotheosis. In reality, if he truly existed, there's a high likelihood that Romulus didn't vanish at all. Rather, he may have died a more mundane death, and the Romans subsequently interred his bones or ashes in this mausoleum. Another possibility is that this may not have even been a tomb *per se*. It might have instead been a shrine of sorts that was built and dedicated to Romulus. Lastly, the ancient authors could have been confused. They may have simply mistaken an unrelated ancient monument for Romulus' resting place.[21]

Regardless of whether the Romans erected a grand tomb for Romulus, Rome's founder was dead, and the Romans were filled with mixed emotions over Romulus' passing. While some were certainly pleased that he was no longer king, others dearly loved him. The sadness plaguing many Romans probably eased in time, but not for Hersilia. She was distraught and in constant agony over losing her husband. She had little desire to continue living without him, and she even pleaded with the gods to allow her to see Romulus once more. Sometime later, while walking on the Quirinal Hill, she apparently received her wish. According to

Ovid, what appeared to be a shooting star swept her up. Thereupon, she disappeared and was transported to the heavens, where she was joyfully reunited with Romulus/Quirinus. Like her husband, the Romans deified her, and she became known as the goddess Hora.[22]

While Romulus and Hersilia allegedly became deities, Rome was left to grapple with more terrestrial issues. The Roman kingdom was without a leader, and it seems that Romulus hadn't anticipated his death at this point because he evidently never endorsed a successor. Therefore, after Rome's subjects absorbed the shock of his untimely death, they began to ponder their city's future. The Senate did as well and began discussing how to replace Romulus and what form of government should be instituted now that they were rid of the tyrannical monarch.

XVII

Interregnum

'Quirites! elect your king, and may heaven's blessing rest on your labours! If you elect one who shall be counted worthy to follow Romulus, the senate will ratify your choice.'

– Unknown Interrex

Romulus' untimely death clearly shocked the Romans. He was a man in his mid-50s, and while this was a ripe old age in antiquity, he was apparently healthy and still full of vigour at the time of his demise. Consequently, most of his subjects weren't anticipating his death, but then again, neither was he. Nevertheless, it happened, and it left the Roman kingdom in disarray because it appears that Romulus hadn't endorsed an heir and initially there was no known consensus candidate who could succeed him.

Even though Romulus may have had a son, named Aollius, there's nothing to suggest that he was a viable candidate or that Rome's system of government was intended to be a hereditary monarchy. In fact, it doesn't seem that there was even an accepted mode of appointing a new king in place, but potential methods would have included gaining the Senate's and the tribe's consent. Thus, if Aollius sought the crown, he presumably needed to gain both bodies' approval in order to be confirmed as Rome's king. However, there's no mention of Romulus' son attempting to succeed his father. This could signify that Aollius was dead, which is plausible given the era's life expectancy and child mortality rate; that he had no interest in ruling, especially considering his father's suspicious disappearance; that he wasn't a realistic candidate for whatever reason; or perhaps the ancient writers were wrong, and Romulus didn't actually have a son. Indeed, Dionysius of Halicarnassus claimed that Romulus died without any children, which could indicate that Aollius either never existed or died sometime before Romulus' apotheosis.[1]

Another possible candidate for the kingship would have been Romulus' *Praefectus Urbi*, Denter Romulius. He had apparently managed affairs in Rome when Romulus empowered him to do so. He was an experienced senator and must have been a competent administrator, but ancient sources do not mention his candidacy. Maybe he had died by this time, was too old to rule, had no desire to succeed Romulus or the senatorial class at large simply didn't care for the man. These are all plausible explanations, but unfortunately, it is impossible to know for certain why he wasn't crowned ruler of Rome.

While Aollius and Denter Romulius evidently weren't leading campaigns to become Rome's next king, many others apparently were. There was an abundance of ambitious men within the patrician class who coveted the crown. Yet few, if any, of these individuals commanded the widespread popularity and respect needed to become Rome's monarch, and for several reasons. First, it was very difficult to succeed their famed founder because no one could compete with his successful record and unquestioned leadership, even if he had grown incredibly tyrannical later in his life. Second, there were surely many candidates, which must have made it difficult to differentiate one from another. Lastly, Rome's most powerful men primarily hailed from one of two large groups, the Sabines and the original Roman colonizers. The oldest set of Roman settlers naturally wanted one of their own to become king, while the Sabines understandably preferred someone of their ethnicity.[2]

Each faction strove to find a candidate from their own ranks who would ensure that their special interests would be addressed. With the Sabines and the initial class of Romans and their descendants competing with each other, it became incredibly challenging for any prospective candidate to obtain the necessary consensus to be appointed king. This unsurprisingly created an impasse, and it slowly appeared that no one would achieve the widespread support needed to replace Romulus.[3]

The ongoing debacle became known as the interregnum, and as time progressed, the government remained in a quasi-suspended state. Eventually, the Senate and probably even the plebeians acknowledged that this level of dysfunction couldn't be sustained indefinitely. Therefore, the Senate introduced and enacted an alternate plan, which conveniently vested additional power in the senators' hands, at least until they could settle on a more permanent government. They instituted a new system and created the role of interrex, who served as the head of state, but the position wasn't a permanent assignment. It rotated among the sitting senators.[4]

In accordance with this system, according to Dionysius, the Senate was divided into groups of ten, called decuries. One person from each decury was chosen at random until a total of ten senators had been appointed. Each of the chosen senators subsequently took turns acting solely as interrex for a period of five days. After all ten had ruled, a new set of ten senators was selected and the process started anew. Thereby, the senatorial class tried to fairly share power among themselves.[5]

This new system seemed to temporarily mollify many senators. It permitted them to attain greater authority and effectively limited the power of the executive branch, which the senators seemed to appreciate, but it was a terribly inefficient mode of governing. After all, it was difficult to successfully promote an agenda in a five-day period, and some senators were simply poor leaders and had no business being the head of state. As a result, this arrangement yielded few positive results other than ensuring that no single person could dominate Rome.[6]

For about a year, the people watched the Senate fumble about as it struggled to rule in five-day terms. The system's cumbersome nature and ineffectiveness was readily apparent, and it frustrated the people. Not only was the form of governance not working well, but the plebeians felt that there was an unwelcome byproduct of replacing the monarchy with this new arrangement. They believed that, instead of having a single king, they now had a host of masters – the members of the Senate – which multiplied their strife. They additionally felt as though the Senate was perpetuating this system so that they could hold onto power and permanently rule as an oligarchy. As such, the people began to loudly insist that the failed experiment end, and they appeared eager to elect a new king.[7]

Their demands grew to such a degree that the Senate could no longer ignore their earnest pleas, but most senators probably admitted that their system of governance was flawed and unrealistic. The Senate had tried to rule but failed miserably, and the senators feared that the people might forcefully wrest power from them and appoint a king on their own accord. Before this possibility could be realized, the Senate ratified a measure that essentially enabled the people to select a new monarch.[8]

This mode of appointing a king also seemed to be the easiest way to find a candidate with the greatest amount of popular support. Still, the Senate didn't want to entirely surrender their hold over the state. So, when the Senate authorized the people to elect a king, the senators included a major caveat: while the people had the right to vote for their preferred monarch, their choice would be considered null and void until the Senate confirmed the candidate. This, in essence, gave the Senate veto power over monarchical appointments.[9]

Once the necessary parties agreed upon this method of selecting a king, the sitting interrex called the tribes together and exclaimed, 'Quirites! elect your king, and may heaven's blessing rest on your labours! If you elect one who shall be counted worthy to follow Romulus, the Senate will ratify your choice.' The people were thrilled that the Senate had bestowed this power upon them and that they would again be ruled by one king rather than many senators. The Senate's supposed act of generosity pleased the masses so much that they passed a motion deferring the privilege of choosing or perhaps nominating the next king to the Senate. The plebeians stated that they trusted that the senators would select a man worthy of ruling Rome. However, following the Senate's previous efforts, it's hard to imagine that the senators truly inspired much confidence.[10]

The senators welcomed the people's proposal, for obvious reasons: it empowered their body to appoint or at least nominate the next king. Yet when the senators reconferred, they unsurprisingly still bickered over who should succeed Romulus and how he should be chosen, which had previously been a sticking point. After some lengthy debate, the senators agreed that the older Roman senatorial faction should select the king, but they endeavoured to seem impartial. As a result, they decided that they should choose someone from neither the Roman nor the Sabine senatorial factions in order to remain unbiased and more easily reach senatorial consensus.[11]

After settling on these ground rules, the senators continued to deliberate and finally nominated and unanimously approved a wise Sabine man named Numa Pompilius, who hailed from Cures, Tatius' hometown. All of this was done without Numa's knowledge. Regardless of his ignorance, he was widely respected and a very good choice. After the Senate selected him, the sitting interrex convened the tribes and announced the Senate's choice. The people were likely pleased that they would have a stable government once more, and they were surely gratified with the Senate's choice, given Numa's popularity. Thereupon, ambassadors travelled to Cures to inform Numa of their decision and to escort him to Rome to assume his role as head of state.[12]

Upon hearing the news, Numa revealed he had no desire to become king or even journey to Rome to contemplate the matter, but eventually, Numa hesitatingly agreed to go to Rome and discuss becoming its leader. Still, he refused to become monarch without first consulting the gods, but after conducting the necessary rites and observing favourable omens, he finally acquiesced and accepted the nomination. At some point afterwards, the people voted and confirmed Numa as their king, and he was officially installed as Rome's monarch.[13]

While there had been a power struggle and an extended period of dysfunction, a monarch again ruled Rome, just as Romulus had prescribed. Indeed, this form of government lasted for centuries, and Rome's eponymous founder would have been mostly pleased by the results. Following Numa Pompilius' peaceful reign, a series of kings ruled Rome and increased the city's influence and domain. Eventually, a man named Lucius Tarquinius, who was later known by the cognomen of Superbus, became king, but his tenure as Rome's monarch was marked by violence and oppression.

The monarchy that Romulus established might have lived beyond Superbus' reign, but one deplorable criminal act caused the system to crumble and changed Rome's course of history forever. One night, Superbus' son, Sextus Tarquinius, headed for the home of a married noblewoman named Lucretia. She naively invited Sextus into her home and prepared dinner for him. She even permitted him to spend the night in one of her spare bedrooms, but this wasn't deemed inappropriate behaviour. It was understood that if a member of the royal family surprisingly dropped by, then the host was expected to treat the prominent guest with hospitality. Regrettably in this case, a vile plot was afoot.[14]

When nearly everyone within the household was asleep, Sextus crept into Lucretia's room, grasping an unsheathed sword. He woke her and demanded that she consent to his carnal desires, but when she steadfastly refused to have sex with him, he threatened to murder her. Again, she bravely rejected his advances and claimed that she welcomed death over cheating on her husband, but this only angered Sextus. Faced with her tenacious defiance, he finally threatened to kill her and one of her male slaves, whom he would strip naked and lay in bed with Lucretia's corpse. He would subsequently tell the world that she had been slain while committing adultery with her servant. The thought of Sextus shamefully sullying her sterling reputation was more than she could bear. As such, she dropped her defences, and Sextus viciously raped her and then withdrew from her home.[15]

Immediately following the despicable act and Sextus' departure, Lucretia became overwhelmed with guilt and fell into despair. She quickly resolved to inform her family of the crime, and upon doing so, she begged them to avenge the offences that she had endured. Then she drew a dagger and fatally plunged it into her heart, and she collapsed lifeless on the floor.[16]

The crime and the spectacle spurred the Romans into action as they united to bring Sextus to justice and dethrone Superbus. Very quickly, while the monarch was away, the mutinous environment spread, and the Roman people officially approved a measure deposing and exiling their king.[17] As King Tarquinius Superbus' people turned against his rule, news of the revolt swiftly spread, and it quickly became unmanageable. Even Superbus' legionaries abandoned the king.[18] Before long, Superbus was without an army or a capital city, leaving him no option but to flee into exile. His son Sextus wasn't so lucky. He escaped to the city of Gabii, where Romulus had purportedly studied many years before, and while there, vigilantes killed Sextus for his atrocities.[19]

By 509 BC, the Romans had ousted Superbus, and the monarchy that Romulus had supposedly created was as dead as its founder. However, the state still remained, and a new, brighter future awaited the Romans. After purportedly enduring a monarchical system of governance for almost 250 years, the Romans opted to institute a republican form of government led by elected magistrates, not kings. The new system resembled the original in certain ways. There was still a Senate and popular assemblies that enjoyed voting powers, but it differed in that the Romans regularly elected the members of the republican executive branch and voted on laws and declarations of war.

The Romans went a step further. They introduced specific reforms to hopefully ensure that no person ever permanently obtained influence approaching that of a king. Two executive officers, called consuls, served concurrently to limit their power, and they could veto one another's actions. This was thought to protect Rome from official malfeasance and those who craved authority. Beyond this, the consuls' terms lasted only one year, and in most scenarios, they could only hold the office once in any ten-year period. This helped insulate the Romans from those who coveted great power and sought to retain it for long periods.[20]

The Romans eventually created more elected posts, and they served different roles, including judges, treasury officials, public works administrators, military leaders and priests. Under this system, the Roman Republic mostly flourished for nearly 500 years. It ultimately gave rise to many successful men, including Cincinnatus, Camillus, Scipio Africanus, Marius, Sulla, Pompey and of course Julius Caesar.

Thanks to a host of individuals, Rome grew into a sprawling state, but in time, its leading men began to ignore the Roman constitution, disregard their fellow citizens' well-being and rely on violence to solve their differences. This fractured and impaired the republican government. Following many tumultuous years, in 27 BC, the Republic finally gave way to an autocracy that was led by emperors. Despots again ruled Rome, but the state remained on stable ground for some time. The empire greatly expanded, at one point stretching from Britain to the Middle

East, but over the centuries, Rome gradually grew decadent and weaker as its foes became stronger. This spelled doom for Rome, and in the fifth century AD, the exhausted Western Roman Empire finally came to an end.

One of Rome's more astounding features was its incredible lifespan. Some 1,200 years passed from Romulus' legendary founding of Rome to the Western Roman Empire's fall. In an ironic but poetically fitting twist of fate, the person who is traditionally considered the last emperor of Rome's Western Empire was an adolescent named Romulus Augustus. He inherited a dying state, which was a hollow shell of its former greatness. He had little chance of returning Rome to its golden days, and instead, he was present for its expiration. While King Romulus and Romulus Augustus shared few similarities, it seems appropriate that Rome's legendary story opened and closed with a teenager named Romulus.[21]

XVIII

Legacy

'What hounds the Romans is bitter fate and the crime of a brother's murder, ever since the blood of innocent Remus flowed into the earth, a curse to his descendants.'

– Horace

Many years after Romulus died, Rome shifted away from the monarchy that he had instituted. In time, Rome became a powerful republic and ultimately an expansive empire, but even as the centuries passed, Romulus' name never diminished from the Romans' consciousness. However, his legacy was and still is complex. Incredible power and legitimacy remained attached to his name, and the Romans revered him in many ways. At the same time, there was also a palpable discomfort with specific chapters of his life. Some ancient writers even appeared to loathe him.

The Romulus legend, if it is to be believed, provided the Romans with a bevy of reasons to be in awe of their eponymous founder. Like many great mythical heroes, he was supposedly the son of a god, but he wasn't the offspring of just any deity. He was a descendent of Mars, the god of war, who was important to the Romans. Being a major deity's scion demanded the Romans' respect and interest for centuries, but less supernatural episodes in Romulus' life likewise impacted his reputation.

While allegedly the son of a Vestal Virgin and Mars, Romulus probably grew up in relative poverty. A humble shepherd raised him, but Romulus' simple upbringing wasn't an impediment to his meteoric rise. Despite his lowly station, he recruited a body of men, joined with his biological grandfather Numitor and placed him back on his throne. This provided Numitor and the Albans with much-deserved justice. Plutarch asserted that Romulus even released his mother from her purported wrongful imprisonment. Later Romans bore great appreciation for bravery, virtuous living and those who advocated for justice. Thus, many lauded Romulus for this behaviour. Even the judgmental Cicero described Romulus as having an 'outstanding reputation for valour and integrity'. Clearly, Cicero wasn't referring to all chapters of Romulus' life because the monarch was guilty of many transgressions.[1]

In fact, Romulus personally marred his legacy quite early in his life. First, he cheated in the augury contest with Remus, and according to some traditions, in a fit of rage, he killed his brother or at least created the policy that led to Remus' death. Romans disdained cheating and, like all societies, believed that murder was a despicable crime, but they considered killing some family members unconscionable. The Romans felt that parricide was especially shameful, but the murder of a sibling must have been nearly as disgraceful, considering the close blood ties.[2] As such, many later Romans never seem to have completely forgiven Romulus for his involvement in Remus' death. Plutarch even claimed that 'no one shall acquit Romulus of unreasoning anger or hasty and senseless wrath in dealing with his brother.' Plutarch concluded that 'there could have been no good reason for his flying into such a passion.' Orosius likewise condemned Romulus for this crime and affirmed that the murder 'ruined the reputation of his reign'. Cicero even remarked, '[Romulus] threw to the winds his brotherly affection and his human feelings, to secure what seemed to him – but was not – expedient.' Horace went a step further and seems to have believed that Romulus and Remus' spat cursed the Romans and may have foreshadowed the civil wars that eventually plagued Rome. He asserted, 'What hounds the Romans is bitter fate and the crime of a brother's murder, ever since the blood of innocent Remus flowed into the earth, a curse to his descendants.'[3]

Not long after Remus' death, Romulus ceremonially founded Rome and became its heralded first king, and accordingly, the Romans were forever indebted to him. Indeed, certain Romans felt as though Romulus was the ideal man to establish Rome and guide it through its infancy because he possessed the specific skills and abilities needed to guarantee its success. Florus even wrote, 'These kings [including Romulus], by a dispensation of fate, possessed just such a variety of qualities as the circumstances and advantage of the State demanded. For where could greater boldness be found than in Romulus? Such a man was needed to seize the kingship.'[4] The Romans felt gratitude toward Romulus for various other reasons too. Cicero commended Romulus for choosing Rome's specific location. He believed that Romulus wisely placed Rome in a district that was close enough to a waterway to foster trade but far enough from the ocean to protect it from waterborne invasions. A positive corollary of Rome's setting was that, according to Cicero, it shielded its society from being corrupted by frequent contact with foreigners.[5]

Later Romans, especially those of the plebeian class, loved tales of purported self-made men who rose from modest beginnings to the apex of society and power. Romulus had done just this. As is still the case today, witnessing everyday men achieving great success gave the proletariat hope, and when these individuals reached the height of their influence, many plebeians believed that they would champion their causes.[6] Indeed, Plutarch praised Romulus for ascending from his lowly station, and even wrote:

> But Romulus has, in the first place, this great superiority, that he rose to eminence from the smallest beginnings. For he and his brother were reputed to be slaves and sons of swineherds, and yet they not only made themselves free, but freed first almost all the Latins, enjoying at one and the same time such most honourable titles as slayers of their foes, saviours of their kindred and friends, kings of races and peoples, founders of cities.[7]

Romulus also created what Cicero dubbed the 'admirable foundation-stones of the state', and by that, Cicero meant the Senate and the use of augury, both of which became mainstays in old Rome that lasted for generations and helped shepherd the city to greatness. However, the ancient Romans traced many of their other beloved, timeworn traditions to Romulus. In fact, he was the first to allow the Romans to vote, and while their democratic power was limited under the monarchy, it may have helped pave the way for Rome's eventual republican form of government.[8]

Some Romans additionally credited Romulus with creating the patrician and equestrian classes, which existed for centuries and whose members eventually became incredibly influential. Romulus also set long-lasting customs, including requiring children to wear a protective amulet, which they called the *bulla*, and the *toga praetexta*. This custom lasted well into the Imperial period. Moreover, Romulus created the forerunners of Rome's legionary standards. While they were humble-looking poles topped with bundles of hay, they evolved and, in time, were adorned with one of multiple animals. Ultimately, because of the statesman and reformer Gaius Marius, the Romans settled on only displaying an eagle atop their standards.[9]

Beyond this, when Romulus appointed the original *Patres* and required that they aid those in need, he may have established a basic version of *clientela*. This was a system of mutual favours that bound the rich and the poor together and built goodwill and trust between the classes. The patrons frequently aided their clients, while the clients often reciprocated in different ways. For many, it was a beneficial arrangement that helped the Romans for hundreds of years.[10]

Romulus established Rome's foundations, laid down basic laws and even built Rome's first walls. Because of Romulus' impactful actions, his reputation recovered to some extent even though he had deceived and may have even murdered Remus. Unfortunately, another shameful moment in Romulus' life was not far behind.[11] To either establish alliances with the neighbouring communities or provide a new generation of Romans, Romulus organized the seizure of a host of virgins from the surrounding cities. Regardless of his reasoning, it was a criminal act that tainted his kingship. As the centuries passed, historians never forgot the abduction. In fact, later Romans struggled to justify the kidnapping and the rapes that likely followed. Orosius, who was clearly no fan of pagans and seemed hostile to Romulus, refused to defend Romulus' role in the affair. Orosius instead claimed that it was 'wicked' and 'shameless', and it is hard to disagree.[12]

At least one unscrupulous Roman, Emperor Caligula, used Romulus' example to justify his own misbehaviour. Supposedly, while attending the marriage of Gaius Calpurnius Piso and Livia Orestilla, Caligula grabbed Livia and absconded with her. The following day, Caligula announced that he had acquired a wife in the same manner that Romulus and his subjects had obtained theirs, kidnapping.[13]

By organizing and ordering the virgins' abduction, Romulus had acted disgracefully once more, but again, he redeemed himself to a degree because of subsequent events. Eventually, the forced marriages became loving unions, and since there were no documented divorces for hundreds of years, the laws that he enacted to fortify marriages apparently did the trick.[14] Another result of the virgins' abduction was that Romulus defeated and incorporated Caenina, Antemnae and Crustumerium into his growing realm, increasing his kingdom's size and might. A massive conflict with the Sabines followed this, which Orosius claimed was 'a fact signifying that foreign and civil wars, always interrelated, would never cease'. Despite Orosius' contention that this was an ominous moment, Romulus consequently merged his city with Tatius and many of his subjects, and the two ruled as equals, as Rome blossomed. Interestingly, many Romans traced the Republic's usage of two concurrent government executives, called consuls, to the dual kingship of Romulus and Tatius.[15]

Aside from these matters, Romulus waged numerous wars. Many of them were defensive, just wars, which ultimately resulted in the Roman city-state's expansion. However, certain ancient writers suggested that Romulus may have, at times, purposefully provoked his enemies to enlarge Rome's domain. Regardless of what initiated the conflicts, each time he defeated a city in war, he mercifully offered to let the defeated people relocate to Rome, become full Roman citizens and enjoy the concomitant benefits. Later Romans, including Tacitus, concluded that this was a shrewd and farsighted method of growing the nascent kingdom. Tacitus even wrote, 'Romulus, on the other hand, was so wise that he fought as enemies and then hailed as fellow-citizens several nations on the very same day.' Later Roman generations even expanded Rome's domain, power and legionary ranks by employing a similar policy.[16]

Romulus grew his kingdom and admitted the newly conquered as citizens, but he also allegedly erected temples and other public works and instituted religious forms. Romulus is even credited with bringing the important cult of Vesta to Rome, where it thrived for hundreds of years. While Romulus may not have been directly responsible for constructing Vesta's temple, ancient historians credited him with building temples to Jupiter Stator and Jupiter Feretrius. The original structures have since vanished with the passage of time, but the cults continued long after Romulus' death. Even the tradition of depositing the *spolia opima* in Jupiter Feretrius' temple, while rare, lived on after Romulus' purported apotheosis. Perhaps the most impressive building project sometimes assigned to Romulus was the creation of the Roman Forum. This remained important to the Romans throughout the Republican and Imperial periods, and its remains can still be admired today.[17]

Romulus ruled much of his tenure as king justly, fortified his kingdom, displayed his cunning on the battlefield, created longstanding traditions and cared for his people. Appian even believed that he governed as a father who genuinely loved his subjects. Unfortunately, his disposition began to change later in his life. Instead of acting with leniency when presiding over criminal cases, he began delivering draconian sentences, including hurling the condemned from the Tarpeian Rock, which must have been a terrifying ordeal. This method of execution survived Romulus for hundreds of years, as the imposing precipice ominously stood as a stark reminder of government officials' willingness to act with cruelty. This wasn't the limit of Romulus' brutality, though. He also ordered his lictors to walk before him, while bearing the *fasces*, which were the signs of his office, to advertise his power. Too frequently, he demanded that they mercilessly use their staves to beat his subjects. Allegedly because of Romulus, the office of lictors and the carrying of the *fasces* lived on in Rome, but the lictors weren't the only group that shadowed Romulus and obeyed his harsh demands. Romulus' 300 Celeres likewise accompanied him and may have participated in his subjects' abuse.[18]

Toward the end of Romulus' reign, he regularly circumvented the Senate, screamed orders at its members and even acted without the people's consent. This irked some but not all of the Romans. Many of the plebeians, especially among the soldiery, loved Romulus and believed that he was some sort of caring demi-god. However, a host of the newly enfranchised Romans felt that he mistreated them and showed favouritism to the older citizens. There may be some truth to this, but Romulus' character devolved in other ways as well. He had originally instituted what was essentially a limited monarchy, but he increasingly acted as an absolute monarch. Indeed, his despotic behaviour tainted the end of his reign, and many later Romans believed that Romulus had become an oppressive tyrant. This tarnished Romulus' reputation even further. Regardless of the unjust brutality that marked the latter portion of Romulus' tenure, he somehow gained redemption again and was rewarded by becoming the god Quirinus. This was an immense promotion that positively influenced how many viewed him.[19]

It was and is difficult to forget Romulus' supposed actions as a despot, and several ancient writers seem to have never entirely excused him for a few dreadful episodes in his life. Still, they couldn't ignore his many alleged contributions that moulded the Roman state, society and religion. As such, Romulus' legacy and the Romans' opinion of him varied but were relatively positive. The Romans predominantly revered him but also strongly disapproved of some of his behaviour. Yet the disappointment couldn't have remained too strong, given that Romulus was deified. After all, it may have been inadvisable for the Romans to publicly hold a serious grudge against the god who supposedly watched over their state.

Some loved Romulus, but others hated him and certainly a sizeable portion held mixed feelings. Despite the diverging opinions related to Romulus, great power and legitimacy was attached to his name long after his death. During the Republican period, many Romans vied to be called another Romulus or a founder of Rome, which would have greatly elevated their stature. Some Romans considered Marcus Furius Camillus the second founder of Rome for ejecting the Gauls after they had sacked Rome. Many regarded Gaius Marius to be Rome's third founder for defeating a menacing barbarian alliance that included the mighty Cimbri. While these later Romans didn't literally establish Rome, they may have saved it from possible destruction, which ushered in a kind of rebirth. The point is that being named another Romulus or called Rome's founder was a prestigious title partly because of Romulus' importance and heroism. In fact, many wished to be viewed in the same glorious light as him.[20]

Julius Caesar was one such person who flirted with being associated with Romulus in several ways. He adopted the cognomen *pater patriae*, or 'father of the fatherland'. Considering that Romulus had been the first to be called *pater urbis* ('father of the city'), Caesar may have embraced the nickname to link himself to Romulus' greatness. Some even considered Caesar 'a Romulus' for his perceived contributions to the state. He shared more than this with Romulus, though. According to the ancient historian Cassius Dio, the Romans permitted – or at least tolerated – Caesar to dress as the kings once did, use a gilded chair as if he were a monarch and employ a large bodyguard similar to the Celeres. Caesar's subjects also authorized him to deposit *spolia opima* in the temple of Jupiter Feretrius as if he had personally slain his enemy's leader, like Romulus had done to Acron. While Caesar didn't technically qualify for this great honour, it elevated his stature and not-so-subtly compared him to Romulus.[21]

Even Emperor Augustus (Octavian), Julius Caesar's adopted son, considered being directly and publicly linked to Romulus. Some of Octavian's fawning adherents suggested that he should adopt Romulus' name, but after serious consideration, Octavian declined the proposal. It was probably a wise decision, given that the Romans of his era abhorred the thought of a Roman king and Octavian strove to appear as though he wasn't essentially a new Roman monarch. Taking the name of Rome's founder and first king would have complicated his plan. Octavian did, however, accept the name of Augustus. It may have been chosen, in part, because of its connection to Romulus. While it loosely means 'majestic one', it was related to augury too, which Romulus had brought to Rome. Perhaps Augustus realized this and chose the name, in part because it was indirectly associated with Romulus.[22]

The attempts to intertwine Romulus' and Augustus' legacies continued after the emperor died. Before and after Augustus' death, it was customary to carry images of celebrated ancestors during funeral processions. Within Augustus' cortege, many paintings of relatives were carted around, but there were also images of Romulus on display. It doesn't seem that this sort of behaviour was limited to Augustus and his funeral directors. In time, participants of these solemn ceremonies exhibited images of Romulus in other notable Romans' funerary processions. This may have served multiple purposes, including augmenting their reputation by closely linking later Romans with Romulus.[23]

Some Romans were far less subtle than Augustus in their promotion of their superficial connections to Rome's lauded founder. Following Romulus' death, there were a host of Romans who received their founder's name. Even the Western Roman Empire's last emperor was called Romulus Augustus, which combined the prestige of two famed Romans. In reality, the only thing poor Romulus Augustus had was nominal power, considering that he briefly ruled over a dying empire. Nevertheless, myriad other Romans were similarly given a name that was ultimately traced to Rome's revered founder.[24]

The Romans celebrated and remembered Romulus in other ways too. They venerated objects and sites associated with his life. The later Romans considered the Ficus Ruminalis, Romulus' cornel tree, his *lituus* and even Romulus' house sacred, and according to the ancient writers, dutiful servants religiously maintained them for centuries. As the god Quirinus, Romulus additionally enjoyed a temple on the Quirinal Hill, with all the trappings and attention due to a great deity. There were many other public reminders of Romulus as well. The eponymous founder was sometimes proudly represented on Roman money. In fact, one of Rome's earliest minted silver coins featured the infants, Romulus and Remus, suckling Lupa, but this was hardly the extent of Romulus' numismatic appearances. He adorned a host of coins minted throughout the Republican and Imperial eras.[25]

Moments in Romulus' life were also commemorated in various kinds of artwork, including that of funerary stelas and sculptures. One such instance occurred in 296 BC after the Romans elected two brothers, Quintus and Gnaeus Ogulnius, to public office. While serving in their official capacity, they commissioned the creation of a sculpture depicting Romulus, Remus and the she-wolf Lupa. Then they publicly displayed it near the Ficus Ruminalis.[26] This wasn't the last piece of art connected to Rome's eponymous founder. Images of Romulus and Remus enjoying Lupa's life-sustaining milk were found carved on tombstones throughout the Roman Empire as late as the fourth century AD. Apparently, having the twins adorn one's final resting place was quite fashionable for a period of time, and it was especially common during Emperor Hadrian's reign (AD 117–138).[27]

While authority and popularity were connected to Romulus' name and image, there were also cautionary tales. When Pompey the Great advocated for a proposal that would have provided him with immense power to sweep the seas of pirates, many Romans believed that he was guilty of a blatant power grab. They felt that the posting would give him far more authority than any one man deserved. Therefore, one of Rome's consuls reminded him of Romulus' life and informed Pompey that if he acted as Romulus had, then he too would meet the same appalling end.[28]

Years later, Julius Caesar likewise received what some believed was a warning from Mark Antony. After Caesar had become Rome's dictator, many worried that he actively considered becoming a king of sorts. As a result, during the Lupercalia festival, which some believed bore a close connection to Romulus, Antony publicly hailed Caesar as king and tried to put a diadem on his head. This was done in the Roman Forum. The Romans viewed this as a place of freedom and liberty during the Republic, and it was a location that Romulus may have created. The setting was important because much of what the Forum represented in the Republican era was antithetical to the notion of a king. According to Cassius Dio, Antony's actions and the location he chose were cleverly intended to remind Caesar of Romulus' fate and the Romans' freedom. Antony meant for the spectacle to encourage Caesar to opt against appointing himself king.[29]

Even though Romulus was imperfect, the Romans largely lauded him as a celebrated visionary, cherished founding father and the god that watched over the state. While ancient historians regularly censured the monarch for his numerous faults, his transgressions didn't overshadow his accomplishments. This is to be expected because Romulus had the tremendous ability to obtain redemption following many of his misdeeds. At no fault of his own, Romulus' early years were marred by disgrace. His mother was a Vestal Virgin who became pregnant, and while many ancients claimed the conception was miraculous, a host of Albans probably frowned upon the illegal pregnancy. Afterwards, Amulius shamefully sentenced Romulus and Remus to death, but they managed to survive because a wolf, or more likely a prostitute, nursed the boys.

Even so, Romulus regained his honour by acting nobly, deposing Amulius and replacing him with the rightful king, Numitor, but occasional periods of disgrace continued. After Romulus cheated in the augury contest and somehow participated in his brother's death, he cleansed himself and his adherents of their crimes. Then he established a city that eventually became one of the world's greatest civilizations. Yet, after its founding, he ordered the theft of a host of nearby virgins, but again, he was able to offset the negative impact on his legacy. He enlarged Rome's boundaries through a series of wars, merged his kingdom with Tatius and instituted many governmental, societal and religious institutions loved by later Romans. However, he again acted contemptibly by ruling as a power-hungry tyrant in the waning days of his reign. Still, he apparently overcame this ignominy, possibly due to his mostly positive body of work as king, and he ultimately became an important deity.

Greatness comes in many forms, whether it stems from battlefield or political successes, bettering the world through innovation or sacrifice, being a model of virtuous living, etc. While an untold number of men and women meet this standard, few, if any, boast an unblemished career, but imperfection doesn't invalidate their accomplishments. Likewise, Rome and Romulus, if the ancient texts can be believed, achieved a remarkable level of greatness that cannot be denied, but Romulus was incredibly flawed and committed numerous misdeeds. While every person should aim to be far more virtuous than Romulus, his biography clearly demonstrates that heroism and glory can be traced to people with woefully defective characters. Regardless of Romulus' copious faults, the Romans always remembered that it was from Romulus' imperfection that the flower of Rome sprouted and flourished for over 1,000 years. In fact, Romulus and Rome itself are examples of how greatness is sometimes borne of disgrace, but the opportunity for redemption often isn't far off.

XIX

Myth

'Fiction is the lie through which we tell the truth.'
– Albert Camus

Rome's foundation story is steeped in myth. At times, it is incredibly challenging to discern what, if anything, is truthful and what is a whimsical fable, and these aggravating difficulties arise at the supposed genesis of Rome's history, the Trojan War. For a considerable time, scholars disregarded the Trojan War as nothing more than a poetic work of fiction. However, that prevailing opinion began to reverse once Heinrich Schliemann excavated the site of Hisarlik, where Troy is thought to have stood. His findings appeared to corroborate portions of the Homeric tradition, which triggered a *volte-face* in academia. Most now admit that there is at least some validity in Homer's works, although there are still a few dissenters.

Despite Schliemann's discoveries and the subsequent revelations, the Trojan War clearly didn't occur as Homer and many other ancient historians claimed. First, aside from the conflict's fictional supernatural storyline, the dating appears to be incorrect. The ancients placed Troy's sacking in the 1180s BC, but archaeological evidence suggests that *circa* 1250 BC might be closer to the correct date. Second, unlike the narrative found within Homer's poems, the civilization at Hisarlik lived on following its collapse, and it fell multiple times in total. This indicates that the Trojan War might not have been a single epic conflict but a series of shorter wars over a much longer period of time. Homer may have simply truncated a string of conflicts into one. Still, there is some truth at the heart of Trojan War legend, and various Roman and Greek historians believed that the war set the stage for Romulus' rise and Rome's founding.[1]

But what about Romulus? Did he actually exist? Most modern historians are naturally sceptical. Some claim that Romulus is 'unhistorical' and merely a 'literary fabrication'. From their perspective, Romulus is little more than a fictional character from a fanciful fairy tale. While this is a strong statement, these same individuals came to their conclusions for understandable, albeit inconclusive, reasons. According to the naysayers, the case against Romulus is pretty simple. They say that the canonical foundation myth follows a familiar structure found in several cultures. It includes many sensational episodes, which simply cannot be true, and the ancient accounts of Rome's founding vary greatly, while some don't even include Romulus at all. Furthermore, the sceptics assert that the traditional dates set for Romulus' reign are wildly inaccurate, and there's a dearth of early evidence supporting the notion of a hero founder named Romulus. Even archaeology, some have claimed, discredits the orthodox Roman foundation myth. Thus, today's historians have largely cast Romulus aside as a fictitious character, but is there really enough evidence to conclude with certainty that Romulus never lived?[2]

For various reasons, the veracity of Romulus' story cannot be disregarded based solely on the supernatural, hard-to-believe elements found within the foundation myth. First, Romulus' biography may have been corrupted after years of being handed down to new generations via the oral tradition as mundane events evolved into spectacular adventures. Second, these incredible episodes might have appeared in the written record because certain ancient writers took great literary licence to bolster their founding hero's reputation by exaggerating his circumstances. Finally, conceivable, ancient alternative versions to the most notable, suspicious events in Romulus' life existed.

For one, the miraculous cause of Romulus and Remus' births – allegedly thanks to the god Mars – would normally be reason to doubt the tale right from the start. Yet the conception legend may have simply been a cover story that masked a much more ordinary event. Some ancient writers attested that Mars didn't ravage Rhea Silvia. Instead, Amulius or one of her admirers actually impregnated her. Still, others implied that Romulus was born out of prosaic circumstances that didn't even include an imprisoned Vestal Virgin. In fact, certain accounts presented

Rome's eponymous founder as Aeneas' son, grandchild or someone else's descendant, and many of these traditions assert that he wasn't conceived with the help of a deity. Each of these certainly present more plausible scenarios than the fable claiming that a god fathered Romulus.[3]

The tale of a wolf named Lupa suckling Romulus and Remus is another questionable portion of the myth that rightly generates healthy scepticism. Wolves have no reason to nurture humans. Rather than care for them, it's more than likely that, as a carnivore, a wolf would devour vulnerable infants, but there were ancient alternatives to the kind-hearted she-wolf legend. This episode might have been easily explained by some ancient historians who claimed that a wolf named Lupa did not suckle the boys. A prostitute did, and the basis for this claim is pretty simple. *Lupa* was a derogatory ancient term that essentially meant whore. This implies that a prostitute fed and looked after the infants. So, in lieu of presenting negative details about Rome's founder, such as a prostitute rearing him, ancient writers may have preferred to create a wolf named Lupa and a fantastic tale. This neatly sidestepped the unbecoming story about the prostitute, which protected Romulus' and his adopted mother's characters. It simultaneously augmented Romulus' reputation by adding this dramatic story, while still seeming to maintain a grain of truth, that is Lupa/*lupa*.[4]

Romulus' supernatural ascension into the heavens at the end of his life spurs further suspicion, and understandably so. According to some traditions, during a storm and an eclipse, the gods called Romulus up to the heavens to live with his father, Mars. Thereupon, he vanished into thin air and left behind no physical trace. Not long after, he became a god, as his apotheosis was complete. The ancients widely circulated this account, but alternative versions also existed, which were simpler and much more credible.

Several traditions present Romulus as an intolerable, power-hungry tyrant, and as a result, some of his subjects felt that his despotic rule had become so unbearable that his reign should be concluded by force. Therefore, these disgruntled Romans waited for a favourable moment to assassinate him. When the opportunity arose, possibly during a storm and/or an eclipse, they secretly slew him, dismembered his body and hid the remains. Perhaps in order to protect themselves from reprisals for their misdeeds, they informed the broader Roman populace that the gods had miraculously transmitted Romulus to the heavens.[5]

For these supernatural episodes in Romulus' supposed life, there were other, more believable versions. Thus, the mere existence of outlandish accounts in the ancient writings does not provide the sceptics with a justified basis to doubt that Rome's eponymous founder once lived. Even so, other evidence needs to be evaluated when determining the validity of the case for or against Romulus. There are a considerable number of known artifacts presented by academics who debate Romulus' possible existence. Unfortunately, though, many of them originate from periods long after Romulus was thought to have resided on the Palatine Hill.

One of the oldest possible pieces of evidence is a fifth-century BC funerary stele in Bologna, Italy, with a bizarre scene on it of a single infant suckling a beast. Is this an early depiction of Romulus and Lupa? Some think so, but the motif of animals nursing humans isn't unique to the Romulus myth. Beyond this, the animal appears to bear feline-like traits. This prompted modern historian T.P. Wiseman to claim that the beast was actually a lion or a panther, which is contrary to the Romulean myth. Moreover, Wiseman asked, if this is supposedly Romulus, then why isn't Remus sitting alongside him? This is a fair, but unsettled, question. Understandably, people differ over the meaning of the stele and what it depicts, but it is really inconclusive evidence at best.[6]

Those who believe that Romulus was indeed a real man waste little time identifying an ornate, fourth-century BC hand-held mirror that was discovered in Bolsena, Italy. On the back of the mirror is a detailed scene of a beast nursing two infants, who are accompanied by a host of other figures. For those who have concluded that this is evidence for Romulus, they claim that this is a very early representation of Romulus, Remus and Lupa, but who are the others on the mirror? Some believe that they are Latinus, past king of the Latins, and a few other individuals who are connected to Rome's fabled history. These same researchers additionally point out on the mirror a woodpecker representing Mars and the Ficus Ruminalis, which are both part of the Romulus myth.

Outline of the Bologna Stele's Lower Relief

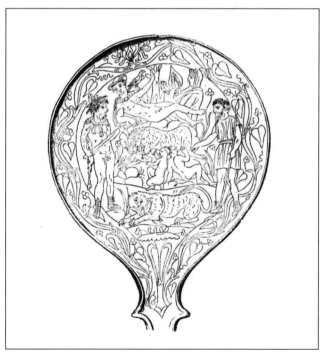

Bolsena Mirror
Source: Roscher, W.H., *Ausführliches Lexikon der Griechischen und Römischen Mythologie* (B.G. Teubner, 1886–1890), pp.1465–66.

Also found on the mirror, they allege, is an owl sacred to Vesta and a second beast, maybe a wolf.[7]

Sceptics, on the other hand, have numerous responses to these assertions. They claim that the mirror doesn't show Romulus and Remus and others from their myth. Instead, there are perfectly acceptable alternatives to these hypotheses. While there are several competing theories, one contends that the children found on the mirror aren't Romulus and Remus but the twin Lares. They were deities who safeguarded the Romans. What's more, many scholars claim that some of the figures surrounding the two infants have little or no relation to the Romulus foundation myth, and they provide several possible identities for them. They also argue that the second beast isn't a wolf but some sort of feline, which has no bearing on Romulus' supposed life. Even if the second animal was a wolf, how would it fit into Romulus' story? It apparently doesn't. There are many theories attempting to decipher what the mirror portrays, but the point is that there are sound, competing views. So, what does the mirror really depict? Unfortunately, at this point, it's impossible to know, but later Roman evidence exists that is less ambiguous.[8]

In 296 BC, the Ogulnius brothers served as Roman aediles, which were elected posts tasked with maintaining public works and overseeing festivals. During their one-year term, they dedicated a statue of the she-wolf, Lupa, giving suck to the infants Romulus and Remus, and it was placed in an area adjacent to the Ficus Ruminalis for all to see.[9] Not long after, in 269/268 BC, the Romans minted silver coins depicting Hercules' head on one side, while the obverse bore an image of Lupa nursing Romulus and Remus. Unlike the aforementioned stele and mirror, no one doubts that the sculpture and coinage were representations of Romulus and Remus.[10]

For some, these two examples are undeniable proof that the canonical version of Romulus and Remus' lives had clearly taken root by this period. Yet if Romulus was real and founded Rome perhaps around 753 BC, then why are there such a small number of artefacts attesting to Romulus' existence prior to this era? There are a couple of explanations. First, many of Rome's oldest creations may have been lost to time. Second, the early Romans were vastly different from their descendants, who had celebrated artists and boasted the expertise and wealth to create grand monuments and images. Consequently, the lack of early physical evidence doesn't close the case against Romulus. It's just a fact about ancient Rome.[11]

Moreover, the Romans cannot be faulted for waiting until 269/268 BC to mint coins featuring their eponymous founder because currency of this kind was fairly new in Rome. In fact, the first silver coinage appeared not long before the Romans placed Romulus's image on their money. So, Romulus was actually displayed on one of Rome's first silver coins. While this is evidence that the Romulus myth was prevalent in the Roman Republic, it still comes hundreds of years following Romulus' purported reign and doesn't necessarily prove that he ever existed, only that the myth existed in the third century BC.[12]

Other issues related to Romulus have given serious researchers pause, including questions surrounding the literary record. First, the earliest extant fragmentary mentions of Romulus appeared 400 or more years subsequent to Rome's supposed founding date. Second, there are many different Roman foundation myths, which sometimes vary considerably. Even when there was general agreement among the writers who recorded the canonical foundation story, there were a multitude of minor inconsistencies between their works.

There is no known written record of an eponymous Roman founder until around the mid-fourth century BC when the writer Alcimus referenced such a person. However, the first history of Rome's foundation wasn't drafted until as late as the third century BC by the Greek writer Diocles of Peparethus. Only later did Fabius Pictor publish his annalistic records, the first known Roman writing detailing Romulus' story. Pictor completed them during the latter half of the third century BC, 500 years or so after Romulus allegedly ploughed Rome's foundational furrow. Once writers published these early accounts, other traditions began to increasingly appear, but some of them bear many discrepancies.[13]

The first known records of Romulus were written long after he had allegedly ascended into the heavens, but this is not the death knell in the case for Romulus. While the Greeks were known for their many writers, for a considerable time, they had little reason to care enough about the Romans to chronicle their history. For the first few hundred years of

Rome's purported existence, it was little more than an insignificant, rural backwater that was quite a distance from mainland Greece. The Greeks at large would have had relatively limited knowledge of Rome. What they did know about the Romans evidently didn't compel them to write about the people whom they undoubtedly viewed as uncivilized oafs living in the backcountry. Thus, it's unsurprising that the Greeks chose not to write, at least on a large scale, about the Romans until they found them more interesting.

As for the Romans, they don't appear to have been prolific writers for much of their early history. They were too often fighting wars and desperately struggling to survive. What's more, there wasn't much of a literary tradition, if any, during Rome's infancy, and there may be good reason or this. While Cicero implied that the Romans had always been literate, and Livy and Dionysius asserted that the Arcadians brought writing to Italy before Romulus was born, modern scholars date Roman literacy to as early as around the 600s BC. Even immediately following that period, writing was probably pretty sparse.[14] Once Rome became more established, they supposedly kept robust documents that recorded much of their history. Unfortunately, according to Livy, little of it still exists because when the Gauls sacked Rome in around 390 BC, a conflagration mostly destroyed the priceless corpus of historical archives, although modern historians doubt whether the sacking was really that destructive. Nevertheless, if true, all of this may explain what appears to be a relatively late arrival of Roman written histories recounting Romulus' life.[15]

While the earliest known recorded accounts about Romulus were 400–500 years after he supposedly founded Rome, other previously existing literature related to Romulus almost certainly existed. It is certainly plausible that Alcimus, Diocles and others drew from earlier writings. Regrettably, these primary sources don't exist in any form today, but it's more than likely that previously written reports were available and influenced many ancient historians. Authors of the earliest known Romulus traditions presumably didn't conceive the story on their own in a vacuum, although it is possible. They may have had predecessors, maybe many. Unfortunately, it is impossible to know from what time period these early sources might have originated. Some modern academics believe that the

Romulus myth sprouted sometime in the sixth or fifth century BC, but it could have just as easily come even earlier and stemmed from real events.

There were likely more than just written histories that the ancient writers used as primary sources too. Pictor and other early historians may have relied on Roman plays that recreated the city's founding. There was also perhaps a rich oral tradition that had been handed down for generations and influenced the early writings about Romulus. As a result, the fact that the known written histories arrived long after Romulus' era is hardly conclusive evidence against his existence.

Romulus' sceptics likely would concede this point, but they are quick to mention that there are numerous foundation legends. Dionysius mentioned that he knew of fourteen different myths, Plutarch referenced thirteen, Festus ten and Servius eight.[16] More recently, T.P. Wiseman even claimed to have found at least 60 distinct legends that still exist. Some of these specifically mention Romulus, while others don't, and many do not differ much from the canonical version. Yet there are various spellings, genealogies and stories assigned to Rome's founding hero. The names include Rhomos, Rhomus, Rhomylos and of course Romulus, which all bear striking similarities to each other. In fact, the majority of the different foundation accounts directly link Rome's establishment to a person whose name was either Romulus or something similar.[17]

There are tales that claim Rome was named for a woman named Rhomé/Roma who persuasively suggested that the Trojans should burn their ships, forcing them to remain in Italy.[18] Others claim that Aeneas' son or a grandson was called Rhomos (or someone similarly named), and he founded Rome. Sometimes Romulus or a derivative thereof is a relative of Aeneas, and other times he isn't. In some traditions, he is Rhea's son, but at least one ancient author stated that Romulus was the son of a slave girl who served the Alban royal family under King Tarchetius' reign. She was impregnated when she had sex with a phallus that magically arose from a hearth. In another legend, Romulus is the son of Latinus and a Trojan woman named Roma. A separate account presents the eponymous founder as Odysseus' son. There are traditions that present Romulus with a twin and some that don't, while others claimed that he had two or even three brothers.[19] Another ancient writer even alleged that

Remus was not killed at all. Rather, he outlived Romulus.[20] Beyond these matters, ancient Greeks and Romans produced multiple foundation dates that ranged from sometime in the 800s to 728 BC. While this isn't an exhaustive list of the myth's variations, it certainly shows their divergence.[21]

Eventually, the Romans settled on what roughly became the orthodox foundation story found in Livy, Dionysius, Plutarch, etc. Most modern historians agree that the canonical version of Rome's foundational legend became widely accepted and adopted no later than the mid-fourth century BC, possibly earlier. They came to this conclusion because of the literary record's dating and the images of Romulus that were created in 296 and 269/268 BC.

However, there are numerous inconsistencies of lesser significance even within the canonical foundation story. Given that much of Rome's earliest writings were reportedly lost around 390 BC and those who chronicled Rome's early history hailed from different parts of the Mediterranean, this is to be expected. Later historians may have been forced to sometimes rely on different sources as well as less than dependable ones. This may reveal why the nature of the many writings appears confused at times. Still, there are those who discount the orthodox tradition and ask which one, if any, of these many different stories is true, considering that they vary to some degree? Sceptics also reasonably inquire why one version should be afforded greater credence than the others? These are fair questions, but while they focus on matters of less importance and nitpick the details, they miss the main point: there is pretty broad agreement among the ancient writers who chronicled the canonical and even heterodox foundation myths that someone, whose name was either Romulus or something similar, played a major role in Rome's founding.[22]

Despite this, for some time, the archaeological evidence seemed to support the theories posed by those who claimed that Romulus was a complete fabrication. It appeared that while the Palatine Hill was inhabited from about 1000 BC, Rome hadn't come into existence as we understand it until maybe 625–550 BC, long after Romulus allegedly lived. Yet this notion has been recently challenged. Archaeologist Andrea Carandini and many others have been conducting excavations in and around Rome for decades. Some of their findings have been fascinating, question the prevailing opinions about Rome and Romulus, and seem, in a way, to support the case for Romulus.[23]

Among the exciting archaeological announcements was the discovery of the remains from a Palatine Hill wall, which dates to around 775–750 BC. Its setting corresponds to the possible location of the wall that Romulus supposedly built. Beyond this, some archaeologists now believe the sanctuary of Vesta to be from around 775–750 BC, and the lowest strata of the Forum's pavement can be dated to as early as roughly 750–700 BC. Excavators have found votive artefacts where the original temple Romulus purportedly built to honour Jupiter Feretrius is thought to have possibly stood, and the relics are from 750–700 BC. When archaeologists examined the area where the Vulcanal once was, they discovered sacred deposits from the late 700s BC. Carandini has also examined and dated what he believes is the Roman royal palace. He concluded that it might have been Romulus' dwelling, in part, because of its location, its relative grandness and its date. Experts believe it to be from around 750–725 BC. Each of these locations is associated in one way or another with the Romulus legend, and the dates roughly coincide with the range given by the ancient authors.[24]

What do these findings mean? They suggest that Rome may be much older than many modern archaeologists and historians have long believed. The discoveries further imply that during Rome's early period, it wasn't merely a smattering of random dwellings but an organized community. It may have boasted walls, a marketplace, shared culture and religious institutions. Still, some critics believe that Carandini's and others' discoveries mean very little. They contend that it is just a happy coincidence that the dates broadly align with the ancient foundation legends. Furthermore, Carandini's detractors claim that it's unsurprising that archaeologists made these finds, given that the region was inhabited since at least 1000 BC. Lastly, they assert that these discoveries do not prove that Romulus ever existed.

Critics of Carandini and his allies make some fair points. The archaeological finds don't necessarily confirm that Romulus was a real person. Nothing has been unearthed that emphatically does so, but the discoveries do seem to corroborate portions of the canonical Romulus tale, which give a degree of credence to segments of the Romulus myth. Some naysayers will likely respond by stating that Romulus was fictitious and was grafted onto previously known true stories about the Palatine wall, Forum, Vulcanal and Temple of Vesta, in a process called Romulization. In all fairness, this isn't out of the realm of possibility.[25]

However, if one is simply trying to determine whether someone with a name resembling Romulus had something to do with Rome's founding, possibly in the eighth century BC, then Carandini's work and other archaeological findings seem to be supporting evidence. Yet it's not very strong, because it doesn't explicitly prove Romulus' existence. It merely appears to confirm, or at least doesn't disprove, certain ancillary portions of the foundation myth, but critics also take aim at the written record to try to confute the Romulus legend.

Yet, at times, modern efforts to invalidate many portions of Romulus' biography seem to unfairly disparage the ancient historians. Nearly every generation vainly believes that they are the most advanced in human history and are closer to intellectual perfection than any other. This kind of haughty notion sometimes leads moderns to disregard our intellectual predecessors as incredibly naïve simpletons. While there have been amazing advancements over the centuries, the ancients possessed the same critical thinking skills that modern humans enjoy.

To assume the ignorance of those from the Roman era and auto-matically accept the veracity of today's prevailing opinion about Rome's founding is quite unfair. Ancient writers like Dionysius, Plutarch, Livy and Cicero were serious, but imperfect, researchers and historians. While they may have sometimes used sources with credibility issues, they strove for accuracy. Indeed, Dionysius claimed to have relied on writers who were 'best accredited'. Regardless of the sources' reputations, serious ancient historians had little reason to lie. When segments of Romulus' story seemed too fantastic to be truthful, Roman and Greek historians often recorded their doubts and included more plausible, known alternatives. However, the ancient writers whose works are still extant, or at least exist in fragmentary form, largely seemed to conclude that

Romulus, or someone with a similar name, may have indeed existed and played a role in Rome's founding. This broad consensus, which spans different time periods, appears to support the theory of an eponymous founder actually existing. Indeed, Plutarch insisted that the notion of such a hero was the 'most authentic tradition'. It's important to remember that these ancient writers and their forebears had access to a host of other historical documents that haven't survived to the modern era, and they lived much closer in time to the epochs that they chronicled than today's researchers. Therefore, they may have been aware of other, much older historical sources and might have had a more accurate grasp over whether Romulus was a historical figure than most modern historians give them credit for.[26]

The ancient writers might have also had non-written sources that traced back to Rome's founding. The Romulean oral tradition may have been alive and well during the lives of Dionysius', Plutarch's, Livy's and Cicero's predecessors. These historians could have relied upon a rich verbal history, giving them a more robust set of sources that moderns cannot access. Admittedly, oral traditions are hardly accurate, which may explain the numerous different versions of Rome's foundation legend. Still, some veracious components may have existed within it and been handed down from generation to generation. This could have ensured the survival of a collective memory of an eponymous founder.

Many modern historians challenge these notions and claim that the oldest part of the Romulus myth originated in the sixth century BC, but this date is arbitrary. Could the Romulus legend have been created as a piece of fiction out of thin air in the sixth century BC? That's definitely a possibility, but there's certainly no hard evidence proving that the tale emerged from nothing during that era. It's at least equally, if not more, plausible that it wasn't. Could Romans from this era, which would have been 250 years or less removed from Rome's possible founding, have been so ignorant of their culture's recent past that they accepted a lie? Again, this could be the case. On the other hand, maybe they knew that there was a sliver of truth to the Romulus legend because their ancestors had somehow kept at least partially accurate accounts of the

Romulean myth alive. To be fair, it is also possible that they knew that the Romulus legend was a work of fiction but over the centuries the Romans accepted it as fact.

Rome's historians may not have had to simply rely on the words of their fathers and grandfathers. There were venerated sites and relics in ancient Rome that the Romans took as proof of Romulus' existence. The ancients supposedly kept Romulus' *lituus*. They knew of the location of the fig tree that may have given Romulus, Remus and Lupa shade, the Ficus Ruminalis or at least its descendant, which the Romans cared for with religious devotion. They additionally maintained the cornel tree that allegedly sprouted from a shaft that Romulus hurled from one hill to another, although again, it must have been the original tree's offspring. Romulus' home, the Casa Romuli, supposedly existed for hundreds of years after his death, and the Romans looked to it as a kind of hallowed temple and preserved it until the fourth century AD. The Lupercal Cave, which has purportedly been rediscovered, was tied to the Romulean myth and was well-known in antiquity and revered. Together, all of these examples provided the ancients with what they believed was concrete supporting evidence for the Romulus myth.[27]

Naysayers are quick to correctly point out that none of these sites, artefacts or revered trees proves the existence of Romulus. For one, the *lituus*, Ficus Ruminalis, cornel tree and Casa Romuli no longer exist, at least in their original state. Even if they did, it would be hard to imagine them directly verifying the Romulus legend. That only leaves the Lupercal Cave that has survived to the modern era, but it doesn't necessarily imply that Romulus was real. The sceptics appear willing to concede that these trees and sites might have been hallowed in antiquity, but the real reason that they were sacred may have predated the Romulus tale. So, when the Romulus legend took root, the Romans incorporated the sacred trees and locations into the newly established Romulus myth and artificially grafted him onto them. This is a distinct possibility, but once more, it's also possible that these stories contained a grain of truth about the existence of an eponymous founder. Maybe it shouldn't be automatically assumed that the ancients were a bunch of bumbling ignoramuses. Perhaps they deserve more credit, and maybe there's a degree of accuracy in some of their writings beyond what many modern historians have proposed.

Despite this possibility, there are a host of theories attempting to explain why the ancients supposedly created a potentially fictional Romulus myth and how it evolved over time. According to a modern theory, as the centuries passed, Rome was given a fantastic founding story, like many celebrated Greek city-states had, and an eponymous founder, which offered Rome further prestige. This, some hypothesize, led to the creation of the Romulus legend. Alternatively, as Plutarch claimed some believed, maybe Rome gained its moniker from the word for strength because it denoted the locals' martial prowess. Another possibility is that Rome was named after the Tiber River's ancient appellation, Rumon. Any of these hypotheses are conceivable.[28]

There's plenty to doubt about the Romulus myth, and quite frankly, much of the supporting evidence for Romulus isn't that strong. Still, those who insist that Romulus is entirely a work of fiction have no definitive basis of support for that assertion, and similarly, those who emphatically insist that Romulus existed simply cannot prove that claim. However, the reality is that it seems far-fetched that Romulus' life, as presented by Dionysius, Livy, Plutarch, Cicero and others, specifically happened in such an implausible way. It's important to remember that it wasn't out of the ordinary for some ancient writers to include exaggerations in their publications. Their works were often a reflection of their own time. They sometimes took poetic licence and used poor, insufficient sources. This may have impacted the veracity of the accounts on which later, more serious historians were forced to rely.

Notwithstanding these limitations, the literary record, while woefully imperfect, is the best extant evidence for Romulus, and Carandini's and others' findings seemingly buttress some of the sources' assertions. Yet, if the question at hand is, 'did someone, whose name was either Romulus or something similar, play a role in Rome's founding around 800–700 BC?', then the answer becomes clearer. There is no shortage of literary and perhaps archaeological evidence appearing to affirmatively answer the question in one way or another. Indeed, the majority of the surviving foundation stories claim that there was some eponymous founder. On the other hand, there's only limited evidence supporting the sceptics' point of view.

It's certainly possible that Rome was named for an ancient word for strength or the Rumon River. However, in light of the written histories and archaeological discoveries, it is at least equally likely that Rome was named for someone integral to its founding. In fact, it is more reasonable to accept that there is a kernel of truth within a legend for which there is ample literary and some archaeological evidence, despite its deficiencies, as opposed to believing in something when there's far less proof. Therefore, the weight of the existing evidence suggests that there might be some validity to the Romulean myths, but it is important to remain sceptical, considering that the evidence is incredibly limited.

Remember for a moment that academics almost universally disregarded the Trojan War and even Troy's existence as pure fiction. This was the widespread, expert opinion of the day even though the ancient writers persistently maintained that the Trojan War occurred. These ancient sources were inconsistent at times and presented fantastic tales, but it turned out that there was some truth in their writings. Heinrich Schliemann and subsequent archaeologists ultimately vindicated the ancient historians. This should serve as a cautionary tale for moderns who cast Romulus aside as a completely fabricated myth. Like Troy, maybe there is some truth at the heart of the Romulus legend.

Bibliography

Carandini, Andrea, *Rome: Day One* (Princeton University Press, Princeton, 2011).

Cornell, T.J., *The Beginnings of Rome* (Routledge, New York, 1995).

Fraschetti, Augusto, *The Foundation of Rome* (Edinburgh University Press, Edinburgh, 2005).

Neel, Jaclyn, *Early Rome: Myth and Society* (Wiley Blackwell, Hoboken, 2017).

Strauss, Barry, *The Trojan War* (Simon and Schuster Paperbacks, New York, 2006).

Wiseman, T.P., *Remus: A Roman Myth* (Cambridge University Press, New York, 1995).

Notes and References

Amm. – Ammianus Marcellinus, *Rerum Gestarum*
Apollod. *Epit.* – Apollodorus, *Epitome*
Apollod. *Lib.* – Apollodorus, *Library*
App. *BC.* – Appian, *The Civil Wars*
App. *Pun.* – Appian, *Punic Wars*
App. *Reg.* – Appian, *Kings*
Cic. *Balb.* – Marcus Tullius Cicero, *For Cornelius Balbus*
Cic. *Div.* – Marcus Tullius Cicero, *On Divination*
Cic. *Leg.* – Marcus Tullius Cicero, *On the Laws*
Cic. *Off.* – Marcus Tullius Cicero, *On Duties*
Cic. *Rep.* – Marcus Tullius Cicero, *On the Republic*
Cic. *Vat.* – Marcus Tullius Cicero, *Against Vatinius*
Dio – Cassius Dio, *History of Rome*
Diod. – Diodorus, *Library of History*
Dion. Hal. – Dionysius of Halicarnassus, *Roman Antiquities*
Eur. *Hel.* – Euripides, *Helen*
Flor. – Florus, *Epitome of Roman History*
Frontin. *Str.* – Frontinus, *Stratagems*
Gel. – Aulus Gellius, *Attic Nights*
Hom. *Il.* – Homer, *Iliad*
Hom. *Od.* – Homer, *Odyssey*
Horace *Ep.* – Horace, *Epodes*
Les. *Il.* – Lesches of Mitylene, *Little Iliad*
Livy – Livy, *History of Rome*
OGR – *Origo Gentis Romanae*
Oros. – Orosius, *Seven Books Against the Pagans*
Ovid *Ars.* – Ovid, *Ars Amatoria*
Ovid *Fast.* – Ovid, *Fasti*
Ovid *Met.* – Ovid, *Metamorphoses*
Phot. *Bib.* – Photius, *Bibliotheca*

Plin. *Nat.* – Pliny the Elder, *Natural History*

Plut. *Cam.* – Plutarch, *Life of Camillus*

Plut. *Comp. Thes. Rom.* – Plutarch, *Comparison of Theseus and Romulus*

Plut. *Mar.* – Plutarch, *Life of Marius*

Plut. *Num.* – Plutarch, *Life of Numa*

Plut. *Pomp.* – Plutarch, *Life of Pompey*

Plut. *Rom.* – Plutarch, *Life of Romulus*

Prop. – Propertius, *Elegies*

Sal. *Cat.* – Sallust, *The War with Catiline*

Sal. *Iug.* – Sallust, *The War with Jugurtha*

Serv. *Aen.* – Maurus Servius Honoratus, *Commentary on the Aeneid of Vergil*

Strab. – Strabo, *Geography*

Suet. *Aug.* – Suetonius, *Life of Augustus*

Suet. *Calig.* – Suetonius, *Life of Caligula*

Suet. *Jul.* – Suetonius, *Life of Julius Caesar*

Tac. *Ann.* – Cornelius Tacitus, *Annales*

Varro *Ling.* – Varro, *de Lingua Latina*

Verg. *Aen.* – Vergil, *Aeneid*

Thuc. – Thucydides, *History of the Peloponnesian War*

Chapter I: Aeneas

Quote: Dion. Hal. 1.58.2 (trans. Earnest Cary).

1. Bryce, Trevor R. 'The Trojan War: Is There Truth behind the Legend?', *Near Eastern Archaeology*, vol. 65, no. 3 (2002), pp.182–95; Korfmann, Manfred, *et. al.*, 'Was There a Trojan War?', *Archaeology*, vol. 57, no. 3 (2004), pp.36–41.
2. Hom. *Il.* 21.441–457.
3. Fraschetti, Augusto, *The Foundation of Rome* (Edinburgh University Press, 2005), p.1.
4. Bryce, Trevor R., 'The Trojan War: Is There Truth behind the Legend?', *Near Eastern Archaeology*, vol. 65, no. 3 (2002), pp.182–95; Foster, B.O., 'The Trojan War Again', *The American Journal of Philology*, vol. 36, no. 3 (1915), pp.298–313; Lord, Albert B., 'Homer, the Trojan War,

and History', *Journal of the Folklore Institute*, vol. 8, no. 2/3 (1971), pp.85–92.

5. Eur. *Hel.* 1; Apollod. *Lib.* 3.10.7–8.

6. Apollod. *Epit.* 2.16.

7. Apollod. *Epit.* 3.3; Hom. *Il.* 7.350–365.

8. Apollod. *Epit.* 3.6; Strauss, Barry, *The Trojan War* (Simon and Schuster, 2006), p.27.

9. Hom. *Il.* 2.800–816, 8.560–565.

10. Bryce, Trevor R., 'The Trojan War: Is There Truth behind the Legend?', *Near Eastern Archaeology*, vol. 65, no. 3 (2002), pp.182–95

11. Hom. *Il.* 2.494–759; Thuc. 1.10.4–5.

12. Hom. *Il.* 3.200–210, 11.135–145; Apollod. *Epit.* 3.28–29.

13. Livy 1.1; Hom. *Il.* 13.460–461.

14. Hom. *Il.* 2.494–759; Thuc. 1.10.4–5; Apollod. *Epit.* 3.29.

15. Apollod. *Epit.* 3.29–32.

16. Apollod. *Epit.* 4.7; Hom. *Il.* 22.131–404.

17. Dion. Hal. 1.46.1.

18. Hom. *Od.* 4.270–275, 8.500–505; Apollod. *Epit.* 5.15.

19. Apollod. *Epit.* 5.16–17; Hom. *Od.* 8.505–515; Les. *Il.* Frag. 1.

20. Apollod. *Epit.* 5.19–23; Dion. Hal. 1.46.1.

21. Verg. *Aen.* 2.268–469; Dion. Hal. 1.46.1–2.

22. Verg. *Aen.* 2.730–1045; Dion. Hal. 1.46.1, 1.47.1; Diod. 7.4.1–2; Ovid *Met.* 13.623–629.
    *Dion. Hal. 1.47.6 states that Aeneas may have had other sons besides Ascanius.

23. Verg. *Aen.* 3.1–20; Livy 1.1; Diod. 7.4.3–4; Dion. Hal. 1.47.4.

24. App. *BC* Frag. 1.1; Verg. *Aen.* 3.1–20; Dion. Hal. 1.47.4; Diod. 7.4.3–4; Ovid *Met.* 13.623–639.

25. Dion. Hal. 1.49.1, 1.51.2, 1.53.3; Ovid *Met.* 13.623–639, 14.1–74; Verg. *Aen.* 1.198–207, 3.192–277; Strab. 5.3.

26. Dion. Hal. 1.9.3, 1.11.1, 1.13.4, 1.17.1, 1.18.2, 1.57.2; Livy 1.1.

27. Livy 1.1; Dion. Hal. 1.57.4, 1.59.1; Ovid *Met.* 14.441.

28. Livy 1.1; Dion. Hal. 1.57.2, 1.59.1.

29. Dion. Hal. 1.59.1–3, 1.60.1; Strab. 5.3; Livy 1.1–2; App. *BC* Frag. 1.1; Verg. *Aen.* 6.756–800; Castagnoli, Ferdinando and Castagnoli,

Fordinande, 'LAVINIUM AND THE AENEAS LEGEND', *Vergilius (1959)*, no. 13 (1967), pp.1–7; Dennison, Walter, 'The Latest Dated Inscription from Lavinium', *Classical Philology*, vol. 5, no. 3 (1910), pp.285–90; Laroche, Roland A, 'The Alban King-List in Dionysius I, 70–71: A Numerical Analysis', *Historia: Zeitschrift Für Alte Geschichte*, vol. 31, no. 1 (1982), pp.112–20.

OGR 12 states that Latinus gave Aeneas 500 *jugera* of land.

*Dion. Hal. 1.59.1 claims the Trojans were given 'about forty stades in every direction of the hill'.

*Dion. Hal. 1.59.3 states that some believed that Lavinium was named after a different woman named Lavinia. She was the first to die of natural causes during Lavinium's construction.

30. Livy 1.1–2; Verg. *Aen*. 6.756–800.
31. Livy 1.2; Dion. Hal. 1.59.2.
32. Livy 1.2; Dion. Hal. 1.43.2, 1.64.1–4; Strab. 5.3; Ovid *Met*. 14.441; Diod. 7.5.2; App. *BC* Frag. 1.1.
33. Dion. Hal. 1.64.4; Livy 1.2; App. *BC* Frag. 1.1; Ovid *Met*. 14.581–608.
34. Dion. Hal. 1.64.4–5 (trans. Earnest Cary); Tilly, Bertha, 'The Identification of the Numicus', *The Journal of Roman Studies*, vol. 26 (1936), pp.1–11.
35. Livy 1.2; Diod. 7.5.2; Ovid *Met*. 14.581–608.

Chapter II: Romulus and Remus

Quote: Plut. *Rom*. 6.2 (tran. Bernadotte Perrin).
1. Livy 1.3.
2. Livy 1.3; Dion. Hal. 1.66.1; Flor. 1.1.4; App. *BC* Frag. 1.2.
3. Livy 1.3; Dion. Hal. 1.66.1; Strab. 5.3; App. *BC* Frag. 1.2; Diod. 7.5.3, 7.5.6; Serv. *Aen*. 8.63.
   *Varro *Ling*. 5.144 and Diod. 7.5.6 claim that Alba Longa was named for the white sow connected to the Aeneas myth.
4. Livy 1.3; Flor. 1.1.4; Dion. Hal. 1.71.2; Diod. 7.5.7.
5. Diod. Frag. 7.5.7; Fraschetti, Augusto, *The Foundation of Rome* (Edinburgh University Press, 2005), p.25.
6. Livy 1.3; Diod. 7.5.12; Dion. Hal. 1.71.4; App. *BC* Frag. 1.3.

7. Plut. *Rom.* 3.2.

   *Strab. 5.3 suggests that Numitor and Amulius may have ruled Alba Longa concurrently for a period.

8. Diod. 7.5.12; Plut. *Rom.* 3.2; Livy 1.3; Dion. Hal. 1.71.4; App. *BC* Frag. 1.3; Strab 5.3.

9. Livy 1.3.

10. Plut. *Rom.* 7.1.

11. Dion. Hal. 1.76.2–3; Strab. 5.3; App. *BC* Frag. 1.3; Livy 1.3.

   *Livy 1.3 states that Amulius murdered Numitor's sons, implying Numitor had at least one son other than Aegestus who was also killed.

12. Plut. *Rom.* 3.2–3; Dion. Hal. 1.76.3.

   *Plut. *Rom.* 3.3 and Dion. Hal. 1.76.3 note that Rhea Silvia was also called Ilia.

13. Plut. *Rom.* 3.2; Dion. Hal. 1.76.3–4; Strab. 5.3; App. *BC* Frag. 1.3; Bennett, Florence M., 'A Theory Concerning the Origin and the Affiliations of the Cult of Vesta', *The Classical Weekly*, vol. 7, no. 5 (1913), pp.35–37.

14. Plut. *Rom.* 12.5; Grafton, A.T. and Swerdlow, N.M., 'The Horoscope of the Foundation of Rome', *Classical Philology*, vol. 81, no. 2 (1986), pp.148–53.

15. Dion. Hal. 1.77.1–2; Plut. *Rom.* 3.3; Livy 1.4.

16. Dion. Hal. 1.77.1–2; Livy 1.4; Flor. 1.1.1; Strab. 5.3; Cic. *Rep.* 6.24; Plut. *Rom.* 12.5; Grafton, A.T. and Swerdlow, N.M., 'The Horoscope of the Foundation of Rome', *Classical Philology*, vol. 81, no. 2 (1986), pp.148–53.

17. Dion. Hal. 1.77.4.

18. Livy 1.4; Dion. Hal. 1.77.1–4.

19. Dion. Hal. 1.77.4.

20. Dion. Hal. 1.78.1.

21. Dion. Hal. 1.78.1–2; Plut. *Rom.* 3.3.

22. Dion. Hal. 1.78.2–3.

23. Dion. Hal. 1.78.3–4.

24. Dion. Hal. 1.78.4; Livy 1.4; Plut. *Rom.* 3.3, 12.5–6; Grafton, A.T. and Swerdlow, N.M., 'The Horoscope of the Foundation of Rome', *Classical Philology*, vol. 81, no. 2 (1986), pp.148–53.

25. Wiseman, T.P., *Remus: A Roman Myth* (Cambridge University Press, 1995), p.23; Carandini, Andrea, *Rome: Day One* (Princeton University Press, 2011), p.36.

26. Plut. *Rom.* 3.3; Dion. Hal. 1.78.4.

27. Dion. Hal. 1.78.5.

28. Dion. Hal. 1.79.2; Livy 1.4; Strab. 5.3; App. *BC* Frag. 1.3.

29. Plut. *Rom.* 3.4; Dion. Hal. 1.79.4; Livy 1.4; Cic. *Rep.* 2.4.

30. Plut. *Rom.* 3.4; Livy 1.4–5; Dion. Hal. 1.31.4, 1.79.4–5; App. *BC* Frag. 1.3.

31. Plut. *Rom.* 3.4; Livy 1.4; Dion. Hal. 1.79.4–5; App. *BC* Frag. 1.3; Ovid *Fast.* 2.381–424.

32. Dion. Hal. 1.79.5; Plut. Rom. 3.5, 4.1; Livy 1.4; Flor. 1.1.2–3; Plin. *Nat.* 15.20.

33. Dion. Hal. 1.32.3–5; Plut. Rom. 4.1; Livy 1.4; Plin. *Nat.* 15.20.

34. Livy 1.4; Plut. *Rom.* 4.2; Dion. Hal. 1.79.6; Cic. *Rep.* 2.4; Flor. 1.1.3; Ovid *Fast.* 2.381–424.

35. Livy 1.4; Plut. *Rom.* 4.3.

36. Plut. *Rom.* 4.2; Dion. Hal. 1.79.6; Livy 1.4.

37. Dion. Hal. 1.79.6–8; Livy 1.4; Flor. 1.1.3; Strab. 5.3.

38. Plut. *Rom.* 6.1; Dion. Hal. 1.79.9–10; Livy 1.4; Cic. *Rep.* 2.4; Flor. 1.1.3; Strab. 5.3.

    *Dion. Hal. 1.84.1–4 alleges that somehow, while Rhea was a Vestal Virgin, she became pregnant, likely through the traditional means. Once she gave birth, her father switched her newborns with others that he had procured. Then he used his remaining influence and wealth to smuggle her infant children out of Alba Longa. He subsequently entrusted them to Larentia and Faustulus to rear.

39. Plut. *Rom.* 6.1, 8.1; Dion. Hal. 1.79.9, 1.82.3.

40. Plut. *Rom.* 4.1, 6.2, and 9.1; Livy 1.4; Cic. *Rep.* 2.4.

41. Cornell, T.J., *The Beginnings of Rome* (Routledge, 1995), p.16; Wiseman, T.P., *Remus: A Roman Myth* (Cambridge University Press, 1995), p.129; Dion. Hal. 1.33.4.

42. Gel. 7.7; Plin. *Nat.* 18.2.

43. Livy 1.4; Cic. *Rep.* 2.4; Plut. *Rom.* 6.2–3; Ovid *Fasti* 2.359–380.

44. Plut. *Rom.* 10.2.

45. Gel. 7.7; Plin. *Nat.* 18.2.
46. Strab. 5.3; Plut. *Rom.* 6.1; Dion. Hal. 1.84.5.
47. Plut. *Rom.* 6.1; Dion. Hal. 1.84.5.
48. Dion. Hal. 1.84.5; Fraschetti, Augusto, *The Foundation of Rome* (Edinburgh University Press, 2005), p.15; Plut. *Rom.* 6.1.
49. Plut. *Rom.* 6.2–3; Cic. *Rep.* 2.4; Dion. Hal. 1.79.11.
50. Flor.1.1.5.
51. Fraschetti, Augusto, *The Foundation of Rome* (Edinburgh University Press, 2005), p.26; Cic. *Div.* 1.3, 1.107–108; Plut. *Rom.* 6.2–3; Dion. Hal. 1.79.10–11; Livy 1.4.
52. Diod. 8.4.1–2; Livy 1.4.

Chapter III: Numitor

Quote: Dion. Hal. 1.80.4 (trans. Earnest Cary).
 1. Plut. *Rom.* 6.3; Livy 1.4.
 2. Dion. Hal. 1.79.12, 1.81.4; Plut. *Rom.* 7.1.
 3. Livy 1.3.
 4. Dion. Hal. 1.79.12.
 5. Dion. Hal. 1.79.12–13; Plut. *Rom.* 7.1; Livy 1.5.
 6. Plut. *Rom.* 7.1.
 7. Plut. *Rom.* 7.1; Dion. Hal. 1.79.13.
 8. Livy 1.5; Plut. *Rom.* 7.1–2; Dion. Hal. 1.79.13.
 9. Plut. *Rom.* 7.2; Dion. Hal. 1.80.2; Livy 1.5.
10. Dion. Hal. 1.80.1; Livy 1.5; Plut. Rom. 21.2–5; Rodriguez-Mayorgas, Ana, 'Romulus, Aeneas and the Cultural Memory of the Roman Republic', *Athenaeum* (2010), vol. 1, pp.89–109; Wiseman, T.P., *Remus: A Roman Myth* (Cambridge University Press, 1995), pp.80–84, 87; Fraschetti, Augusto, *The Foundation of Rome* (Edinburgh University Press, 2005), pp.18–23.
11. Dion. Hal. 1.80.2–3; Livy 1.5.
12. Dion. Hal. 1.79.13–14; Plut. *Rom.* 7.2.
13. Dion. Hal. 1.80.3; Plut. *Rom.* 8.1; Livy 1.5.
14. Dion. Hal. 1.80.4, 1.81.1; Plut. *Rom.* 8.1.
15. Dion. Hal. 1.81.1; Livy 1.5; Plut. *Rom.* 8.5–6.

16. Plut. *Rom.* 7.2.
17. Plut. *Rom.* 7.2–3; Dion. Hal. 1.81.2.
18. Plut. *Rom.* 7.3–4; Dion. Hal. 1.81.3–4; Livy 1.5.
19. Plut. *Rom.* 7.4–7 (trans. Bernadotte Perrin); Dion. Hal. 1.81.4; Livy 1.5.
20. Plut. *Rom.* 7.7; Livy 1.5; Diod. 8.3.
21. Dion. Hal. 1.81.5–6, 1.82.1–3 (trans. Earnest Cary).
22. Dion. Hal. 1.82.3–4; Plut. *Rom.* 8.1–2.
23. Plut. *Rom.* 8.2–3; Dion. Hal. 1.82.4–6, 1.83.1.
24. Dion. Hal. 1.82.6, 1.83.1–2 (trans. Earnest Cary).
25. Plut. *Rom.* 8.4.
26. Dion. Hal. 1.83.2.
27. Plut. *Rom.* 8.5; Dion. Hal. 1.83.2–3.
    *Dion. Hal. 1.83.2–3 states that a man, possibly confused with the same from Plut. *Rom.* 8.5, was sent to Numitor to bring him back to Amulius' palace and keep him under guard there.
28. Plut. *Rom.* 8.6.
29. Plut. *Rom.* 8.5–6; Livy 1.6.
    *Dion. Hal. 1.83.3 states that their target was the citadel, but Livy 1.5–6 contends that they were primarily focused on capturing the palace instead.
30. Plut. *Rom.* 8.6; Dion. Hal. 1.83.3; Livy 1.5–6.
31. Plut. *Rom.* 8.6; Diod. 8.3; Dion. Hal. 1.83.3; Livy 1.5; Flor. 1.1.5; Strab. 5.3; Ovid *Fasti* 3.43–86.
    *Dion. Hal. 1.84.6–8 presents an alternative version. It states that Numitor masterminded the coup from the beginning. He purposefully fomented discord among the shepherds, hoping to incite a crime against his men. Once this happened he demanded the criminals be tried, which allowed a large body of men to enter Alba Longa. Upon which, he informed Romulus and Remus of their heritage and persuaded them and many others to overthrow Amulius.
32. Plut. *Rom.* 9.1; Plut. *Comp. Thes. Rom.* 5
33. Livy 1.6; Plut. *Rom.* 9.1; Flor. 1.1.5; Strab. 5.3.
34. Plut. *Rom.* 9.1; Dion. Hal. 1.85.1.
35. Livy 1.6; Plut. *Rom.* 9.1; Dion. Hal. 1.85.1–2; Flor. 1.1.5.

*Dion. Hal. 1.85.1–2 states that Numitor may have first suggested that Romulus and Remus should found a colony.

36. Livy 1.6, 1.9; Plut. *Rom.* 9.1–2; Dion. Hal. 1.85.1; Flor. 1.1.5.

37. Everitt, Anthony, *The Rise of Rome* (Random House Trade Paperbacks, 2012), p.18.

38. Livy 1.6; Dion. Hal. 1.85.2.

39. Dion. Hal. 1.85.2–3; Plut. *Rom.* 9.1; Livy 1.6; Flor. 1.1.5–6; Strab. 5.3.

Chapter IV: Remoria

Quote: Livy 1.6 (trans. Rev. Canon Roberts).

 1. Dion. Hal. 1.85.2–4.

 2. Plut. *Rom.* 9.2; Dion. Hal. 1.85.2–3; Flor. 1.1.10.

 3. Livy 1.6; Plut. *Rom.* 9.1, 9.4; Dion. Hal. 1.85.2, 1.85.5–6.

 4. Cic. *Rep.* 2.5–6.

 5. Strab. 5.3; Cic. *Rep.* 2.7–9.

 6. Cic. *Rep.* 2.7–9; Cornell, T.J., *The Beginnings of Rome* (Routledge, 1995), pp.48, 55.

 7. Dion. Hal. 1.85.4–5.

 8. Dion. Hal. 1.85.3–6, 1.87.3; Wiseman, T.P., *Remus: A Roman Myth* (Cambridge University Press, 1995), pp.114–17.

 9. Plut. *Rom.* 9.4; Dion. Hal. 1.85.2, 1.85.5–6.

10. Dion. Hal. 1.85.6; Cornell, T.J., *The Beginnings of Rome* (Routledge, 1995), p.72; Wiseman, T.P., *Remus: A Roman Myth* (Cambridge University Press, 1995), pp.7, 114–17; Plut. *Rom.* 9.4; Cic. *Div.* 1.107.
     *There are multiple spellings of Remoria, including Remuria and Remonion. Wiseman, T.P., *Remus: A Roman Myth* (Cambridge University Press, 1995), p.7.

11. Dion. Hal. 1.85.6; Plut. *Rom.* 9.4; Fraschetti, Augusto, *The Foundation of Rome* (Edinburgh University Press, 2005), p.36.

12. Dion. Hal. 1.85.6; Livy 1.6.

13. Livy 1.6; Cic. *Rep.* 2.12; Dion. Hal. 1.85.6.

14. Dion. Hal. 1.85.5, 1.86.1; Livy 1.6.

15. Dion. Hal. 1.86.1.

16. Plut. *Rom.* 9.5–7; Dion. Hal. 1.86.1; Livy 1.6; Flor. 1.1.6; Cic. *Rep.* 2.5; Cic. *Div.* 1.3, 1.107–108; Cic. *Vat.* 8.20.

17. Dion. Hal. 1.86.1–2.

18. Dion. Hal. 1.86.1–2; Plut. *Rom.* 9.5; Livy 1.6; Flor. 1.1.6; Cic. *Div.* 1.3; Cic. *Rep.* 2.5; Cic. *Vat.* 8.20.

    *Cic. *Div.* 1.107 reports that Ennius claimed Romulus watched for the vultures from the Aventine Hill.

19. Plut. *Rom.* 22.1–2.

20. Dion. Hal. 1.86.3.

21. Dion. Hal. 1.86.3; Plut. *Rom.* 9.5.

22. Dion. Hal. 1.86.3–4; Plut. *Rom.* 9.5; Livy 1.7; Flor. 1.1.6.

23. Dion. Hal. 1.86.4 (trans. Earnest Cary); Livy 1.7.

    OGR 23.2–4 states that Romulus didn't forward a message that summoned Remus, but when Remus saw six vultures, he delivered the news to Romulus. However, Romulus declared that he would show him twelve vultures. Then they appeared and were accompanied by lightning, and Romulus taunted Remus.

24. Dion. Hal. 1.86.4, 1.87.1; Livy 1.7.

25. Livy 1.7; Dion. Hal. 1.87.1.

26. Dion. Hal. 1.87.4.

    *Dion. Hal. 1.87.1–3 states that there was a battle but asserts that Remus died in the battle. Dion. Hal. 1.87.4 states that Celer slew Remus after leaping over the fortifications, but there is no mention of a large-scale battle. Plut. Rom. 10.1–2 seems to combine both Dion. Hal. 1.87.1 and 1.87.4. Livy 1.7 states that somehow Remus was killed in a tumult, which could allude to a battle. Livy 1.7 later includes the account of Remus leaping over the fortifications and being slain.

27. Dion. Hal. 1.87.4; Diod. 8.6.1; Plut. *Rom.* 10.1.

28. Dion. Hal. 1.87.4 (trans. Earnest Cary); Plut. *Rom.* 10.1; Diod. 8.6.1–2 (trans. Charles L. Sherman).

29. Livy 1.7 (trans. Rev. Canon Roberts); Plut. *Rom.* 10.1; Diod. 8.6.1–3; Dion. Hal. 1.87.4; Flor. 1.1.8; Ovid *Fast.* 4.807–862; Strab. 5.3; Oros. 2.4; Cic. Off. 3.41.

    * Ovid Fast. 4.807–862 states that Celer used a shovel to kill Remus.

30. Dion. Hal. 1.87.4; Livy 1.7; Plut. *Rom.* 10.1; Flor. 1.1.8; Diod. 8.6.3.

31. Plut. *Rom.* 10.2.
32. Dion. Hal. 2.13.2.
33. Dion. Hal. 1.87.1.
    *Serv. Aen. 6.779 claims that the two factions began fighting over the settlement's name.
34. Dion. Hal. 1.87.1–3; Plut. *Rom.* 10.1–2; Oros. 2.4.
35. Dion. Hal. 1.87.3.
36. Plut. *Rom.* 11.1; Dion. Hal. 1.87.2–3; Ovid *Fast.* 4.835–4.856 (trans. Jaclyn Neel); Kyle, Donald G., *Spectacles of Death in Ancient Rome* (London and New York, Routledge, 2001), pp.128–54.
37. Kyle, Donald G., *Spectacles of Death in Ancient Rome* (London and New York, Routledge, 2001), pp.128–54; Cornell, T.J., *The Beginnings of Rome* (Routledge, 1995), pp.33–36; Ovid *Fast.* 5.455–492.
38. Plut. *Rom.* 11.1; Dion. Hal. 1.87.2–3.
39. Ovid *Fast.* 5.419–492 (trans. James George Frazer).
40. Scheid, John, *An Introduction to Roman Religion* (Indiana University Press, 2003), pp. 50, 169; Ovid *Fast.* 5.419–493 (trans. James George Frazer).
41. Dion. Hal. 1.87.3.
42. Gel. 7.7; Plut. *Rom.* 4.3.
    *Gel. 7.7 discloses that some other sources claim that Larentia made the Roman people her heirs rather than solely Romulus.

Chapter V: Parilia

Quote: Dion. Hal. 2.3.8 (trans. Earnest Cary).
 1. Dion. Hal. 1.87.3; Serv. *Aen.* 1.276.
 2. Dion. Hal. 1.88.1.
 3. Serv. *Aen.* 1.276.
 4. Dion. Hal. 1.88.1.
 5. Dion. Hal. 1.88.1.
 6. Dion. Hal. 1.88.1.
 7. Plut. *Rom.* 11.1–2, 12.1–6; Dion. Hal. 1.88.2–3; Tac. *Ann.* 12.24. Grafton, A.T. and Swerdlow, N.M., 'The Horoscope of the Foundation of Rome', *Classical Philology*, vol. 81, no. 2 (1986), pp.148–53.

*Plut. Rom. 12.2 states that the foundation may have occurred on the 30th of the month.

8. Plut. *Rom.* 11.1–3, 19.7; Dion. Hal. 1.88.2; Tac. *Ann.* 12.24; Ovid *Fast.* 4.809–826; Tac. *Ann.* 12.24.

9. Dion. Hal. 1.88.2–3; Livy 1.7; Plut. *Rom.* 12.1;

10. Plut. *Rom.* 9.3; Livy 1.8; Flor. 1.1.8–9.

11. Livy 1.8; Plut. *Rom.* 9.3; Flor. 1.1.8–9; Dion. Hal. 1.85.2, 2.15.3.
    * Livy 1.8 and Plut. Rom. 9.3 appear to disagree over whether the asylum was built by Romulus and Remus or by Romulus after Remus' death.

12. Dion. Hal. 2.14.1.

13. Dion. Hal. 2.3.1.

14. Dion. Hal. 2.3.8 (trans. Earnest Cary)

15. Dion. Hal. 2.4.1–2 (trans. Earnest Cary)

16. Dion. Hal 2.5.1–2, 2.6.1–3.

17. Dion. Hal. 2.6.1, 2.14.1; Fraschetti, Augusto, *The Foundation of Rome* (Edinburgh University Press, 2005), p.67.

18. Ovid *Fast.* 1.27–44, 3.43–166, 5.53–80; Dion. Hal. 2.18.2; Fraschetti, Augusto, *The Foundation of Rome* (Edinburgh University Press, 2005), p.73; Smith, William, *A Dictionary of Greek and Roman Antiquities* (John Murray, 1875); Livy 1.7.
    *Some ancient writers disagreed on the length of the Romulean year and the number of months. See Plut. *Num.* 18.3 and Smith, William, 'Calendarium', *A Dictionary of Greek and Roman Antiquities* (John Murray, 1875).

19. Plut. *Rom.* 13.1; Dion. Hal. 2.14.1–2; Ovid *Fast.* 6.65–88.

20. Plut. *Rom.* 9.3, 13.1.

21. Plut. *Rom.* 13.1; Dion. Hal. 1.85.3, 2.12.1, 2.13.1; Livy 1.8; Cic. *Rep.* 2.14; Sal. *Cat.* 6.5; Flor. 1.1.15; Ovid *Fast.* 5.53–80.

22. Dion. Hal. 2.8.1, 2.9.1–2, 2.12.1–3, 2.13.1, 2.14.2; Plut. *Rom.* 13.1–3; Livy 1.8; Cic. *Rep.* 2.14.
    *Plut. Rom 13.1 claims that Romulus called the original senators patricians rather than *Patres*.

23. Plut. *Rom.* 13.3–5; Phot. *Bib.* 57.

24. Plut. *Rom.* 13.5–6; Verboven, K.S., 'Clientela, Roman Republic', *The Encyclopedia of Ancient History* (2012); Dion. Hal. 2.9.2.

25. Verboven, K.S., 'Clientela, Roman Republic', *The Encyclopedia of Ancient History* (2012); Plut. *Mar.* 5.4; Plut. *Rom.* 13.6; Dion. Hal. 2.10.3.
26. Livy 1.8; Dion. Hal. 2.14.1–2, 2.24.1.
27. Livy 1.8; Dion. Hal. 2.29.1.
28. Dion. Hal. 2.14.3.
29. Var. *Re. Rust.* 1.10.
30. Livy 1.8–9; Plut. *Rom.* 9.2–3, 14.2; Flor. 1.1.8–9; Dion. Hal. 1.85.2; Strab. 5.3; Flor. 1.1.10.
31. Livy 1.9; Flor. 1.1.10; Strab. 5.3; Plut. *Rom.* 14.5; Dion. Hal. 2.31.1.

Chapter VI: Consualia

Quote: Plut. *Rom.* 14.5 (trans. Bernadotte Perrin,).
1. Livy 1.9; Plut. *Rom.* 14.2; Strab. 5.3; Flor. 1.1.10.
2. Livy 1.9; Dion. Hal. 2.30.2; Plut. *Rom.* 14.2.
3. Livy 1.9 (trans. Rev. Canon Roberts); Dion. Hal. 2.30.2; Flor. 1.1.10; Wiseman, T.P., 'The Wife and Children of Romulus', *The Classical Quarterly*, vol. 33, no. 2 (1983), pp.445–52.
4. Livy 1.9; Plut. *Rom.* 9.2; Dion. Hal. 2.30.2.
5. Livy 1.9; Plut. *Rom.* 16.3.
6. Livy 1.9; Dion. Hal. 2.30.3; Plut. *Rom.* 14.3–4.
   * Plut. *Rom.* 14.1 states that Romulus abducted the maidens because he wanted to provoke a war, not because he needed them for procreation. Supposedly, seers had said if Rome diligently followed a warlike path, then in time, it would become the world's greatest city.
7. Livy 1.9; Dion. Hal. 2.31.1; Plut. *Rom.* 14.1–2.
8. Dion. Hal. 2.30.2–3.
9. Livy 1.9; Plut. *Rom.* 14.4; Dion. Hal. 2.30.3; Wiseman, T.P., 'The Wife and Children of Romulus', *The Classical Quarterly*, vol. 33, no. 2 (1983), pp.445–52.
10. Plut. *Rom.* 14.1, 14.3; Dion. Hal. 2.30.3, 2.31.1; Livy 1.9; Cic. *Rep.* 2.12; Flor. 1.1.10; Strab. 5.3.
11. Dion. Hal. 1.33.2; Scheid, John, *An Introduction to Roman Religion* (Indiana University Press, 2003), pp.49–50.
12. Livy 1.9; Plut. *Rom.* 14.4; Dion. Hal. 2.30.3.

13. Livy 1.9.
14. Plut. *Rom*. 14.1, 14.4; Dion. Hal. 2.30.4, 2.31.1; Livy 1.9; Cic. *Rep*. 2.12; Strab. 5.3; Flor. 1.1.10.
15. Livy 1.9; Dion. Hal. 2.30.3–5; Plut. *Rom*. 14.4–5.
16. Plut. *Rom*. 14.5.
17. Livy 1.9; Plut. *Rom*. 14.5; Dion. Hal. 2.30.5; Cic. *Rep*. 2.12; Strab. 5.3; Flor. 1.1.10; Oros. 2.4.
18. Plut. *Rom*. 15.1–5; Plut. *Pomp*. 4.4; Livy 1.9; Bierkan, Andrew T., Sherman, Charles P. and Stocquart Jnr, Emile, 'Marriage in Roman Law', *The Yale Law Journal* 16.5 (1907), pp.303–27; Hersch, Karen Klaiber, 'Introduction To The Roman Wedding: Two Case Studies', *The Classical Journal*, 109.2 (2014), pp.223–32.
19. Livy 1.9; Plut. *Rom*. 14.5; Dion. Hal. 2.30.5.
20. Dion. Hal. 2.30.4.
21. Livy 1.9; Dion. Hal. 2.30.5.
22. Plut. *Rom*. 14.1, 14.6; Dion. Hal. 2.30.6; Cic. *Rep*. 2.12; Wiseman, T.P., 'The Wife and Children of Romulus', *The Classical Quarterly*, vol. 33, no. 2 (1983), pp.445–52.
23. Strab. 5.3; Livy 1.10.
24. Plut. *Rom*. 14.1, 14.6; Dion. Hal. 2.30.6; Cic. *Rep*. 2.12.
25. Livy 1.9–10; Dion. Hal. 2.30.5.
26. Livy 1.9–10.
27. Dion. Hal. 2.30.6; Livy 1.9; Plut. *Rom*. 14.6, 19.6; Cic. *Rep*. 2.12; Oros. 2.4.
28. Bierkan, Andrew T., Sherman, Charles P. and Stocquart Jnr, Emile, 'Marriage in Roman Law', *The Yale Law Journal*, 16.5 (1907), pp.303–27; Hersch, Karen Klaiber, 'Introduction To The Roman Wedding: Two Case Studies', *The Classical Journal*, 109.2 (2014), pp.223–32.
29. Plut. *Rom*. 14.6–7, 18.5; Dion. Hal. 2.45.2; Livy 1.11.
30. Plut. *Rom*. 16.2; Livy 1.9–10.
31. Plut. *Rom*. 16.2–3.
32. Livy 1.10.
33. Livy 1.10; Plut. *Rom*. 16.3; Dion. Hal. 2.32.2.
34. Dion. Hal. 2.36.3; Plut. *Rom*. 19.7; Livy 1.13.
35. Livy 1.10, 1.13; Dion. Hal. 2.32.1–3, 2.36.3; Plut. *Rom*. 17.2.

36. Dion Hal. 2.33.1.

37. Ovid *Fast*. 2.425–452 (trans. James George Frazer).

Chapter VII: Caenina

Quote: Plut. *Rom*. 16.3 (trans. Bernadotte Perrin).

1. Dion. Hal. 2.33.1; Livy 1.10.
2. Plut. *Rom*. 17.1; Dion. Hal. 2.33.1; Livy 1.11.
3. Plut. *Rom*. 17.1.
4. Dion. Hal. 2.33.1; Livy 1.10; Plut. *Rom*. 16.3, 17.1.
5. Plut. *Rom*. 16.3–4; Livy 1.10.
6. Dion. Hal. 2.33.1-2; Livy 1.10; Plut. *Rom*. 16.3; Kress, M. and Talmor, I., 'A New Look at the 3:1 Rule of Combat through Markov Stochastic Lanchester Models', *The Journal of the Operational Research Society*, vol. 50, no. 7 (1999), pp.733–44.
7. Dion. Hal. 2.33.2; Livy 1.10.
8. Dion. Hal. 2.33.2.
9. Plut. *Rom*. 16.4; Dion. Hal. 2.33.2.
10. Goldsworthy, Adrian, *The Complete Roman Army* (Thames & Hudson, 2003), pp.26–27; Livy 8.8.
11. Plut. *Rom*. 16.4.
12. Plut. *Rom*. 16.4; Dion. Hal. 2.33.2; Livy 1.10; Flor. 1.11.
13. Plut. *Rom*. 16.4; Dion. Hal. 2.33.2; Livy 1.10.
14. Dion. Hal. 2.33.2; Livy 1.10; Plut. *Rom*. 16.4; Flor. 1.1.11.
    * Dion. Hal. 2.33.2 states that the second battle with Acron and the bout between the kings occurred after Romulus sacked Caenina.
15. Plut. *Rom*. 16.4; Dion. Hal. 2.34.1.
16. Plut. *Rom*. 16.4.
17. Plut. *Rom*. 16.4; Flor. 1.1.11; Cic. *Rep*. 2.15–16; Dion. Hal. 2.28.3.

Chapter VIII: Antemnae and Crustumerium

Quote: Livy 1.11 (trans. Rev. Canon Roberts).

1. Livy 1.11; Dion. Hal. 2.34.1.
2. Livy 1.11; Plut. *Rom*. 17.1; Dion. Hal. 2.34.1.

* Plut. *Rom.* 16.6 and 17.1 suggests that Rome enjoyed a triumph before it warred with Antemnae.

3. Plut. *Rom.* 16.5–6; Dion. Hal. 2.34.1–2; Livy 1.10.
4. Dion. Hal. 2.34.1–3; Plut. *Rom.* 16.6; Livy 1.10.
5. Dion. Hal. 2.34.3; Plut. *Rom.* 16.6.
6. Livy 1.38.
7. Dion. Hal. 2.34.4; Livy 1.10 (trans. Rev. Canon Roberts); Plut. *Rom.* 16.6; Flor. 1.11.
8. Livy 1.10; Plut. *Rom.* 16.7.
9. Dio. 44.4.3.
10. Livy 1.11.
11. Dion. Hal. 2.35.1–6; Liv 1.11; Plut. *Rom.* 16.4, 17.1.
12. Dion. Hal. 2.35.2–6 (trans. Earnest Cary).
13. Dion. Hal. 2.36.1; Livy 1.11; Plut. *Rom.* 17.1.
14. Dion. Hal. 2.36.1; Livy 1.11; Plut. *Rom.* 17.1.
   *Plut. *Rom.* 17.1 states that Crustumerium banded together with Antemnae and Fidenae in a single battle against Rome.
   *Flor. 1.1.10. implies that the Romans battled and defeated the Veientes around this time.
15. Dion. Hal. 2.36.1.
16. Dion. Hal. 2.36.1.
   *Livy 1.11 presents a different version of the conflict with Crustumerium. The Crustumerians were demoralized by Caenina and Antemnae's swift defeats. When the legionaries ultimately battled with Crustumerium at an unknown location, the Crustumerians responded feebly, giving the Romans an easy victory and control of their city.
17. Dion. Hal. 2.36.1; Livy 1.11; Plut. *Rom.* 17.1.
18. Dion. Hal. 2.36.2.
19. Dion. Hal. 2.36.3; Plut. *Rom.* 17.2.

Chapter IX: Tarpeia

Quote: Dion. Hal. 2.39.2–3 (trans. Earnest Cary).
1. Dion. Hal. 2.36.3.
2. Dion. Hal. 2.36.3, 2.37.4; Livy 1.11.

3. Dion. Hal. 2.37.1, 2.38.2.
4. Dion. Hal. 2.37.2.
5. Dion. Hal. 2.37.5.
6. Carandini, Andrea, *Rome: Day One* (Princeton University Press, 2007), pp.108–09.
7. Dion. Hal. 2.37.3–5.
8. Dion. Hal. 2.38.1; Strab. 5.3.
9. Dion. Hal. 2.38.1.
10. Dion. Hal. 2.38.1; Plut. *Rom.* 17.2.
11. Dion. Hal. 2.38.2; Livy 1.11; Plut. *Rom.* 17.2.
    *Plut. Rom. 17.5 states that some believed that Tarpeia was an abducted maiden and Tatius' daughter.
12. Dion. Hal. 2.38.3–4 (trans. Earnest Cary); Plut. *Rom.* 17.2; Flor. 1.1.12.
13. Dion. Hal. 2.38.4.
14. Dion. Hal. 2.38.4; Livy 1.11; Varro *Ling.* 5.41.
15. Dion. Hal. 2.38.4–5, 2.39.2; Livy 1.11; Plut. *Rom.* 17.2–3.
    *Prop. 4.4.15–94 claims that Tarpeia lusted after Tatius and surrendered the fortress in order to become his wife.
16. Dion. Hal. 2.39.1.
17. Dion. Hal. 2.39.1; Plut. *Rom.* 17.2; Livy 1.11.
18. Dion. Hal. 2.39.3, 2.40.1–2, 2.41.1; Livy 1.11; Plut. *Rom.* 17.3–4; Flor. 1.1.12–13.
19. Dion. Hal. 2.40.1–3; Plut. *Rom.* 17.3–5, 18.1; Flor. 1.1.12.
20. Dion. Hal. 2.41.1.

Chapter X: Tatius

Quote: Livy 1.13 (trans. Rev. Canon Roberts).
1. Livy 1.12.
2. Dion. Hal. 2.41.1.
3. Dion. Hal. 2.41.2; Plut *Rom.* 18.2.
4. Dion. Hal. 2.41.2.
    * Dion. Hal. 2.41.1 states that there were two major battles between the Romans and Sabines.
    * Plut. *Rom.* 18.2–7 seems to suggest there was only one major battle.

* Livy 1.12 also seems to suggest that there was only one major battle.

* There is also disagreement over the battle's order of events.

5. Dion. Hal. 2.41.2–3, 2.42.1.
6. Dion. Hal. 2.42.1–2.
7. Livy 1.12, 1.22; Plut. *Rom.* 18.5.
8. Dion. Hal. 2.42.2–3; Flor. 1.1.13.
9. Dion. Hal. 2.42.2–5.
10. Dion. Hal. 2.42.4–6; Livy 1.12.

    *Plut. *Rom.* 18.4 asserts that the Lacus Curtius gained its name under different circumstances. According to Plutarch, at the onset of the Sabine/Roman war, Mettius Curtius charged on his horse faster than his army. During his advance, his horse became lodged in a marsh, and it was ultimately named for him.

    *Livy 1.12 doesn't mention the single combat. Livy only recorded that Curtius lost control of his horse and dived into the lake for safety. Livy suggests this bout occurred at a later point.
11. Dion. Hal. 2.43.1–2; Plut. *Rom.* 18.5.
12. Dion. Hal. 2.43.2–3.
13. Dion. Hal. 2.43.3–4; Livy 1.12 (trans. Rev. Canon Roberts); Plut. *Rom.* 18.6–7; Flor. 1.1.13.
14. Dion. Hal. 2.43.4–5; Livy 1.12; Plut. *Rom.* 18.7.
15. Dion. Hal. 2.44.1–3.
16. Dion. Hal. 2.45.1–6.
17. Dion. Hal. 2.45.6, 2.46.1.
18. Dion. Hal. 2.46.1.
19. Plut. *Rom.* 18.7, 19.1; Livy 1.12–13.
20. Livy 1.13 (trans. Rev. Canon Roberts); Plut. *Rom.* 19.1–5; Flor. 1.1.14.
21. Livy 1.13; Plut. *Rom.* 19.2–7. Flor. 1.1.14.
22. Dion. Hal. 2.46.1–2; Livy 1.13; Plut. *Rom.* 19.7–8; Flor. 1.1.14; Cic. *Rep.* 2.13; Oros. 2.4; Strab. 5.3.
23. Dion. Hal. 2.46.2, 2.47.1; Livy 1.13; Plut. *Rom.* 19.7, 20.1; Flor. 1.1.14–15; Cic. *Rep.* 2.13; Cic. *Balb.* 13.31.
24. Dion. Hal. 2.46.3.
25. Dion. Hal. 2.52.5.
26. Livy 1.13.

Chapter XI: Duarchy

Quote: Livy 1.13 (trans. Rev. Canon Roberts).

1. Dion. Hal. 2.50.1; Plut. *Rom.* 20.4.
2. Plut. *Rom.* 20.5–6; Ovid *Met.* 15.552–621; Dion. Hal. 2.50.1.
3. Dion. Hal. 2.50.1; Plut. *Rom.* 20.4.
4. Plut. Rom. 22.3; Dion. Hal. 2.7–29.

   *Plut. Rom 22.3 seems to state that many laws were enacted after merging with the Sabines.

   *Dion. Hal. 2.9–29 states otherwise.
5. Dion. Hal. 2.50.1.
6. Serv. *Aen.* 7.709.
7. Plut. *Rom.* 20.1, 20.4; Dion. Hal. 2.47.2.
8. Plut. *Rom.* 20.1–2; Livy 1.13; Dion. Hal. 2.7.2; Cic. *Rep.* 2.14; Flor. 1.1.15.

   *Livy 1.13 states that they were named the Ramnenses, Titienses and Luceres, and they were not tribes but centuries of knights.
9. Plut. *Rom.* 20.2; Dion. Hal. 2.22.3.
10. Plut. *Rom.* 20.2; Livy 1.13; App. *Pun.* 112–113; Cic. *Rep.* 2.14. Dion. Hal. 2.7.3–4, 2.14.3.
11. Dion. Hal. 2.21.3, 2.22.1, 2.23.1–2.
12. Livy 1.43.
13. Livy 1.13, 1.15; Plut. *Rom.* 26.2; Plin. *Nat.* 33.9; Dion. Hal. 2.64.3.
14. Plut. *Rom.* 22.3. Dion. Hal. 2.25.2–6.
15. Dion. Hal. 2.25.2–7; Plut. *Rom.* 22.3.

    *Dion. Hal. 2.25.3 claims that Romulus forbade divorces.
16. Plut. *Comp. Thes. Rom.* 6; Gel. 4.3; Dion. Hal. 2.25.7.
17. Plut. *Rom.* 20.3, 22.3; Dion. Hal. 2.25.5.
18. Plin. *Nat.* 14.14; Dion. Hal. 2.25.6.
19. Plut. *Rom.* 22.4; Phot. *Bib.* 57; Oros. 5.16
20. Plut. *Rom.* 20.3.
21. Dion. Hal. 2.15.2, 2.26.1–4, 2.27.1–2.
22. Dion. Hal. 2.29.1.
23. Dion. Hal. 2.29.1; Cic. *Rep.* 2.16.
24. Plut. *Rom.* 14.7.
25. Plut. *Rom.* 20.1.

26. Plut. *Rom.* 21.1; Livy 8.8.
27. Plut. *Rom.* 21.1; Cic. *Rep.* 2.13.
28. Plut. *Rom.* 21.1–4; Scheid, John, *An Introduction to Roman Religion* (Indiana University Press, Bloomington and Indianapolis), p.51.
29. Cic. *Div.* 1.3; Cic. *Rep.* 2.13, 2.16; Plin. *Nat.* 14.14, 18.2; Gel. 7.7.
30. Dion. Hal. 2.50.2; Tac. *Ann.* 12.24; Plut. *Rom.* 18.4; Livy 1.13.
31. Dion. Hal. 2.50.2.
32. Dion. Hal. 2.28.1–3.
33. Dion. Hal. 2.50.3; Flor. 1.1.13; Ovid *Fast.* 6.791–794.
34. Dion. Hal. 2.50.3; Plut. *Rom.* 22.1; Plin. *Nat.* 16.86.
    *Plut. Rom. 22.1 states that Numa Pompilius may have been responsible for instituting the cult of Vesta in Rome.
35. Dion. Hal. 2.50.3.
36. Tac. *Ann.* 6.11; Dion. Hal. 2.12.1.

Chapter XII: Cameria

Quote: Dion. Hal. 2.51.4 (trans. Earnest Cary).
1. Dion. Hal. 2.50.4–5.
2. Dion. Hal. 2.50.4; Cic. *Rep.* 2.15–16.
3. Dion. Hal. 2.50.4–5.
4. Dion. Hal. 2.50.5, 2.54.2; Plut. *Rom.* 24.3.
5. Dion. Hal. 2.50.5.

Chapter XIII: Laurentum

Quote: Dion. Hal. 2.51.1 (trans. Earnest Cary).
1. Dion. Hal. 2.51.1–2, 2.52.2.
2. Livy 1.14; Plut. *Rom.* 23.1; Dion. Hal. 2.51.1.
    *Dion. Hal. 2.51.1 claims that the targeted people were from Lavinium, not Laurentum.
3. Plut. *Rom.* 23.1–2; Dion. Hal. 2.51.1, 2.51.1–3.
4. Dion. Hal. 2.51.3.
5. Dion. Hal. 2.51.3; Plut. *Rom.* 23.1; Livy 1.14.
    *Plut. Rom. 23.1 states that the Sabines may have never attacked any shepherds. Rather they came upon a group of Laurentian ambassadors

who were headed to Rome for whatever reason, and the Sabines resolved to rob them and nothing more. When they refused to surrender their belongings to the robbers, the Sabine bandits slew them.

6. Dion. Hal. 2.51.3; Plut. *Rom.* 23.1.
7. Dion. Hal. 2.51.3.
8. Dion. Hal. 2.52.1; Plut. *Rom.* 23.1.
9. Dion. Hal. 2.52.1, 2.52.4.
10. Dion. Hal. 2.52.1–3.
11. Dion. Hal. 2.53.1.
12. Dion. Hal. 2.52.3; Livy 1.14.
13. Dion. Hal. 2.52.3; Plut. *Rom.* 23.2; Livy 1.14; Strab. 5.3; Oros. 2.4.
    *Oros. 2.4 claimed that Romulus had actually murdered Tatius.
    *Dion. Hal. 2.52.4 presents an alternative account in which Tatius travelled to Lavinium not for a sacrifice but to ask for the Sabine criminals to be forgiven. During his speech, he was stoned to death.
14. Dion. Hal. 2.52.5; Plut. *Rom.* 23.2–3.
15. Dion. Hal. 2.52.5; Plut. *Rom.* 23.2–3; Plin. *Nat.* 14.14.
    *Plut. *Rom.* 23.2 suggests that Tatius' killers travelled alongside Romulus back to Rome.
16. Dion. Hal. 2.53.1; Plut. *Rom.* 23.3; Livy 1.14.
17. Plut. *Rom.* 24.1–2.
18. Dion. Hal. 2.53.1; Plut. *Rom.* 23.3, 24.2; Livy 1.14.
19. Dion. Hal. 2.53.1.
20. Plut. *Rom.* 24.2.
    *Plut. *Rom.* 24.1–2 claims that the plague, blood rain and punishment of the killers happened at a later date, after the war with Fidenae.
21. Plut. *Rom.* 23.3–4; Livy 1.14.
22. Tac. *Ann.* 1.54; Tac. *Hist.* 2.95.
23. Dion. Hal. 2.53.1; Cic. *Rep.* 2.14; Strab. 5.3; Plut. *Rom.* 23.4.

Chapter XIV: Fidenae

Quote: Livy 1.14 (trans. Rev. Canon Roberts).
1. Plut. *Rom.* 23.5.
2. Dion. Hal. 2.53.2, 2.53.4, 3.27.1; Livy 1.14; Plut. *Rom.* 17.1, 23.5–6.

3. Dion. Hal. 2.53.2; Livy 1.14; Plut. *Rom.* 23.5–6.
4. Dion. Hal. 2.53.2.
5. Dion. Hal. 2.53.2; Livy 1.14; Plut. *Rom.* 23.5–6.
6. Plut. *Rom.* 23.6; Livy 1.14.
7. Dion. Hal. 2.53.2–3; Plut. *Rom.* 23.6; Livy 1.14.
8. Dion. Hal. 2.53.2.
   *Livy 1.14 claims that Romulus didn't wait. He rushed with his legions to confront the Fidenates. Livy also doesn't mention seeking a peaceful solution. Rather Livy seems to imply Romulus immediately leading troops toward Fidenae.
9. Dion. Hal. 2.53.2–3.
10. Dion. Hal. 2.53.3.
    *Dion. Hal. 2.53.3 claims that the Romans' initial response consisted of plundering, followed by attempting to return to Rome.
    *Livy 1.14 implies that the Romans quickly sought battle with the Fidenates without partaking in the initial plundering mentioned by Dionysius.
11. Dion. Hal. 2.53.3.
    *Dion. Hal. 2.53.3 states that the Romans were preparing to begin their trek back home after their plundering raids.
12. Dion. Hal. 2.53.3; Plut. *Rom.* 23.6; Livy 1.14.
13. Livy 1.14; Plut. *Rom.* 23.6.
    *Dion. Hal. 2.53.3 makes no mention of Romulus' plans for an ambush or the subsequent battle. Rather, Dionysius briefly mentioned a fierce set-piece battle followed by the Romans flooding into Fidenae and sacking the town.
    *Plut. *Rom.* 23.6; Livy 1.14 do not mention the battle recorded by Dionysius either. Thus, there were either two battles (one recorded by Dionysius and one recorded by Livy and Plutarch) or, more likely, the ancient authors provided different accounts of the same battle.
14. Livy 1.14; Frontin. *Str.* 2.5.1; Plut. *Rom.* 23.5.
15. Livy 1.14; Frontin. *Str.* 2.5.1; Dion. Hal. 2.53.3.
16. Livy 1.14; Frontin. *Str.* 2.5.1; Plut. *Rom.* 23.6; Dion. Hal. 2.53.3.
17. Livy 1.14; Plut. *Rom.* 23.5–6; Dion. Hal. 2.53.3–4.

18. Plin. *Nat.* 16.5.
19. Dion. Hal. 2.53.4; Plut. *Rom.* 23.6.
20. Cic. *Rep.* 2.14.
21. Dion. Hal. 2.54.1; Plut. *Rom.* 24.2.
22. Dion. Hal. 2.54.1–2; Plut. *Rom.* 24.2–3.
23. Plut. *Rom.* 24.3.
24. Dion. Hal. 2.54.2; Plut. *Rom.* 24.3.

Chapter XV: Veii

Quote: Livy 1.15 (trans. Rev. Canon Roberts).

1. Dion. Hal. 2.54.3; Plut. *Rom.* 25.1; Livy 1.15.
2. Plut. *Rom.* 25.2.
3. Dion. Hal. 2.54.3–55.6; Plut. *Rom.* 25.2–5; Livy 1.15; Oros. 2.4
   *Plut. *Rom.* 25.2–5 stated that the Veientes marched in two columns, one toward Romulus and one to Fidenae. The Veientes captured the latter, but Romulus ultimately defeated both detachments. Thereupon Veii requested Romulus' peace terms.
   *Livy 1.15 claimed that the Veientes invaded Rome's domain for the sake of plunder. Romulus then raised and army, but the Veientes had left Rome's realm by the time Romulus and his legionaries were mobilized. So they marched toward Veii whereupon Veii's army attacked the Romans but lost the battle. The Romans returned home but laid waste to Veii's territory on the way. After this episode, the Veientes sued for peace.
   *Oros. 2.4 asserted that Romulus purposefully provoked the Veientes, who were insignificant at the time, in order to spark the conflict.
4. Dion. Hal. 2.54.3–4.
5. Dion. Hal. 2.55.1–2.
6. Dion. Hal. 2.55.2; Livy 1.15.
7. Dion. Hal. 2.55.3–4; Plut. *Rom.* 25.2–5; Livy 1.15.
8. Plut. *Rom.* 25.5; Dion. Hal. 2.55.4–5.
9. Dion. Hal. 2.55.4–6; Plut. *Rom.* 25.4–5; Livy 1.15.
10. Dion. Hal. 2.55.6.
11. Livy 1.15; Plin. *Nat.* 3.9; Dion Hal. 2.16.2.

Chapter XVI: Apotheosis

Quote: Plut. *Rom.* 28.2 (trans. Bernadotte Perrin).

1. Plut. *Rom.* 27.1.
2. Dion. Hal. 2.56.3; Plut. *Rom.* 26.1, 27.1–2; Livy 1.15; Plut. *Num.* 2.2.
3. Dion. Hal. 2.56.3.
4. Livy 1.15.
5. Plut. *Rom.* 26.2; Plin. *Nat.* 33.9; Livy 1.15.
6. Plut. *Rom.* 26.2.
7. Plut. *Rom.* 26.1–2; Plin. *Nat.* 9.63.
8. Dion. Hal. 2.56.3; Plut. *Rom.* 27.2.
9. Dion. Hal. 2.56.3–4; Plut. *Rom.* 27.2; Plut. *Num.* 2.2.
10. Dion. Hal. 2.56.4–6; Plut. *Rom.* 27.3–7; Livy 1.16; Ovid *Fast.* 2.475–511; Cic. *Rep.* 6.24; Fraschetti, Augusto, *The Foundation of Rome* (Edinburgh University Press, 2005), p.94.
    *Dion. Hal. 2.56.5 states that new citizens, rather than senators, may have huddled around Romulus.
11. Dion. Hal. 2.56.2, 2.56.7; Plut. *Rom.* 27.7–8, 29.7; Livy 1.16; Flor. 1.1.16–17.
12. Dion. Hal. 2.56.4–5; Plut. *Rom.* 27.5–8; Livy 1.16.
    *Dion. Hal. 2.56.5 claimed that some believed new citizens killed Romulus, not the senators.
13. Dion. Hal. 2.56.4–5; Flor. 1.1.17; Fraschetti, Augusto, *The Foundation of Rome* (Edinburgh University Press, 2005), pp.103, 105; Plut. *Rom.* 27.5–8; Livy 1.16; Abbott, Jacob, *Romulus* (Timeless Classic Books, 2010), p.143.
14. Plut. *Rom.* 28.1–2; Livy 1.16; Cic. *Rep.* 2.20; Cic. *Leg.* 1.3; Flor. 1.1.18; Fraschetti, Augusto, *The Foundation of Rome* (Edinburgh University Press, 2005), p.89.
    *Cic. *Rep.* 2.20 stated that Proculus was actually a pauper.
15. Plut. *Rom.* 28.1–2 (trans. Bernadotte Perrin).
16. Plut. *Rom.* 28.2; Livy 1.16 (trans. Rev. Canon Roberts); Cic. *Rep.* 2.20; Cic. *Leg.* 1.3; Flor.1.1.18
17. Plut. *Rom.* 28.1–3; Livy 1.16.
18. Plut. *Rom.* 28.3, 29.1–2; Ovid *Fast.* 2.475–511.

19. Fraschetti, Augusto, *The Foundation of Rome* (Edinburgh University Press, 2005), p.94; Plut. *Rom.* 29.2.
20. Plut. *Rom.* 29.2; Fraschetti, Augusto, *The Foundation of Rome* (Edinburgh University Press, 2005), p.94.
21. Horace *Ep.* 16.13–14; Fraschetti, Augusto, *The Foundation of Rome* (Edinburgh University Press, 2005), pp.91–93; Cornell, T.J., *The Beginnings of Rome* (Routledge, 1995), pp.94–95.
22. Ovid *Met.* 14.829–851.

Chapter XVII: Interregnum

Quote: Livy 1.17 (trans. Rev. Canon Roberts).
1. Dion. Hal. 3.1.4.
2. Livy 1.17.
3. Livy 1.17.
4. Dion. Hal. 2.57.1; Livy 1.17; Cic. *Rep.* 2.23.
5. Livy 1.17; Dion. Hal. 2.57.1–2.
   *Plut. *Num.* 2.6 states that the terms of each interrex were not five days but only twelve hours (six by day and six by night). Furthermore, Plutarch made no mention about the senators being divided into decuries. The senators simply took turns ruling over the state for twelve-hour increments.
6. Plut. *Num.* 2.7; Cic. *Rep.* 2.23–24; Dion. Hal. 2.57.3.
7. Livy 1.17; Dion. Hal. 2.57.3; Plut. *Num.* 3.1.
8. Livy 1.17.
9. Livy 1.17; Dion. Hal. 2.57.3.
10. Livy 1.17 (trans. Rev. Canon Roberts); Dion. Hal. 2.57.3–4.
    *Dion. Hal. 2.57.3–4 claims that the people were authorized to choose what form of government they wished to live under.
11. Dion. Hal. 2.58.1.
12. Dion. Hal. 2.58.2–3; Livy 1.18; Plut. *Num.* 3.2–4; Cic. *Rep.* 2.25.
13. Plut. *Num.* 5.2–5, 6.1, 7.1–3; Cic. *Rep.* 2.25.
14. Livy 1.57–58; Dion. Hal. 4.64.2, 4.64.5.
15. Livy 1.58; Dion. Hal. 4.64.5, 4.65.1–4; Cic. *Rep.* 2.46; Flor. 1.7.11.

16. Livy 1.58, 1.59; Dion. Hal. 4.66.1–3, 4.67.1–4, 4.70.1–5; Cic. *Rep.* 2.46; Flor. 1.7.11.

17. Livy 1.59–60; Dion. Hal. 4.76.3–4, 4.84.2; Cic. *Rep.* 2.46.

18. Livy 1.59–60; Dion. Hal. 4.85.1–3.

19. Livy 1.60; Dion. Hal. 4.85.4; Cic. *Rep.* 2.46.

20. Livy 1.60.

21. Heather, Peter, *The Fall of the Roman Empire* (Oxford University Press, 2006), p.429.

Chapter XVIII: Legacy

Quote: Horace, *Ep.* 7.17–20 (trans. T.P. Wiseman).
 1. Plut. *Comp. Thes. Rom.* 5; Cic. *Rep.* 2.18 (trans. Niall Rudd).
 2. Plut. *Rom.* 22.4; Oros. 5.16.
 3. Plut. *Comp. Thes. Rom.* 3 (trans. Bernadotte Perrin); Oros. 2.4 (trans. Roy J. Deferrari); Cic. *Off.* 3.41; Horace *Ep.* 7.17–20 (trans. T.P. Wiseman); Fraschetti, Augusto, *The Foundation of Rome* (Edinburgh University Press, 2005), p.31.
 4. Flor. 1.8.1–2 (trans. E.S. Forster).
 5. Cic. *Rep.* 2.5–11 (trans. Niall Rudd).
 6. Sal. *Iug.* 63.7, 73.3–7, 85.32; Sal. *Cat.* 23.
 7. Plut. *Comp. Thes. Rom.* 4 (trans. Bernadotte Perrin).
 8. Cic. *Rep.* 2.17 (trans. Niall Rudd).
 9. Plut. *Rom.* 8.6, 20.3; Plin. *Nat.* 10.5; Livy 1.8, 1.13; Plut. *Rom.* 13.1; Dion. Hal. 2.8.3; Plin. *Nat.* 33.9.
10. Plut. *Rom.* 13.5–6; Verboven, K.S., 'Clientela, Roman Republic', *The Encyclopedia of Ancient History* (2012).
11. Plut. *Rom.* 11.2–3, 22.3; Dion. Hal. 1.88.2, 2.7–29.
12. Plut. *Rom.* 14.1–2; Livy 1.9; Dion. Hal. 2.30.2; Oros. 2.4 (trans. Roy J. Deferrari).
13. Suet. *Calig.* 25; Dio. 59.8.7.
14. Dion. Hal. 2.25.7.
15. Oros. 2.4 (trans. Roy J. Deferrari).
16. Oros. 2.4; Tac. *Ann.* 11.24 (trans. Alfred John Church, William Jackson Brodribb, Sara Bryant).

17. Dion. Hal. 2.34.4, 2.50.2–3; Livy 1.10, 1.12; Plut. *Rom.* 16.6–8, 18.6–7, 22.1.

18. Phot. *Bib.* 57; Cic. *Rep.* 2.16; Dion. Hal. 2.29.1, 2.56.3; Plut. *Rom.* 26.2.

19. Plut. *Rom.* 26.1–2, 27.1–2; Dion. Hal. 2.56.3–4; App. *BC* 2.16; Plut. *Comp. Thes. Rom.* 2.

20. Livy 4.20, 5.49, 7.1; Plut. *Cam.* 1.1; Plut. *Mar.* 27.5.

21. Suet. *Jul.* 85; Livy 1.16, 5.49; Dio. 44.4.2–5, 44.6.1–3; Fraschetti, Augusto, *The Foundation of Rome* (Edinburgh University Press, 2005), pp.110–12; Scott, Kenneth, 'The Identification of Augustus with Romulus-Quirinus', *Transactions and Proceedings of the American Philological Association*, vol. 56 (1925), pp.82–105.

22. Suet. *Aug.* 7.2; Scott, Kenneth, 'The Identification of Augustus with Romulus-Quirinus', *Transactions and Proceedings of the American Philological Association*, vol. 56 (1925), pp.82–105.

23. Dio. 56.34.2; Tac. *Ann.* 4.9.

24. Amm. 2.8.

25. Livy 1.4; Fraschetti, Augusto, *The Foundation of Rome* (Edinburgh University Press, 2005), p.16; Plut. *Rom.* 20.5, 22.1–2, 29.2; Montzamir, Patrice' 'Romulus, Remus, Tarquinius Priscus and Servius Tullius', Academia.edu, pp.1–13; Donlan, Walter, 'The Foundation Legends of Rome: An Example of Dynamic Process', *The Classical World*, vol. 64, no. 4 (1970), pp.109–14; Wiseman, T.P., 'Remus, A Roman Myth' (Cambridge University Press, New York), 25 August 1995, p.72; Bremmer, Jan, 'ROMULUS, REMUS AND THE FOUNDATION OF ROME', *Bulletin of the Institute of Classical Studies* 34 (July 1987), pp.25–48.

26. Livy 10.23.

27. Milovanović, Bebina and Nemanja, Mrđić, 'The She-Wolf Motif with Romulus and Remus on a Tomb Stela of an Augustal from Viminacium', *Bollettino di Archeologia On Line*, Special Volume, Poster Session 3 (2010), pp.90–94.

28. Plut. *Pomp.* 25.4.

29. Dio. 46.19.6–7; Fraschetti, Augusto, *The Foundation of Rome* (Edinburgh University Press, 2005), p.109.

Chapter XIX: Myth

Quote: This quote is disputed but is traced to a handwritten manuscript page from 'The Stranger', Editorial Board, 'The Guardian view on the value of fiction: read lies, and learn the truth', *The Guardian*, 28 August 2015.

1. Bryce, Trevor R., 'The Trojan War: Is There Truth behind the Legend?', *Near Eastern Archaeology*, vol. 65, no. 3 (2002), pp.182–95; Korfmann, Manfred, *et. al.*, 'Was There a Trojan War?', *Archaeology*, vol. 57, no. 3 (2004), pp.36–41; Foster, B.O., 'The Trojan War Again', *The American Journal of Philology*, vol. 36, no. 3 (1915), pp.298–313; Lord, Albert B., 'Homer, the Trojan War, and History', *Journal of the Folklore Institute*, vol. 8, no. 2/3 (1971), pp.85–92.

2. Neel, Jaclyn, *Early Rome: Myth and Society* (Wiley Blackwell, 2017), p.56; Rodriguez-Mayorgas, Ana, 'Romulus, Aeneas and the Cultural Memory of the Roman Republic', *Athenaeum*, vol. 98 (2010), pp.89–109; Bremmer, Jan, 'Romulus, Remus and the Foundation of Rome', *Bulletin of the Institute of Classical Studies* (1987), pp.25-48.

3. Dion. Hal. 1.77.1; Plut. *Rom.* 2.2–4.

4. Plut. *Rom.* 4.3; Livy 1.4; Dion. Hal. 1.84.4.

5. Dion. Hal. 2.56.4.

6. Neel, Jaclyn, *Early Rome Myth and Society* (Wiley Blackwell, 2017), p.104; Wiseman, T.P., 'Remus, A Roman Myth' (Cambridge University Press, New York), 25 August 1995, p.65.

7. Carandini, Andrea and Sartarelli, Stephen, 'Rome: Day One' (Princeton University Press, Princeton, New Jersey), 25 July 2011, pp.38–39.

8. Wiseman, T.P., 'Remus, A Roman Myth' (Cambridge University Press, New York), 25 August 1995, pp.67–71; Wiseman, T.P., 'Reading Carandini', *The Journal of Roman Studies*, vol. 91 (2001), pp.182–93; Wiseman, T.P., 'The She-Wolf Mirror: An Interpretation', *Papers of the British School at Rome*, vol. 61 (1993), pp.1–6.

9. Livy 10.23; Montzamir, Patrice, 'Romulus, Remus, Tarquinius Priscus and Servius Tullius, Academia.edu., pp.1–13. Donlan, Walter, 'The Foundation Legends of Rome: An Example of Dynamic Process', *The Classical World*, vol. 64, no. 4 (1970), pp.109–14; Wiseman, T.P., 'Remus, A Roman Myth' (Cambridge University Press, New York),

25 August 1995, p.72; Rodriguez-Mayorgas, Ana, 'Romulus, Aeneas and the Cultural Memory of the Roman Republic', *Athenaeum*, vol. 98 (2010), pp 89–109; Bremmer, Jan, 'ROMULUS, REMUS AND THE FOUNDATION OF ROME', *Bulletin of the Institute of Classical Studies* 34 (July 1987), pp.25–48.

10. Rodriguez-Mayorgas, Ana, 'Romulus, Aeneas and the Cultural Memory of the Roman Republic', *Athenaeum*, vol. 98 (2010), pp.89–109; Montzamir, Patrice, 'Romulus, Remus, Tarquinius Priscus and Servius Tullius', Academia.edu, pp.1–13; Donlan, Walter, 'The Foundation Legends of Rome: An Example of Dynamic Process', *The Classical World*, vol. 64, no. 4 (1970), pp.109–14; Wiseman, T.P., 'Remus, A Roman Myth' (Cambridge University Press, New York), 25 August 1995, p.72; Bremmer, Jan, 'ROMULUS, REMUS AND THE FOUNDATION OF ROME', *Bulletin of the Institute of Classical Studies* 34 (July 1987), pp.25–48.

11. Montzamir, Patrice, 'Romulus, Remus, Tarquinius Priscus and Servius Tullius', Academia.edu, pp.1–13.

12. Wiseman, T.P., 'Remus, A Roman Myth' (Cambridge University Press, New York), 25 August 1995, p.156; Montzamir, Patrice, 'Romulus, Remus, Tarquinius Priscus and Servius Tullius', Academia.edu, pp.1–13; Bremmer, Jan, 'ROMULUS, REMUS AND THE FOUNDATION OF ROME', *Bulletin of the Institute of Classical Studies* 34 (July 1987), pp.25–48.

13. Wiseman, T.P., 'Remus, A Roman Myth' (Cambridge University Press, New York), 25 August 1995, pp.1–2, 110; Plut. *Rom.* 8.7.

14. Cic. *Rep.* 2.18; Livy 1.7; Dion. Hal. 1.33.4; Cornell, T.J., *The Beginnings of Rome* (Routledge, 1995), pp.10, 16.

15. Livy 6.1.

16. Dion. Hal. 1.72–73; Plut. *Rom.* 1–2; Fest. 326–9L; Serv. *Aen.* 1.273; Wiseman, T.P., 'Review', *The Classical Journal*, vol. 107, no. 2 (2012), pp.248–50.

17. Wiseman, T.P., 'Remus, A Roman Myth' (Cambridge University Press, New York), 25 August 1995, p.44.

18. Plut. *Rom.* 1.2–3; Dion. Hal. 1.72.2; Donlan, Walter, 'The Foundation Legends of Rome: An Example of Dynamic Process', *The Classical World*, vol. 64, no. 4 (1970), pp.109–14.

19. Plut. Rom. 2.1–6; Dion. Hal. 1.72.1–6; Donlan, Walter, 'The Foundation Legends of Rome: An Example of Dynamic Process', *The Classical World*, vol. 64, no. 4 (1970), pp.109–14; Montzamir, Patrice, 'Romulus, Remus, Tarquinius Priscus and Servius Tullius', Academia.edu, pp.1–13; Wiseman, T.P., 'Remus, A Roman Myth (Cambridge University Press, New York), 25 August 1995, p.54.

20. *OGR* 23.6.

21. Neel, Jaclyn, *Early Rome Myth and Society* (Wiley Blackwell, 2017), p.11; Rodriguez-Mayorgas, Ana, 'Romulus, Aeneas and the Cultural Memory of the Roman Republic', *Athenaeum*, vol. 98 (2010), pp.89–109; Cornell, T.J., *The Beginnings of Rome* (Routledge, 1995), p.72.

22. Montzamir, Patrice, 'Romulus, Remus, Tarquinius Priscus and Servius Tullius', Academia.edu, pp.1–13; Rodriguez-Mayorgas, Ana, 'Romulus, Aeneas and the Cultural Memory of the Roman Republic, *Athenaeum*, vol. 98 (2010); Bremmer, Jan, 'ROMULUS, REMUS AND THE FOUNDATION OF ROME', *Bulletin of the Institute of Classical Studies* 34 (July 1987), pp.25–48.

23. Cornell, T.J., 'The Beginnings of Rome: Italy and Rome from the Bronze Age to the Punic Wars' (Routledge, 1 edition, New York), 7 October 1995, p.72; Carandini, Andrea and Sartarelli, Stephen, 'Rome: Day One' (Princeton University Press, Princeton, New Jersey), 25 July 2011, p.117; Fraschetti, Augusto, *The Foundation of Rome* (Edinburgh University Press, 2005), p.54.

24. Carandini, Andrea and Sartarelli, Stephen, 'Rome: Day One' (Princeton University Press, Princeton, New Jersey), 25 July 2011, pp. 70, 87, 89, 91, 96; Wiseman, T.P., 'Review', *The Classical Journal*, vol. 107, no. 2 (2012), pp.248–50; Slayman, Andrew and Merola, Marco, 'Were Romulus and Remus Historical Figures?', *Archaeology*, vol. 60, no. 4 (July/August 2007), pp.22–27.

25. Neel, Jaclyn, *Early Rome Myth and Society* (Wiley Blackwell, 2017), p.5.

26. Dion. Hal. 1.45.4 (trans. Earnest Cary); Plut. Rom. 2.1 (trans. Bernadotte Perrin).

27. '"Mythical Roman Cave" Unearthed', *BBC News*, BBC, 20 November 2007, news.bbc.co.uk/2/hi/europe/7104330.stm.; Rodriguez-Mayorgas, Ana, 'Romulus, Aeneas and the Cultural Memory of the Roman

Republic', *Athenaeum*, vol. 98 (2010), pp 89–109; Fraschetti, Augusto, *The Foundation of Rome* (Edinburgh University Press, 2005), pp.16–17; Plut. *Rom.* 20.6.

28. Plut. *Rom.* 1.1; Serv. *Aen.* 8.63; Cornell, T.J., *The Beginnings of Rome* (Routledge, 1995), p.69.

Index